American Drama 1945–2000

Blackwell Introductions to Literature

This series sets out to provide concise and stimulating introductions to literary subjects. It offers books on major authors (from John Milton to James Joyce), as well as key periods and movements (from Old English literature to the contemporary). Coverage is also afforded to such specific topics as Arthurian Romance. All are written by outstanding scholars as texts to inspire newcomers and others: non-specialists wishing to revisit a topic, or general readers. The prospective overall aim is to ground and prepare students and readers of whatever kind in their pursuit of wider reading.

Published

1	John Milton	*Roy Flannagan*
2	Chaucer and the Canterbury Tales	*John Hirsh*
3	Arthurian Romance	*Derek Pearsall*
4	James Joyce	*Michael Seidel*
5	Mark Twain	*Stephen Railton*
6	The Modern Novel	*Jesse Matz*
7	Old Norse–Icelandic Literature	*Heather O'Donoghue*
8	Old English Literature	*Daniel Donoghue*
9	Modernism	*David Ayers*
10	Latin American Fiction	*Philip Swanson*
11	Re-Scripting Walt Whitman	*Ed Folsom and Kenneth M. Price*
12	Renaissance and Reformations	*Michael Hattaway*
13	The Art of Twentieth-Century American Poetry	*Charles Altieri*
14	American Drama 1945–2000	*David Krasner*

American Drama
1945–2000

An Introduction

David Krasner

Blackwell
Publishing

© 2006 by David Krasner

BLACKWELL PUBLISHING

350 Main Street, Malden, MA 02148-5020, USA
9600 Garsington Road, Oxford OX4 2DQ, UK
550 Swanston Street, Carlton, Victoria 3053, Australia

The right of David Krasner to be identified as the Author of
this Work has been asserted in accordance with the UK Copyright,
Designs, and Patents Act 1988.

First published 2006 by Blackwell Publishing Ltd

2 2007

Library of Congress Cataloging-in-Publication Data

Krasner, David, 1952–
American drama 1945–2000 : an introduction / David Krasner.
p. cm.—(Blackwell introductions to literature)
Includes bibliographical references and index.
ISBN: 978-1-4051-2086-9 (hardcover : alk. paper)
ISBN: 978-1-4051-2087-6 (pbk. : alk. paper)
1. American drama—20th century—History and criticism.
I. Title. II. Series.

PS352.K73 2006
812′.5409—dc22
2005030632

A catalogue record for this title is available from the British Library.

Set in 10/13pt Meridien
by Graphicraft Limited, Hong Kong
Printed and bound in Great Britain
by TJ International Ltd, Padstow, Cornwall.

The publisher's policy is to use permanent paper from mills that operate a
sustainable forestry policy, and which has been manufactured from pulp
processed using acid-free and elementary chlorine-free practices. Further-
more, the publisher ensures that the text paper and cover board used have
met acceptable environmental accreditation standards.

For further information on
Blackwell Publishing, visit our website:
www.blackwellpublishing.com

Contents

List of Illustrations   vi
Acknowledgments   vii

Introduction   1

1 Politics, Existentialism, and American Drama,
   1935–1945   4

2 Money is Life: American Drama, 1945–1959   27

3 Reality and Illusion: American Drama, 1960–1975   62

4 Mad as Hell: American Drama, 1976–1989   100

5 The Body in Pain: American Drama, 1990–2000   147

Notes   183
Selected Bibliography   192
Index   195

Illustrations

1 Arthur Miller's *Death of a Salesman*, drawing by Joseph
Hirsch   52
2 Playbills, author's collection, courtesy of the Hatch-Billops
Collection   68
3 Edward Albee's *Who's Afraid of Virginia Woolf?*, courtesy
of Kansas City Repertory Theatre (formerly Missouri
Repertory Theatre)   78
4 Sam Shepard's *True West*, courtesy of Kansas City
Repertory Theatre (formerly Missouri Repertory Theatre)   111
5 Tony Kushner's *Angels in America*, author's collection   162
6 August Wilson's *Two Trains Running*, courtesy of Kansas
City Repertory Theatre (formerly Missouri Repertory
Theatre)   165

Acknowledgments

I want to thank Andrew McNeillie for inviting me to write this book. The editors and staff at Blackwell – Emma Bennett, Brigitte Lee, Karen Wilson, and Astrid Wind – have provided support and encouragement. Professor James V. Hatch of the Hatch-Billops Collection, Laura Muir, Director of Communications of the Kansas City Repertory Theatre, and Michael Wilson, Artistic Director of the Hartford Stage, have generously offered photographs. I am very grateful to Steven Bayne for his editorial advice, to my mother, and to my wife Lynda, who tolerates my obsessive-compulsive writing habits. The book was published with the assistance of the Frederick W. Hilles Publication Fund of Yale University. The arguments in this book have been tested in the classroom. I thank the students in Five American Playwrights class (Mamet, Shepard, Wilson, Kushner, and Vogel), and Edward Albee class at Yale University. Their intellectual generosity and enthusiasm stimulated memorable sessions. Finally, I want to thank American playwrights, without whom this book could not have been written.

Introduction

This book examines American drama from 1945 to 2000. By "American drama" I mean plays by playwrights from the United States representing what might be called the "American experience." American drama conforms to no fixed set of rules; playwrights create independently, are informed by different concerns, and explore multiple ideas. Any consideration of a national literature benefits by the diversity this entails. Nevertheless, the creation of a national genre requires the recognition of conceptual coherence. Themes and motifs emerge because dramatists discover in the American experience a mirroring of their own attitudes and apprehensions. The world offers modes of experiences from which it is possible for dramatists to forge analyses and apply them creatively. The writers discussed here are responding to, and attempting to make sense of, the realities of America. My aim is to provide perspectives on American drama from which to evaluate its themes. The plays considered are therefore examples of broader movements. I have found it necessary at times to dwell at length on certain dramas even at the expense of foreshortening the focus on others, in order to emphasize my points and effectively engage in the themes presented here. While every effort will be made to consider as many dramas as possible, the goal is to present ideas and thematic connections rather than blanket coverage. This means some plays and playwrights will regrettably be ignored.

   The book is divided chronologically, emphasizing the importance of history on American drama. Chapter 1 considers selected plays from 1935 to 1945 that set the groundwork for what followed. Each proceeding chapter is attentive to four interrelated dynamics based on a period's particular context. Chapter 2 (1945–1959) examines plays in which characters desire to belong to the mainstream; chapter 3 (1960–1975) explores dramas that rebel against mainstream norms; chapter 4 (1976–1989) analyzes characters who rage; and chapter 5 (1990–2000) takes up plays that emphasize the body. The designated chapters are a synthetic account of American drama, with some plays and playwrights admittedly falling outside the scope of this conceptual framework. Acknowledging exceptions, I nevertheless believe the four conditions to be fundamental to the development of American drama and provide a way to navigate this large and diverse field. It is hoped that the assertions put forward in this book will prove useful to scholars and practitioners. My objective is to present perspectives from which not only researchers, but also directors, actors, designers, and playwrights may evaluate the dramas examined here.

One additional point: American dramas were influenced by theatrical production. The dramatists in this study engaged self-consciously in creating interesting theatre. All commingled with actors, directors, and designers whom they depended on to produce their works. Their dramas served as veritable blueprints for theatrical production. While most of the dramas were what one might call "realistic," situating their characters in time and place as though they were real people living in a specific environment, the dramatists also imaginatively presented reality through the prism of theatricality. They held a mirror up to nature, but configured reality based on their theatrical objectives. Playwrights, in other words, wrote for the stage and not for the page. Although the focus here is on drama rather than performance, emphasis will be placed on the fact that every play was (and still is) intended for performance. While spatial limitations prevent an analysis of production history, every effort will be made to note the importance of production – staging practices, acting styles, and design concepts – whenever possible. For consistency, production dates refer to the New York openings unless otherwise stated.

Several superb books on American drama already exist. They are catalogued in the bibliography and I have profited greatly from them. The magnitude of Gerald Bordman and Thomas Hischak's comprehensive multi-volume chronology of American theatre stands out, as does Don Wilmeth and Christopher Bigsby's exemplary three-volume *Cambridge History of American Theatre*. Kudos belongs to Bigsby in particular for the concreteness of his presentations as well as the thoughtfulness of his analysis. His insights into Arthur Miller are nonpareil. The Blackwell *Companion to Twentieth-Century American Drama* represents over thirty exemplary scholars who examine a capacious range of playwrights, themes, and periods of American drama. Their ideas have inspired my thinking. I have no intent to challenge the analyses of other thinkers or works, but rather will explore the influence of history, philosophy, art, music, culture, literature, race, gender, ethnicity, and politics on American drama, in the hope of attaining some understanding of how these concepts bear on the creation of a national literature and genre.

CHAPTER 1

Politics, Existentialism, and American Drama, 1935–1945

ALL: STRIKE, STRIKE, STRIKE!!

Clifford Odets, *Waiting for Lefty* (1935)[1]

SIMON STIMSON: Yes, now you know. Now you know! That's what it was to be alive. To move about in a cloud of ignorance; to go up and down trampling on the feelings of those . . . of those about you. To spend and waste time as though you have a million years. To be always at the mercy of one self-centered passion, or another. Now you know – that's the happy existence you wanted to go back to. Ignorance and blindness.

Thornton Wilder, *Our Town* (1938)[2]

America's Great Depression (1929–1941) brought uncertainty but also artistic possibility. The narrator, Tom, in Tennessee Williams's ground-breaking play *The Glass Menagerie* (1945) describes the bewilderment and miasma of the previous decade: "I turn back time. I reverse it to that quaint period, the thirties, when the huge middle class of America was matriculating in a school for the blind. Their eyes had failed them, or they had failed their eyes, and so they were having their fingers pressed forcibly down on the fiery Braille alphabet of a dissolving economy."[3] The ruptured social fabric jolted Americans into a new self-awareness; as the world irrevocably changed, so the artistic repres-entation changed. The Great Depression led to an unprecedented self-examination of what it meant to be an American. Theodore Dreiser, for example, observed in 1936 that the period forced Americans to reexamine their bedrock concepts of individualism and freedom, as well as rethink the highfalutin notions of the "self-made man, pioneers, this is the best country in the world and you ought to be proud you were born here, the stars and stripes, etc."[4] Such skepticism yielded a new social awareness and a desire to uncover the roots of economic collapse.

In an effort by dramatists from 1935 to 1945 to create a theatrical language that would capture the desperation and prevailing hardships, two types of plays emerged. The first challenged adverse social conditions. The playwrights of this group were progressives who starkly highlighted the conditions of the poor. The second type examined a version of existentialism indigenous to America. These playwrights, influenced by the rising interest in European existentialism, concentrated on the nature of individualism or individuals who, through their actions, examined life's meaning and value. For the progressives, the economic woes prompted artists and writers to reconstruct events salient to the Depression. Documentary reportage, such as Arthur Arent's 1938 play *One Third of a Nation* (sponsored by the Federal Theatre Project's *Living Newspaper*) ushered in proletarian-style drama. "Social problem plays," such as Clifford Odets's *Waiting for Lefty* in 1935, examined the consequences of economic devastation. These dramatists additionally sought a vernacular that would replicate the machine age, urban living, and fast-paced "jazz age" of their time. For the existentialists, plays generally brought into focus American small-town family life, which illuminated the meaning of "being an American." The consequences of the Depression and world war reflected a sense that America had peered into the abyss, and that Americans had to reevaluate their actions in the face of futility. Moral certainty, which had characterized American melodrama prior to the 1930s, gave way to a sense of contingency. There arose a feeling that life was unpredictable. In *Existential America*, George Cotkin remarks that for French existentialists Sartre and Camus, Americans "lacked a sense of anguish about problems of existence, authenticity, and alienation," problems of general concern among Europeans. American materialism and optimism was believed to gainsay the gloom and doom representing European plays and literature. However, the American psyche during the mid-twentieth century, Cotkin contends, contained "certain darker and deeper elements" that were made evident by American art, literature, and drama.[5] Thornton Wilder's *Our Town* (1938) and *The Skin of Our Teeth* (1942), Robert Sherwood's *The Petrified Forest* (1935), and William Saroyan's *The Time of Your Life* (1939) exemplified plays partaking in a self-examination of community and a reevaluation of morality. The plays of the progressives and the existentialists laid the foundation of American drama for the second half of the twentieth century.

Clifford Odets's *Waiting for Lefty* is important for several reasons. One of the most significant political dramas of its time, it was produced by the Group Theatre, which would become the most innovative theatre company of the 1930s. Opening in January 1935 at the Civic Repertory Theatre in New York as a benefit for the left-leaning *New Theatre Magazine, Waiting for Lefty* concerns a number of taxi drivers awaiting the return of their representative, Lefty Costello. As the men debate whether to strike or not, they learn that Lefty has been murdered. Their reaction is to unite in demanding better wages and working conditions. This play captured the imagination of a generation seeking to galvanize the political aims of the "Popular Front." The "Popular Front," Michael Denning contends, was a "broad social movement" emerging from the economic crisis of 1929 that incorporated "workers' theatres, proletarian literary magazines, and film industry unions" yielding a social democratic agenda.[6] The standing room-only crowd at the Civic Repertory Theatre, along with the actors at the opening of *Waiting for Lefty*, shouted "Strike" at the conclusion. Energized by the performance, the actors and audience together spilled out into the streets of New York demanding economic justice for the working class. The spontaneous reaction was largely due to the drama's intensity as well as an actual taxi-cab strike ongoing in New York. The play became the standard-bearer of workers' theatre across the nation.

The play began as a workshop project for the Group Theatre. Founded in 1931 by producer Cheryl Crawford and directors Lee Strasberg and Harold Clurman, the Group consisted of disillusioned actors, directors, and designers. Reacting against Broadway's triviality, they produced a theatre of social change. They advanced a new type of play and performance style that coincided with new aesthetic theories. Influenced by the Moscow Art Theatre's 1923 and 1924 tours through the United States, the Group Theatre instilled a naturalistic acting style centered on verisimilitude and social activism that marked a widespread shift in aesthetic values. The style developed by the Moscow Art Theatre's artistic director, Konstantin Stanislavsky, inspired Strasberg and Clurman to incorporate psychological depth, emotional connection, and three-dimensional characterizations within an American medium. Through Stanislavsky's influence, the American acting style known as the "Method" took firm hold. Playwrights began writing dialogue to fit the "Method." The vernacular expressed the realistic demands of actors seeking Stanislavskian veracity. American actors and playwrights, however, added a distinction to Stanislavsky's system. The music of African American jazz and the indigenous vernacular of the blues had influenced American dramatists and performers for some time. Popular in the 1920s, by the mid-1930s jazz and blues records saturated American culture. Originating from turn-of-the-century Ragtime, the syncopated rhythms, improvisatory style, heightened energy, and jazz melodies characteristic of African American blues became integral to American acting style, and in turn influenced written dialogue. Odets's *Waiting for Lefty*, in particular, illustrates these influences.

The brief one-act play consists of five scenes and an introduction intended to show what the Depression had done to the American worker. The first scene takes place in the apartment of Joe and Edna. Joe Mitchell is a cab driver down on his luck; Edna, his wife, has put their two children to bed when Joe arrives virtually empty-handed despite a day's work. The stage is bare; their furniture had been repossessed that afternoon because Joe was unable to keep up with the payments. Joe enters and immediately feigns ignorance. But Edna's no-nonsense attitude punctures his façade. Pleading for understanding, he makes the case that he is doing his best. Edna, the driving force in the scene, argues that the family is barely making ends meet and that he must take action. Joe is circumspect. He tries to keep Edna at bay, to no avail:

JOE: You don't know a-b-c, Edna.
EDNA: I know this – your boss is making suckers outa you boys every minute. Yes, and suckers out of all the wives and the poor innocent kids who'll grow up with crooked spines and sick bones. Sure, I see in the papers, how good orange juice is for kids. But damnit our kids get colds one on top of the other. They look like little ghosts. Betty never saw a grapefruit. I took her to the store last week and she pointed to a stack of grapefruits. "What's that?" she said. My God, Joe – the world is supposed to be for all of us. (10)

The text reveals Odets's left-leaning ideology, the pragmatic emphasis on doing things, and jazz syncopation. Edna stresses action over passivity; for her, doing eclipses reflection and defeatism. The children see orange juice but cannot drink it. Poverty and squalor are not abstractions, but rather the result of real adversity. Edna's point is grounded in the pragmatic belief that action can change reality, and words have little if any value unless supported by actions and results. In addition, the rhythm of Edna's speech is suggestive of jazz. It is energetic and direct ("your boss is making suckers outa you boys every minute"). She emphasizes time ("every minute") to suggest a drumming tempo. Her vernacular is tough and unsentimental as her discourse accelerates. The rhythm of the dialogue mimics the mechanisms of industrial society. Joel Dinerstein contends that "Jazz was the nation's popular music in the Machine Age (1919–45) because its driving, syncopated rhythms reflected the speeded-up tempo of life produced by the industrialization in the American workplace and the mechanism of urban life." Jazz, he adds, "also reflected the hopes of African Americans for finding a new life outside the South."[7] For similar reasons this expression of hope as well as the driving rhythm was picked up by white immigrants.

Lillian Hellman's *The Children's Hour* (1934) ran for 691 performances, becoming one of the most successful shows of 1935, and enjoyed revivals during the 1940s. Along with Odets's *Waiting for Lefty* it exudes social awareness. The drama explores small-town prejudices. Karen Wright and Martha Dobie are teachers who have built their own grade-school. They become victims of a rumor by a willfully destructive student, Mary. The rumor that Karen and Martha share an "unnatural" relationship spreads. Students withdraw from the school and the marriage of Karen and Dr. Joe Cardin is called off. The play's strength is its characterization of the two principals, Karen and Martha. Despite their being upstanding citizens with substantial contributions to the community to their credit, the mere suggestion of homosexuality stigmatizes them. In the final act, Joe Cardin departs Karen's home. Martha feels the sting of her friend's rebuff. Karen proposes that they run away and start anew. But Martha cautions Karen that "There'll never be any place for us to go. We're bad people. We'll sit. We'll be sitting the rest of our lives wondering what's happened to us. You think this scene is strange? Well, get used to it; we'll be here a long time."[8] Unable to contain her secret, Martha confesses her love. Her guilt eventuates in suicide. Homophobia surfaces as well in Tennessee Williams's *Cat on a Hot Tin Roof* (1955). While it remains uncertain in *Children's Hour* whether Martha's confession of love is actual or driven by despair (or a consequence of both), it is, as in *Cat on a Hot Tin Roof*, the root cause of public disgrace. Hellman and Williams cast a critical perspective on American provincialism; the Midwest in *Children's Hour* and the South in *Cat on a Hot Tin Roof* are exposed for their philistine intolerance. Hellman's future plays, such as *The Little Foxes* (1939), continued to address American avarice, bigotry, and small-mindedness.

The 1935 season presented another significant play, Langston Hughes's *Mulatto*, which ran for 373 performances. Despite a lack of critical support and a questionable rewriting of the last act by the producer Martin Jones, the popularity of its message made it an important development in African American drama (the play was adapted into an opera, *The Barrier*, by Jan Meyerowitz in 1951). Hughes was influential in creating the Karamu Playhouse in Cleveland (known first as the Gilpin Players, named after the actor Charles Gilpin), and he helped shape African American theatres in Los Angeles and New York (the Harlem Suitcase Theatre, just to take one example). Known primarily as a poet and essayist, Hughes was nonetheless a prolific playwright, writing protest plays such as *Scottsboro Limited* (1931), which examined the trial of nine black men falsely accused of rape in Alabama. He fought against job discrimination and unemployment by writing such plays as *Angelo Herndon Jones* (1936), *The Organizer* (1938), and *Don't You Want to Be Free* (1938). During this productive period he also wrote satires such as *Scarlet Sister Barry* (1938) and *Limitations of Life* (1938). Later he offered a gospel musical protesting racial injustice in *Tambourines to Glory* (1963).

Mulatto, based partly on Hughes's short story *Father and Son*, takes place on a Georgia plantation during the 1930s. Colonel Norwood is a brackish white patriarch of three children by his black mistress, Cora (performed by Rose McClendon, one of the leading actresses and producers of African American theatre). Norwood's stubbornness and racism conflict with his paternal feelings; he condescends toward his three children – William, the oldest, Sallie, the youngest, and Robert, an 18-year-old, precocious and rebellious – yet he supports them financially. Robert has the temerity to challenge his father's authority by entering their home through the front door. Robert's sense of entitlement – he believes in his privilege owing to his birthright – leads to a conflict over what it means to be black or white in a racist society. Robert and Norwood clash bitterly, and the ensuing animus results in Norwood's death. *Mulatto* also reflects indirectly the story of Thomas Jefferson and Sally Hemings, Jefferson's slave mistress. Jefferson's long relationship with Hemings produced a family of mixed-race children. Though never explicitly mentioned, the Jefferson connection seems clear. Hughes's play, along with Hellman's *Children's Hour*, is an attack on prejudice and narrow-mindedness.

The year 1935 produced another landmark drama, Clifford Odets's *Awake and Sing!* Produced again by the Group Theatre, the play (originally titled *I Got the Blues*, which reflects the influence of blues aesthetics) examines a lower-middle-class Jewish family living in the Bronx during the Depression. Odets writes that "All the characters in *Awake and Sing!* share a fundamental activity: a struggle for life amidst petty conditions."[9] Bessie Berger, the family matriarch, lives in fear of poverty and destitution; her uxorious husband Myron is an ineffectual nebbish. Their two children, Hennie and Ralph, desire to do better than merely grovel for minimum wage. Their grandfather, Jacob, is an ex-barber and armchair revolutionary; his passions are reading Marx and playing Caruso records. Moe Axelrod is a boarder in their home, a World War I veteran who lost a leg and acquired a cynical outlook on life. He loves Hennie, but his bitterness thwarts his capacity to express emotion. Hennie becomes pregnant by a stranger who abandons the neighborhood. In desperation, Bessie and Myron finagle Max Feinschreiber, a lonely greenhorn immigrant in love with Hennie, to marry her and avoid opprobrium. Once married, they convince Max that Hennie's child is actually his. Blinded by his love and desire to belong in America, Max marries Hennie and accepts the ruse that he fathered the child.

Like *Waiting for Lefty*, the play's power lies in its rhythmic language. Odets incorporates the fast pace of urban living, the sardonic and richly metaphoric Jewish humor, and the driving energy of a restless world. Characters (especially Bessie) frequently refer to the Depression – "furniture on the sidewalk" is a constant refrain – and the hand-to-mouth existence it has accrued in its wake. Jacob instills in his grandchildren the hope that beyond the craven desire for a buck there might be a socialist utopia. But he pushes his point too far, and his daughter Bessie, enraged, destroys his Caruso records. At the end of Act II Jacob climbs to the tenement roof and jumps. He hopes that his life insurance policy will provide a better existence for his grandson Ralph. Act III centers on the arrival of the insurance claims inspector; Bessie wants Ralph to share the policy's three thousand dollars, but Ralph balks. In her effort to persuade her son, Bessie's language is a melting pot conveying the poetic and sarcastic inflection characteristic of Yiddish and guilt-inducing sacrifice mixed with jazz rhythm.

> BESSIE: Ralphie, I worked too hard all my years to be treated like dirt. It's no law we should be stuck together like Siamese twins. Summer shoes you didn't have, skates you never had, but I bought a new dress every week. A lover I kept – Mr. Gigolo!   (95)

Bessie relentlessly urges Ralph to share the money; her point is blunt. Ralph expresses a less cynical vision in the face of Bessie's nihilism.

> BESSIE: If I didn't worry about the family who would? On the calendar it's a different place, but here without a dollar you don't look the world in the eye. Talk from now to next year – this is life in America.
> RALPH: Then it's wrong. It don't make sense. If life made you this way, then it's wrong!   (95)

For Odets, the grim business of living in a capitalist world forces people into a survivalist mode. He understands that life in the Great Depression was undermining the fabric of human relationships. People became hard; to survive, they had to grow estranged. Odets captures not merely the sorrowful results of economic collapse, but also the unsparing isolation that entraps people into selfishness and greed. When Bessie becomes impatient with her father, she destroys his one pleasure in life, his Caruso records. Smashing the records disheartens the old man, who commits suicide. However, he left a three thousand dollar insurance policy for his grandson because he believed that his vitality would inspire social change. Ralph understands his mother's fears, but he also knows that his grandfather left the money for altruistic reasons. It is noteworthy that the significance of "life insurance" as a narrative device is found in Robert Sherwood's 1935 play *The Petrified Forest* and is repeated in two of the most important plays to be dealt with in the next chapter: Arthur Miller's *Death of a Salesman* (1949) and Lorraine Hansberry's *A Raisin in the Sun* (1959).

Ralph's restless energy reveals a desire for happiness beyond mere scrounging. His talk of collectives is lukewarm Marxism rather than Communist dogma. One of Odets's great strengths in this play – a play presaging the work of two future American playwrights, Arthur Miller and David Mamet – is its representation of Jewish chutzpah. The characters display survival tactics as well as an arsenal of wit, guile, and verve. The characteristics of Jews living in urban America resurface in Miller's and Mamet's work. When Jacob argues with his son-in-law, Myron, and his successful businessman son, Morty, about politics and religion, he anticipates Miller's dream of existence transcending money worship. But he also criticizes the forthcoming avidity that will become evident in Mamet's salesmen of *Glengarry Glen Ross* sixty years later.

> JACOB: So you believe in God . . . you got something for it? You! You worked for all the capitalists. You harvest the fruit from your labor? You got God! But the past comforts you? The present smiles on you, yes? It promises you the future something? Did you found a piece of earth where you could live like a human being and die with the sun on your face? Tell me, yes, tell me. I would like to know myself. But on these questions, on this theme – the struggle for existence – you can't make an answer. The answer I see in your face . . . the answer is your mouth can't talk. In this dark corner you sit and you die. But abolish private property!   (73)

Odets regarded the nuclear family, based on the model of the male breadwinner and the organizing capacity of trade unions, as the principal instrument of social improvement. At the end of *Awake and Sing!*, Ralph evokes a socialist alliance of workers, saying, "It's a team down at the warehouse," and "with enough teams together maybe we'll get steam in the warehouse so our fingers don't freeze off. Maybe we'll fix it so life won't be printed on dollar bills" (97). The rat-race mentality that saturates Miller's *Death of a Salesman* in the next decade and Mamet's *Glengarry Glen Ross* in the 1980s is indebted to Odets. The bitterness of life "printed on dollar bills," which is the trademark of Odets's work, is recreated in Mamet's huckster salesmen of *Glengarry* and greedy film producers in *Speed-the-Plow* (1988). The image of land conveyed in Jacob's speech above – "Did you found a piece of earth where you could live like a human being" – is deliberately praised in the past tense ("found") but couched as a question for the present and future. The speech marks the discrimination against Jews throughout Europe, where ownership of land was forbidden. The "fruit" symbolism in *Awake and Sing!* (Act I ends with Moe Axelrod saying, "What the hell kind of house this is it ain't got an orange!!") implies the earth's riches denied by anti-Semitism. Fruit belongs to the land; once an agrarian people enjoying the produce of the earth, Jews under

Christian rule in Europe were denied access to land ownership. They were forced to develop over two thousand years the merchandizing skills and talents for trade and commerce that made possible their survival. Success depended on "shylock" business savvy in order to live in a world of limited opportunities. Morty in *Awake and Sing!* epitomizes the successful Jewish businessman; as Bessie says, "Ralph should only be a success like you, Morty. I should only live to see the day when he rides up to the door in a big car with a chauffeur and a radio. I could die happy, believe me" (66). But for Odets Uncle Morty's success costs him his soul. He will never have a family nor discover happiness; instead, he will live to chisel like Mamet's characters more than a half century later. Morty's first line in the play begins Act II; while receiving a haircut from his father, Bessie enters and says: "Dinner's in half an hour, Morty." Morty replies: "I got time" (59). His success has purchased leisure time, but Morty finds little in the having of it. He is always scheming for his next sale, his next line of clothing. It is in the characters of Hennie, Ralph, and Moe Axelrod that Odets stakes his faith in the future. Moe's language captures that of the "tough guy with a heart" image popular in the 1930s. In the end he elopes with Hennie. Odets presents a hopeful, and a more sentimental, view than Miller and Mamet, but he is clearly their forebear. His immigrant characters are freighted with the burdens and scars of their shtetl life; for them the new world is a sign of hope, but only if they act.

Odets's *Golden Boy* (1937) followed in the tradition of plays that critiqued American avarice and class stature, such as Eugene O'Neill's *The Hairy Ape* (1922) and *The Great God Brown* (1926), Elmer Rice's *The Adding Machine* (1923), Sophie Treadwell's *Machinal* (1928), and John Howard Lawson's *Success Story* (1932). In his study of post-World War I drama, Ronald Wainscott observes that during this period "the onslaught of the industrial complex, the destruction of manners, and the creation of a crass, consumer world" led many American theatre artists to regard "their transforming world as a way of life destroyed, a culture dispossessed." Consequently, many dramas reproduced "the confusion, anger, nihilism, celebration, and reactionism inevitable under such circumstances."[10] Odets's *Golden Boy* exploits these concepts raised by the dramas of the 1920s, adding new facets to issues that roiled during the 1930s.

Produced by the Group Theatre, *Golden Boy* concerns the conflict of Joe Bonaparte, who must decide whether to pursue the violin or become a prizefighter. The backdrop is the same lower-middle Bronx milieu as Odets's *Awake and Sing!,* only now the immigrants are Italian rather than Jewish. For Bonaparte, music and pugilism symbolize the choices of beauty on the one hand, and wealth on the other. Tom Moody, a fight promoter, tries to persuade Joe to fight, while Joe's family encourages his artistic pursuits. Moody uses his girlfriend, Lorna Moon, as temptress; she draws Joe into the fight game over the protests of his family. The scene between Joe and Lorna typifies Odets's ability to weave together rhythmic language, inner conflict, and social aspirations. The two characters sit on a park bench one evening.

> LORNA: Success and fame! Or just a lousy living. You're lucky you won't have to worry about those things. . . .
> JOE: Won't I?
> LORNA: Unless Tom Moody's a liar.
> JOE: You like him, don't you?
> LORNA: (*After a pause.*) I like him.
> JOE: I like how you dress.[11]

Odets's language is taut. Lorna views the alternatives: boxing means "success and fame," while music is little more than a "lousy living." Joe's attraction to Lorna (who epitomizes the era's "whore with a heart of gold"), coupled with his insecurities (he is self-conscious about being "cross-eyed"), yields characterizations reflective of the times. Frustrated by social conditions, Americans looked for shortcuts. Joe's desire to fight rather than live artistically is indicative of a world where the need to survive trumps beauty. Joe's dilemma was shared by many who abandoned their dreams in order to gain the brass ring. Joe fights with a fury that leads to catastrophe. Despite Odets's naive conclusion (the play ends with Joe and Lorna crashing their car after Joe kills his opponent), what he successfully portrays is the image of the working-class immigrant overwhelmed by social conditions. Unable to resolve the conflict between old world values and new world ostentation, symbolized in *Golden Boy* by Joe's desire for fast and expensive cars, Odets's play projects a sense of helplessness.

Another social drama, Maxwell Anderson's *Winterset* (1935), marks a unique venture. A verse play like those of Gertrude Stein, *Winterset* takes place in the poor section of a Brooklyn dockyard. Loosely based on the 1927 execution of Sacco and Vanzetti, the story revolves around the 17-year-old son, Mio, whose father, Romagna, was falsely executed. Mio returns to the neighborhood where the alleged crime took place seeking justice, but also falls in love with Miriamne, the sister of the only actual witness to the crime. The poetic dialogue in *Winterset* conveys the cacophonous world of gangsters, tenements, and surreal improbabilities. The play's ambience is suffused with injustice and violence. The lovers, Mio and Miriamne, consign themselves to death under a hail of bullets by gangsters trying to squelch their quest for justice. The play introduced to the theatre one of America's great set designers, Jo Mielziner. In an effort to accentuate the possibility of hope amidst tragedy, Mielziner's design for the play stressed the overarching Brooklyn Bridge. The initial stage directions obscured the bridge, or at least showed little interest in visualizing it. Mielziner, Mary Henderson writes, "wanted to turn the scene around so that the bridge would be visible as it soared toward an unseen landing and its majestic architecture could represent, perhaps, a metaphor for hope and faith."[12]

Several more plays of the period emphasize the social conditions of the Depression and leftist politics. Among them are: Marc Blitzstein's musical *The Cradle Will Rock* (1937), John Steinbeck's adaptation of his novel of two drifters, *Of Mice and Men* (1937), and Sidney Kingsley's portrait of the working class in his *Dead End* (1935), based on the real-life location of the upper-class River House on East Fifty-Second Street juxtaposed beside a slum. Yet, despite the left-wing proclivity of several dramatists and others looking to experiment in form, the period's dramas primarily reinforced traditional values. Philip Barry's three-act comedy *The Philadelphia Story* (1939) takes place among upper-crust society and mildly pokes fun at the romantic antics of the wealthy. The story revolves around the divorce and new marriage of Tracy Lord (played by Katharine Hepburn), and underscores the lighthearted sexual misadventures of those without a care in the world. John van Druten's *I Remember Mama* (1943) takes a nostalgic look back at Norwegian immigrants living in 1910. The play extols the virtues of self-sacrifice, dedication, and the value of staying "true" to your family. A struggling writer, Katrin, learns that her Mama is the deserving heroine of her stories. Howard Lindsey and George S. Kaufman worked up a play from the *New Yorker* sketches of Clarence Day, producing one of the longest-running hits in American theatre. *Life with Father* opened in 1939 and ran for 3,224 consecutive performances. Its success can be attributed to its avuncular, blustering, but inoffensive "Father," who refuses to see the value of being baptized. Eventually he reneges, though he retains his loveable recalcitrance and masculine pride. The play's setting takes place during the late 1880s, when it was thought traditional values should go unquestioned. "Father" lords over his family on Madison Avenue, dolling out axioms of fiscal responsibility. He says, for example, to the Mayor of New York, "If you can't run this city without raising taxes every five minutes you'd better get out and let somebody who can."[13] Although the play's male chauvinism and offensive comments about African Americans are inexcusable, the comedy provided a respite for a nation exhausted by the Depression and the anxieties of an impending war. Its nostalgic glance at the late nineteenth century, a seemingly more subdued and passive time, must have been a welcome relief from the complexities of the Depression. Moss Hart and Kaufman, in their play *You Can't Take It with You* (1936), succeed at much the same thing. The play involves an eccentric family, the Vanderhofs. One member of the family manufactures firecrackers in the cellar, another practices ballet in the living room, and Grandpa collects snakes and refuses to work or pay his back taxes that are 23 years in arrears. What holds together this essentially plotless play is the romance between Alice, the granddaughter, and her wealthy boyfriend, Tony. This comedy filled Broadway with humor and escapism in an effort to maintain sanity during an unstable time. At the play's conclusion Tony's father, Kirby, has come to take his son away from the Vanderhof mayhem. Grandpa defends his family's way of life against the rat-racing Wall Street mentality that Kirby represents. He asks Kirby why he keeps working when he hates his job and his life, and Kirby replies:

KIRBY: Why do I keep on – why, that's my business. A man can't give up his business.
GRANDPA: Why not? You've got all the money you need. You can't take it with you.

Grandpa suggests that Kirby follow his lead and "have a lot of fun. Time enough for everything – read, talk, visit the zoo now and then [. . .] even have time to notice when spring comes around."[14] Kirby finds Grandpa Vanderhof's thinking "dangerous philosophy" and downright "un-American" (309). The play affirms Grandpa's view that the unadorned life is desirable over the hurly-burly business world. The lighthearted comedies of the period balanced against the stark reality of the times.

Another group of playwrights arose, encouraging a reevaluation of ethical and philosophical values. Thornton Wilder's 1938 three-act play *Our Town* takes place in Grover's Corners, New Hampshire. Each act is presented in 1901, 1904, and 1913, respectively. On the surface Wilder provides a nation weary of the Depression with a welcome nostalgic look at bucolic America. Druten's drama, *I Remember Mama*, also creates its own nostalgic mood. Yet Druten's play remains sentimental, framed in flashbacks by the main character Katrin and centering on her Norwegian immigrant family. Wilder's play grows caustic; while the first two acts create a homespun atmosphere, with the Stage Manager serving as narrator as well as orchestrating the stage action, the last act admonishes the wasted lives of the town's inhabitants. The provincialism of the New Hampshire characters is shown in the third act by setting the scene in a graveyard in which the characters reminisce over their squandered hopes and unfulfilled dreams.

Characters in *Our Town* describe their lives; as Mr. Webb, publisher and editor of Grover's Corners newspaper, remarks, the town is "lower middle class: sprinkling of professional men . . . ten percent illiterate laborers. Politically, we're eighty-six per cent Republicans; six per cent Democrats; four per cent Socialists; rest, indifferent."[15] For a New Hampshire town at the turn of the century, this demographic, Webb goes on to say, creates a "Very ordinary town, if you ask me. Little better behaved than most. Probably a lot duller" (26). What makes the play theatrical is that Wilder has the Stage Manager address the audience directly, and strategically places actors in the audience sometimes challenging the characters. In the first act a character named "Belligerent Man at Back of Auditorium" says, "Is no one in town aware of social injustices and industrial inequality?" (27). "This is the way we were," the Stage Manager informs us; "in our growing up and in our marrying and in our living and in our dying" (35). Act II centers around the courtship of George and Emily, while Act III occurs after Emily dies in childbirth.

Robert Sherwood's 1935 drama *The Petrified Forest* takes place at a roadside café, the "Black Mesa Bar-B-Q," which serves as a gas station and lunch room at a crossroad in the eastern Arizona desert. The inhabitants of this sleepy town meet two outsiders: the first is Alan Squier (played by Leslie Howard), an existentialist philosopher described in the stage directions as a man with "an afterglow of elegance" but also "condemned." The second is the menacing Duke Mantee (played by Humphrey Bogart), a hardened gangster described as "vaguely thoughtful," and like Squier, "unmistakably condemned."[16] Mantee is on the run, stopping at the diner to regroup his gang after a heist during which several people were killed. The play's significance is in the relationship between Squier and Mantee; they are the flip side of the same personality. Squier admires Mantee's coolheaded ability to make decisions despite the threat of death. Squier inveighs against the world to Gabby, the idealistic female who falls in love with him. Moved both by her love and by her idealism, and in an effort to find purpose in his own meaningless world, Squier strikes a bargain with Mantee. He sets up an insurance policy for Gabby without her knowing, and when Mantee is ready to pull out from the diner and make a run for it he agrees to kill Squier, making it appear part of Mantee's murderous banditry rather than a planned suicide. His arrangement elicits Mantee's understanding. Though Squier is educated and speaks eloquently, Mantee grasps Squier's predicament intuitively.

> SQUIER: You'd better come with me, Duke. I'm planning to be buried in the Petrified Forest. I've been evolving a theory about that that would interest you. It's the graveyard of the civilization that's been shot from under us. It's the world of outmoded ideas. Platonism – patriotism – Christianity – romance – the economics of Adam Smith – they're all so many dead stumps in the desert. That's where I belong – and so do you, Duke. For you're the last great apostle of rugged individualism. Aren't you?
> (*Duke has been calmly defoiling a cigar, biting the end off, and lighting it.*)
> DUKE: Maybe you're right, pal. (49)

The existential desire to find meaning in the world drives Squier to make his bargain with Mantee. Sherwood, observes Mark Fearnow, "transformed into action and character his sense of dissolution of American culture. The 'survival' motif of the 1930s permeated his work, as fossils from the earth's civilized past wander rather desperately through a newly barbaric world."[17] Symbolically, both Squier and Mantee converge at the point of life's purpose and value. Life and death, as the existentialists maintain, are never far apart, and both characters share this awareness. It is significant that Squier takes out a life insurance policy as a hedge against life's meaninglessness. As the New Deal came into view, the world of literature and drama began to rely on life insurance in its narratives. This reflected the period's interest in Social Security. Historian David Kennedy contends that the New Deal "pattern can be summarized in a single word: security." Wallace Stevens added to this, noting that "We may well be entering into an age of insurance."[18] The period's drama and literature explored the idea of "human worth"; death now afforded living possibilities – security – for survivors. Clifford Odets and Robert Sherwood, and later Arthur Miller and Lorraine Hansberry, examine life's value resulting from a New Deal society that had taken up these concepts.

William Saroyan's *The Time of Your Life* (1939) takes place in "Nick's," what Saroyan describes as "an American place: a San Francisco water-front honky-tonk."[19] The central character is Joe, an independently wealthy ne'er-do-well who, like Squier in his aimlessness, spends his days at the bar watching the world pass. He is generous, dispensing money freely and treating everyone unlucky to a drink or cash. Throughout the play, characters come to the bar to listen to music or bemoan their fallen state of affairs. For Saroyan, the bar is the world in microcosm, as well as a place where time is examined. The author explores how people spend time; at the beginning of Act II Joe meets Mary, someone he has never spoken to or seen before. They are never-theless soulmates, people who understand life's alienation but are helpless to change it. Mary asks Joe why he drinks, and Joe explains:

> JOE: Twenty-four hours. Out of the twenty-four hours at least twenty-three and a half are – my God, I don't know why – dull, dead, boring, empty, and murderous. Minutes on the clock, *not time of living*. It doesn't make any difference who you are or what you do, twenty-three and a half hours of the twenty-four are spent waiting. (75)

Saroyan's homage to the barfly is a reversal of the many temperance plays that existed before and during Prohibition (*Ten Nights in a Barroom*, for example). Prohibition had only been repealed for seven years when *The Time of Your Life* opened in 1939. The bar, Saroyan seems to suggest, is a place where down-and-outers find solace. The play is filled with the presence of a singer who cannot sing, a comedian who is not funny, a prostitute who aspires to be a burlesque star, and other assorted outcasts filled with illusions. Like Eugene O'Neill's *The Iceman Cometh* (written around the same time), the bar's ambiance can be a place of fantasy and self-deception. Unlike *Iceman Cometh*, Saroyan's world is gentle; however, Saroyan takes the passage of time seriously. When asked about work and life, Joe waxes philosophically:

> JOE: (*Slowly, thinking, remembering.*) What? What-not? That means this side, that side. Inhale, exhale. What: birth. What-not: death. The inevitable, the astonishing, the magnificent seed of growth and decay in all things. Beginning, and end. That man, in his own way, is a prophet. He is one who, with the help of beer, is able to reach that state of deep understanding in which what and what-not, the reasonable and the unreasonable, are one. (90)

Despite Saroyan's boozy sentimentalism, his play lays the groundwork for the bar as a locus of existential contemplation. Saroyan's "passage-of-time" shares much with Edward Hopper's paintings such as the *Automat* (1927) or *Room in New York* (1932). Hopper's works capture alienation American style; for both Saroyan and Hopper, lone individuals are enveloped in inertia. Despite the American pioneer spirit, both artists illustrate solitary disappointment. Rather than optimism, Hopper portrays a disconnected world, epitomized by the specter of a lone individual hunched over her coffee cup in *Automat*, or two figures existing in separate worlds in *Room in New York*: the man engrossed in his newspaper, the woman lazily fingering the piano. Saroyan is more sentimental than Hopper; his brand of existentialism possesses some hope. Neither Saroyan nor Hopper, however, shares Henry David Thoreau's enthusiasm for isolation and solitude in *Walden*, although they do share a sense of what Thoreau called "lives of quiet desperation." Saroyan and Hopper consider aloneness and silence as painfully fallow. Where Saroyan departs from Hopper is in his belief in the possibility that some human connection, however momentary, is genuine.

Wilder's *The Skin of Our Teeth* (1942) symbolizes the American ability to persevere during hard times. Each act centers on the Antrobus family – father, mother, son, daughter, and their maid, Sabina – and each of the three acts depicts a historical catastrophe. In the first act, the family comes face to face with the ice age as it encroaches on their home; the second act parallels Noah as the flood nears; and the third act takes place during the aftermath of a devastating war. The play's opening in 1942 gives the final act real-life significance. Wilder humorously theatricalizes the play by having actors talk directly to the audience. He adds to the humor by including deliberate theatrical "mistakes" in the text, such as missed cues and sick actors needing stage managers to replace them. These devices serve as relief from the seriousness of the play's intent. In 1942 the war was just beginning; audiences needed a breather. Wilder created the appropriate balance of comedy and drama. The play demonstrates the ingenuity, resourcefulness, and upbeat spirit of the Antrobuses amidst impending doom. As Sabina says at the opening:

> SABINA: We've managed to survive for some time now, catch as catch
> can, the fat and the lean, and if the dinosaurs don't trample us to
> death, and if the grasshoppers don't eat up our garden, we'll all live
> to see better days, knock on wood.[20]

Sabina's credo of survival is echoed throughout the play. She says: "Don't forget that a few years ago we came through the depression by the skin of our teeth! One more tight squeeze like that and where will we be?" (126). This line serves as the cue for the mother's entrance, but since the mother misses the cue, Sabina has to repeat her entire monologue. The catastrophe is an oblique reference to the ongoing war, but the tension is made palatable by the theatrical gag of actors missing cues. Sabina throws down her dust cloth and says to the audience:

> SABINA: I can't invent any words for this play, and I'm glad I can't. I
> hate this play and every word in it. As for me, I don't understand a
> single word of it, anyway [...] Besides, the author hasn't made up
> his silly mind as to whether we're all living back in caves or in New
> Jersey today, and that's the way it is all through.   (127)

The conflict in the play is between father and son. Their struggle is accentuated by the son's peevishness and puerility, and the troubles brought about by his violence. Henry represents America's aggressive and immature side; his unbridled rage is countered by his father's ethical sensibility. However, in the second act the father loses his moorings and flirts with Sabina. He threatens to leave and break up the family. During a political campaign in the second act, Antrobus says: "The watchword of the closing year was: Work. I give you the watchword for the future: Enjoy Yourselves" (172). Wilder combines American ideals of Puritan work ethic and the search for happiness, but he also shows the pitfalls of temptation. Sabina, who now plays the role of a "Fortune Teller" on the boardwalk (the act takes place by the sea just before the flood), warns Antrobus and the audience: "Your youth, – where did it go? It slipped away while you weren't looking. While you were asleep. While you were drunk" (179). During the romantic scene between Sabina/Fortune Teller and Antrobus, a head-strong Sabina declares that she will not "play the scene." Turning to the audience, she says: "I'm sorry. I'm sorry. But I have to skip it. In this scene, I talk to Mr. Antrobus, and at the end he decides to leave his wife, get a divorce at Reno and marry me. That's all" (195). The act concludes with Antrobus ushering all the animals, two by two, onto boats.

The third act begins with an amusing problem: some of the actors have "taken ill" from food poisoning while noshing during inter-mission. The stage manager, dresser, and costumer must assume some of the roles so that the show can continue. The major point of the act, however, is the end of the unnamed "war." The play repeatedly declares that the war is over but that the peace will be as difficult to negotiate as the war was to win. The imbroglio between father and son comes to light in a heated exchange. Henry, a soldier who has risen in the ranks and has become the enemy, declares: "The first thing to do is burn up those old books; it's the ideas he [his father] gets out of those old books that . . . that makes the whole world so you can't live in it" (229). Antrobus counters Henry's belligerence with a speech reflecting American liberal values:

GEORGE: How can you make a world for people to live in, unless you've first put order in yourself? Mark my words: I shall continue fighting you until my last breath as long as you mix up your idea of liberty with your idea of hogging everything for yourself. I shall have no pity on you. I shall pursue you to the far corners of the earth. You and I want the same thing; but until you think of it as something that everyone has a right to, you are my deadly enemy and I will destroy you. (236)

Henry's voracious appetite for materialism and autonomy must be balanced, as the playwright suggests, against the community's needs as a whole. The play defines the rationale for war based on American liberal ideals of individual freedom along with social equality. George Antrobus struggles to find a reason to carry on; he epitomizes everything "American" – hopeful and doubtful, strong-willed yet conscious of others, tempted by wealth and pleasure but also admiring of knowledge and fair play. His words at the play's conclusion are rooted in American work ethic and the struggle to make a new world:

> GEORGE: I know that every good and excellent thing in the world stands moment by moment on the razor-edge of danger and must be fought for – whether it's a field, or a home, or a country. All I ask is a chance to build new worlds and God has always given us that. [. . .] We've come a long ways. We've learned. We're learning. And the steps of our journey are marked for us here. (245)

George Cotkin comments on the play, saying that it "captures the eternal interplay between finite and infinite, with survival through the turmoil of existence." He contends that Wilder takes spectators "to the edge of an existential abyss but then retreats, showing the audience a nicely lit exit sign that offers an alternative to Kierkegaard's anguished leap of faith. In Wilder's work, the tragedy of existence is eased instead by a belly laugh, a polite shock of recognition, or a chuckle at the foibles of humankind."[21] Cotkin is correct, but only up to a point; American existentialists like Wilder, unlike their European counterparts, do not consider the world unremittingly bleak. Wilder, like other American dramatists of this era, borrows European ideas of questioning human aims and embracing the knowledge that, as Sartre would have it, existence precedes essence. However for Wilder, contra Sartre, existence is hardly a dire landscape causing us to succumb to nausea. Like Beckett, whose tramps in *Waiting for Godot* exist in a wasteland with little hope of Godot's arrival, the Antrobuses live in a precarious world awaiting catastrophe. Unlike Beckett, Wilder stakes his belief in American ingenuity and resourcefulness, the get-up-and-go spirit that can overcome obstacles. This view does indeed show audiences what Cotkin calls a "nicely lit exit sign" which relieves the burden of finality. But Americans in general avoid dwelling on Kierkegaardian anguish, preferring instead conscious resilience and fortitude. The American poet and essayist Delmore Schwartz wrote in 1948 that *"Existentialism means that no one else can take a bath for you."*[22] Schwartz is referring to Heidegger's notion that no one can die for you, but he uses the bath metaphor rather than death as a way of interjecting tongue-in-cheek humor. A bath, Schwartz says, "is a daily affair, at least in America." He implies that for Americans the contemplation of life and death is not in itself morbid. Americans take life's inevitability and give it a good spin (or wash). In Wilder's world, the family unit is reengaged – son is reconciled and father returns to the fold – because for Wilder the American dream of the family unit is what can pull people through hardship. Wilder's view stakes its terrain on the traditional heterosexual family. This fact, albeit conventional, cannot conceal his existentialism, but suggests an American hopeful version of it. With Beckett, audiences are offered a recycling of nothingness; characters replay their fruitless search for Godot without closure. In the hands of Wilder and other American playwrights, something can be made from nothing, even if that something requires improvisation, and results, however vague, can be obtained. The Antrobuses believe that they can do more than merely endure, endurance being the hallmark of Beckettian "I can't go on, I will go on." Their optimism may be perceived by some as foolish; still, Wilder captures the "American-ness" of his existentialism.

A bleaker view of Americanism consistent with European existentialism can be found in the works of several African American dramatists. This is the result of deeply entrenched segregation, lynching, and the economic condition that gave rise to the expression of blacks as always "first fired, last hired."[23] The period from 1935 to the 1959 of Lorraine Hansberry's play *A Raisin in the Sun* falls between two high watermarks of African American culture, the Harlem Renaissance and the Black Arts Movement. The period 1935 to 1959 has received far less attention than these two great epochs. However, two noteworthy plays, Theodore Ward's *Big White Fog* (1938) and the stage adaptation of Richard Wright's novel *Native Son* (1941, co-written with Paul Green), established the groundwork for future dramas. *Big White Fog* depicts the lower-working-class Mason family living in Chicago during the early 1920s and the early 1930s in the last act. Victor Mason, the father, is enlisted in the Garvey Movement and becomes one of its leaders. Led by the messianic charisma of Marcus Garvey, the Garvey Movement surfaced after World War I as a black separatist movement seeking economic and social independence. Victor is a devout Garveyite, but when he depletes the family savings to support Garvey's Back-to-Africa mission, he costs his family opportunities. His son is denied entry into college owing to poverty and racism, and his daughter is forced into prostitution with a white man in order to survive. The third act takes place amidst the Depression, at a time when the family is facing eviction and the Garvey Movement has already disintegrated. The family turns to the socialists for help (it was a common refrain in the black community during the Depression that if faced with eviction, people would cry out "Get the Reds," meaning gather up the Communists who usually protested evictions and frequently forced landlords to back down). This is, in fact, what happens in the play; the family has twenty days to come up with the rent, and when it fails to do so, the Communists come to its aid. Victor, at the end, is shot and killed defending his furniture as it is being carried away by the police.

Chicago is also the setting for Richard Wright's social drama *Native Son*. Produced in 1941 with Canada Lee in the leading role of Bigger Thomas (Lee was also in *Big White Fog* and the 1944 play *Anna Lucasta* for the American Negro Theatre), the play portrays the bullying, uneducated, yet self-consciously aware Thomas whose unequivocal anger at whites and at his hopelessness ends in death. Taking a job as a chauffeur for a wealthy white family, he accidentally smothers the family's blind daughter. The daughter, desiring to go "slumming," has Thomas drive her and her boyfriend to a honky-tonk in a black neighborhood. She is drunk, forcing Thomas to carry her to her bedroom when they return home late. As she moans, Thomas fears for his life when he hears someone entering the house (a black man carrying a blind white woman to her bedroom might instantly produce a lynching rope). Terrified by the potential for accusations or worse, he covers her mouth in panic and accidentally smothers her. Knowing explanations to be useless, he is on the run for his life. Thomas is eventually caught, tried, convicted, and executed.

Although Wright broke from the Communist Party in 1943, his *Native Son* (1940 novel, 1941 play) is a model representation of socialism and existentialism in literature. Cotkin reminds us that "Wright's pathos depended upon the gritty realism with which he evoked the pain and inauthenticity forced upon African Americans." But Wright was also an "existentialist before he knew such a thing existed."[24] Influenced by Fyodor Dostoevsky, Wright's Bigger Thomas, like

Raskolnikov in *Crime and Punishment*, tests the limits of his actions and moral responsibility. For Wright, the added factor of race and the backdrop of social oppression inform the dramatic potential. Bigger Thomas possesses greater rage than Lorraine Hansberry's Walter Lee Younger in *A Raisin in the Sun*, but both Bigger and Walter Lee keenly feel the injustice that comes from being a dreamer and an outsider. Both *Big White Fog* and *Native Son*, plays set in Chicago, laid the groundwork for Hansberry's Chicago-based play. We will observe how the social protest dramas and plays of existentialism helped develop the American concept of the outsider, as American dramatists emerged from World War II poised to challenge the received wisdom of values and traditions.

CHAPTER 2

Money is Life: American Drama, 1945–1959

AMANDA: *Go to the movies, go! Don't think about us, a mother deserted, an unmarried sister who's crippled and has no job! Don't let anything interfere with your selfish pleasure! Just go, go, go – to the movies!*
TOM: *All right, I will! The more you shout about my selfishness to me the quicker I'll go, and I won't go to the movies!*
Tennessee Williams, *The Glass Menagerie* (1945)[1]

WILLY: *Does it take more guts to stand here the rest of my life ringing up a zero?*
BEN: *(Yielding.)* That's a point, William. *(He moves, thinking, turns.) And twenty thousand – that* is *something one can feel with the hand, it is there.*
Arthur Miller, *Death of a Salesman* (1949)[2]

TYRONE: *Thirty-five to forty thousand dollars net profit a season like snapping your fingers! It was too great a temptation.*
Eugene O'Neill, *Long Day's Journey into Night* (1956)[3]

MAMA: *Son – how come you talk so much 'bout money?*
WALTER: *(With immense passion.) Because it is life, Mama!*
MAMA: *(Quietly.) Oh – (Very quietly.) So now it's life. Money is life. Once upon a time freedom used to be life – now it's money. I guess the world really do change . . .*
WALTER: *No – it was always money, Mama. We just didn't know about it.*
Lorraine Hansberry, *A Raisin in the Sun* (1959)[4]

Tennessee Williams's *The Glass Menagerie* (1945) and Lorraine Hansberry's *A Raisin in the Sun* (1959) begin and end this chapter because they raise ethical concerns reflecting an American way of life.

They are similar to Arthur Miller's *Death of a Salesman* (1949), Eugene O'Neill's *Long Day's Journey into Night* (written during the early 1940s and produced in 1956), O'Neill's *The Iceman Cometh* (also written during the 1940s and produced in 1946), and Williams's *A Streetcar Named Desire* (1947) and *Cat on a Hot Tin Roof* (1955) in that they portray characters experiencing financial, and therefore emotional, crises. They additionally take up related family issues and social injustice with a candor hardly imaginable before on the American stage. Most significantly, they examine characters trying to overcome obstacles to prosperity and happiness. The quotes above from Williams's *The Glass Menagerie* and Hansberry's *A Raisin in the Sun* in particular reveal striking similarities in dialogue between adult sons Tom and Walter Lee, and their mothers Amanda Wingfield and Lena Younger. Both sons long for something more than their mundane lives. Both mothers cling to traditions of family they observe collapsing around them. Tom in *The Glass Menagerie* and Walter Lee in *A Raisin in the Sun* are united by restlessness, desire for financial independence, and dreams of escaping their provinciality. Even the titles of both plays poignantly accentuate a simple feature – a glass menagerie or a raisin in the sun (the latter drawn from Langston Hughes's poem) – thereby calling attention to the mutual theme of ordinary people's struggles. This chapter examines selected plays from 1945 to 1959 depicting the American Dream. While others made their mark, five playwrights – O'Neill, Miller, Williams, Hansberry, and William Inge – are dominant. If the dramatists of the previous chapter forged plays from the progressive righteousness of agitprop drama (*Waiting for Lefty*, for example), and from the portrayal of the existential outsider (*The Time of Your Life*), mid-century American playwrights ripened in the shadow of the Depression to combine the twin elements of 1930s art – social consciousness and being on the margins – in creating protagonists seeking mainstream acceptability.

From 1945 to 1959 America may be remembered for its Ozzie-and-Harriet complacency, military supremacy, anti-Communism, and economic recovery. During the Depression the banking system collapsed and unemployment ran rampant; by comparison, the late 1940s and 1950s enjoyed unprecedented prosperity, and the end of the war catapulted the nation from the periphery of international politics to the position of global superpower. Upward mobility was a fact of economic life, and returning soldiers demanded their share of the American

Dream. This idea of upward mobility is well described by James Truslow Adams, who wrote in 1931 that the "American dream of a better, richer, and happier life for all our citizens of every rank" is "the greatest contribution we have made to the thought and welfare of the world."[5] The desire for an improved life was given impetus by the passing of America's financial crisis. After the war, cities expanded into suburbs to accommodate the influx of returning soldiers eager to enjoy a robust middle class. Increased availability of affordable housing accelerated migration to the suburbs. Having endured the Great Depression and having served their country, soldiers felt they earned the incumbent rewards of the American Dream.

However, not everyone had access to the Dream. The Allied victory left the United States as a model for the world (or at least that was how America saw itself). Yet racial segregation made a mockery of the nation as the so-called paradigm of freedom. Individuals were alienated not only because of race, but owing to discrimination of gender, social class, physical handicap, age, or mental state as well. Dramatists of the era sought to expose these inequities. Many American playwrights from 1945 to 1959 molded their politics from their experiences during the Depression. Even Lorraine Hansberry, younger than her dramatist colleagues Miller, Williams, O'Neill, and Inge, developed her social consciousness from the 1930s and 1940s. Their ideas were formulated on what Henry Wallace called in 1942 "the century of the common man."[6] In contrast to Henry Luce's 1941 *Life Magazine* essay titled "The American Century," Wallace gave expression to the idea of a "people's revolution." Combining the rhetoric of populism and New Deal progressivism, Wallace fashioned an alternative to Luce's imperialistic notion of the American century. Yet, for many American playwrights, the promise of equal opportunity was a cruel deception. Their aim was to expose inequities and bring those on the margins into the fold of American prosperity. Williams's *The Glass Menagerie*, the period's signature play, focuses on one character's restless longing for freedom and his guilty conscience for having attained it at the expense of his family. It also depicts the adversity associated with physical handicap and age, as well as an acute feeling for the hardship of its era.

The Glass Menagerie is the story of a fatherless family during the Depression. It takes place during the 1930s, and is told through the recollections of its narrator, Tom Wingfield. It is, Williams says repeatedly, a "memory" play; the events unfold in the past as Tom describes them in the present. Amanda Wingfield (played originally by the much-heralded actress Laurette Taylor) is an aging Southern belle and matriarch to her children, Tom and Laura. Williams describes her as a "little woman of great but confused vitality clinging to another time and place" (vii). Tom, a wannabe writer, works at a monotonous job; Williams notes that "his nature is not remorseless, but to escape from a trap he has to act without pity" (vii). Amanda's daughter, Laura, is bright but taciturn, spending hours indoors arranging her glass menagerie collection. A childhood illness, likely polio, has left one leg shorter than the other. She is also somewhat agoraphobic. Laura, Williams says, fails to make contact with reality "till she is like a piece of her own glass collection, too exquisitely fragile to move from the shelf" (vii).

The driving force is Amanda, who fears for Laura's future. Her concerns are well founded; Laura, though intelligent, is too sensitive and ill equipped for a competitive world. Social Security and government support have yet to be legislated. In an age of unbridled capitalism, the world had little use for shy and disabled people who collect glass figurines. The portrayal of Laura's disability almost certainly resonated with Americans who had recently lost their President. During Roosevelt's four terms in office (1933–1945), disability was an obvious stigma; Roosevelt attempted to obscure the full extent of his incapacity for fear of shattering his political career. Laura, however, is poor and powerless. Amanda insists that Tom support her. Tom, however, is distressed with his own unproductive life (he can hardly find time to write) as well as with his mother's unremitting criticism. Aware that Tom is unlikely to remain Laura's caretaker, Amanda encourages what she calls a "gentleman caller" for her daughter. Despite her own gentleman suitors during her youth at "Blue Mountain," Amanda married a man who, she says sarcastically, worked for the phone company and fell in love with "long distance." Like father like son, Tom will eventually abandon the family, too.

Williams describes the play's setting as "one of those vast hive-like conglomerates of cellular living-units that flower as warty growths in overcrowded urban centers of lower middle-class population and are symptomatic of the impulse of this largest and fundamentally enslaved section of American society to avoid fluidity and differentiation and to exist and function as one interfused mass of automatism" (3). This claustrophobic-induced conformity makes Tom restless. A likely stand-in for the author himself, Tom desires to break free. A photograph of the father hangs on the upstage wall; the image of abandonment haunts him and his mother. Audiences reported that Laurette Taylor's performance as Amanda was so believable that whenever she turned upstage to view the picture, even though her face was out of view, audiences could sense anger in the movement of her spine.

Amanda enthuses over all the "gentleman callers" Laura will receive, fantasizing an entourage of beckoning men. Laura knows this to be an illusion her mother conjures to boost family morale. Laura reminds her mother that "I'm just not popular like you were in Blue Mountain. . . . (*Tom utters another groan. Laura glances at him with a faint, apologetic smile. Her voice catching a little.*) Mother's afraid I'm going to be an old maid" (12). Like Willy Loman, the discarded, old, and ineffectual salesman in Arthur Miller's *Death of a Salesman*, Laura's "old maid" condition and physical infirmity leave her vulnerable. She knows that she must depend on her brother, or "the kindness of strangers," for survival. Desperate to find her a source of income, Amanda enrolls her daughter in secretarial school, Rubicam's Business College, but the pressure she feels exposed in public overwhelms her. Criticized by her teacher the first day of class, Laura bolts to the bathroom, throws up, leaves, and never returns. Afraid to tell her mother, she pretends to leave for class every morning, taking long walks to museums and the zoo instead. When Amanda finds out, she bluntly echoes Honoré de Balzac's 1847 novel, *Cousin Bette*, which also depicts spinsters and dependence: "What is there left but dependency all our lives? I know so well what becomes of unmarried women who aren't prepared to occupy a position. I've seen such pitiful cases in the South – barely tolerated spinsters living upon the grudging patronage of sister's husband or brother's wife! – stuck away in some little mouse-trap of a room – encouraged by one in-law to visit another – little birdlike women without any nest – eating the crust of humility all their life!" (19). In saying so, Amanda reflects an anxiety much like Billie Holiday in her well-known song "God Bless the Child" (1941). It, too, emphasizes independence and self-sufficiency, because generosity has its limits. The lyrics – "crust of bread and such, you can help yourself but don't take too much" – confirm what Amanda knows too well: "Mama may have, and Papa may have, but God bless the child that's got its own."[7]

Tom describes his mother's efforts to sell renewal subscriptions over the phone for "a magazine for matrons" called *The Homemaker's Companion*, a journal that offers the hope of success with family and life. Her home and life are a failure: a runaway husband, recalcitrant son, dependent daughter, and economic deprivation. The irony is inescapable; Amanda sells what she fails to do in life. Yet Amanda is a saleswoman, and in this she shares a profession with two other important characters of this period, Hickey in O'Neill's *The Iceman Cometh* and Willy in Miller's *Death of a Salesman*. For these three, salesmanship symbolizes something besides selling "things": Hickey sells reality; Willy essentially sells himself, or his self-delusions; and Amanda sells glamour. Each of these "items" belongs to a vision of the American Dream. Upstage of Amanda, Williams's stage directions call for a screen image of a "Glamour Magazine Cover" while Amanda is on the phone "spotted in the dim stage": "Ida Scott," Amanda says, "We *missed* you at the D. A. R. last Monday! . . . Well, I just happened to notice that your subscription to the *Companion*'s about to expire! . . . Heavens – I think she hung up!" (23). Amanda has little choice but to carry on in an effort to survive.

Amanda and Tom bicker over Tom's desire to go to the "movies," which provide him with much-needed fantasy. He, however, agrees that something has to be done about Laura. He locates what he thinks is a suitable "gentleman caller." While Amanda makes plans for the expected visitor, Jim, Tom urges caution. He notes that Laura "is very different from other girls" (58) because she "lives in a world of her own – a world of – little glass ornaments, Mother" (59). But Amanda remains undeterred, believing that Tom's friend is the one. Jim is Tom's workmate at the factory, the "high school hero" (61) who failed to live up to his stardom. Jim patronizingly refers to Tom as "Shakespeare," because Tom writes poetry in his spare time. Other workers regard Tom suspiciously for his "difference" (although never stated overtly, it is likely that Tom is gay), but Jim offers his friendship.

Jim exudes optimism despite hard times. He epitomizes the American spirit of defiance in the face of adversity. He warmly greets his hostess, Amanda, who has planned a costly dinner. Despite the electricity having been turned off (Tom failed to pay the bill), Jim amuses everyone with his upbeat mood. He is taking a course in public speaking, he believes in the future, and he fails to let the Depression discourage him. After dinner Jim and Laura sit alone by candlelight. Jim envisions his life: prosperity looms, or so he thinks. Laura listens admiringly. As the scene unfolds his upbeat attitude becomes infectious. She shares her glass collection, even offering a piece as a gift. Eventually they kiss. But Jim's secret is revealed: he is already engaged to be married. Jim, it turns out, is an opportunist. As the painful reality comes into view, Amanda accuses Tom of knowing this beforehand. Tom pleads innocence, but he is unable to persuade his mother, who, out of frustration, criticizes aggressively. Tom leaves, never to return.

Among the many revolutionizing features of this play was the inventive scenery designed by Jo Mielziner. Williams and Mielziner wanted a production transcending pictorial realism. They created a theatrical space that captured the individual interior world of the characters. Instead of detailed and real-world minutiae, Mielziner aimed for abstraction, suggestion, and minimalism. Mielziner, Mary Henderson contends, "wanted to 'design with an eraser' (his favorite aphorism) so that a play's poetry could be released into a theatre space like a genie out of a bottle. In *The Glass Menagerie*, as in *Winterset*, he had not only found such a play but a far better one than he had ever encountered in his career."[8] In order to underscore the play's poetry and visualize an interior–exterior, past–present stage picture, Mielziner experimented with the concept of "simultaneity." The interior of the family space occurring in the past, and the exterior representing Tom's narration in the present, demanded a dual foreground–background experience. Mielziner implemented a scrim or screen device, casting a thin gloss or haze over the interior setting. The scrim accentuated the web-like sense of entrapment as well as the sense of memory. In *The Glass Menagerie*, Thomas Postlewait observes, the "exterior–interior dynamic, which invites various psychological, social, moral, and metaphysical interpretations in dualistic, often polarized terms, is expressed spatially and temporally," yielding "an essential conflict between motion and stasis, change and permanence." Williams's characters are "usually caught between their conflicting needs for freedom and security." This conflict, Postlewait alleges, is captured "in a stage environment that divides space simultaneously into areas of expansive openness and areas of confinement."[9] The set took on the space of Tom's divided psyche, too; the ability to observe him moving from past to present and interior to exterior without clumsy set changes aided the ability to absorb the notion of a present haunted by the past.

The concluding scene of *The Glass Menagerie* provides a moving example of how past and present intersect. Tom, in the exterior foreground downstage, considers his last day at home, the day of the gentleman caller debacle. The interior stage area portrays Laura and Amanda putting away dinner. Amanda and Laura are in a sense frozen in Tom's mind, their ordinary activities framed and repeated in his memory. The image of the candles flickering and Laura's moth-like movements sear his psyche. Although he tries to forget, Tom discovers bits of memory like bits of glass, particularly when he passes a store window "filled with pieces of colored glass." The vision jolts his recollection. The memory of candles, which the family had to use because Tom deliberately failed to pay the electric bill, is not only conveyed in the character's mind but also depicted theatrically. Tom contemplates the interior world of sister and mother as they clear the table: "I reach for a cigarette, I cross the street, I run into the movies or a bar, I buy a drink, I speak to the nearest stranger – anything that can blow your candles out!" As Laura bends over the candles, he says, "for nowadays the world is lit by lightning! Blow out your candles, Laura – and so good-bye. (*She blows the candles out.*)" (124). The combination of human frailty and concern for the marginalized, so typical of all of Williams's work, casts light on his female characters and the lyrical texture of the language. Poetic devices communicate the unfamiliar; if Williams illuminates Southern lyricism, it is to reveal the full extent of poetry in everyday speech. It emphasizes the delicacy of people like Laura. Laura's fascination with glass figures is a measure of her sensitivity. Other indices of her personality – extreme shyness and physical handicap – create a network of associations that are designed to haunt Tom's memory as well as ours. As we will observe, Blanche in *A Streetcar Named Desire*, Maggie in *Cat on a Hot Tin Roof*, Amanda, and Laura are much alike.

Wallace Stevens remarked that we live by "necessary fictions" while striving for "a new knowledge of reality."[10] This condition is apropos of Eugene O'Neill's plays, especially *The Iceman Cometh*, which illuminates the "necessary fictions" of self-deception. Although one of the most celebrated playwrights during the 1920s and 1930s, by the late 1930s critics contended that O'Neill's talents had dissipated. Nothing could have been further from the truth. From 1939 until the end of his writing career in 1943 (illness having curtailed his ability to function during the last decade of his life, 1943–1953), O'Neill wrote four plays: *The Iceman Cometh, Long Day's Journey into Night, A Moon for the Misbegotten*, and the one-act *Hughie*. All were produced after 1945

(*Long Day's Journey into Night* and *Hughie* posthumously), and all were initially received lukewarmly. It was not until the 1950s that *The Iceman Cometh* and *Long Day's Journey into Night*, with the aid of director José Quintero and actor Jason Robards, began to receive the attention they deserved.

The Iceman Cometh (1946) takes place in 1912, over 24 hours, in Harry Hope's waterfront gin mill. It serves cheap whiskey – the "last-resort variety" – and also serves as a rooming house and intermittent whorehouse. It is the last stop for an assortment of intoxicated dropouts. The play centers on Harry Hope's birthday celebration, but the real excitement occurs with the arrival of Theodore Hickman ("Hickey"). Hickey enters ready with cash to share with the whores and drunkards. His periodic appearances are eagerly anticipated by the barflies because he has a reputation for spending money, knows how to binge, and inebriates into a stupor. Unlike the others, he maintains an otherwise middle-class life, complete with wife Evelyn, respectable sales job, and retains temperance while at work. At Harry's bar, however, Hickey forgoes conformity, releasing his pent-up frustrations. However, this time Hickey's arrival forebodes change.

From his first appearance Hickey makes it clear that he is "off the stuff," as he says. Instead of raising hell, cheating on his wife, and drinking with his fellow bohemians, he comes with a single purpose: to strip away the illusions, what he calls "pipe dreams." The "pipe dream" is the epitome of the American Dream, inspiring an illusion of false hope (hence the metaphor "Hope's bar"). Each habitué dreams of returning to his former glory. The bar patrons will never admit to the F. Scott Fitzgerald axiom that there are "no second acts in America" (or at least they will never admit it out loud). For them, the "second act" contains their illusions in a nutshell: one day they will emerge from the bar restored to their former glory. The fact is, several characters hardly even knew success; but this matters little, as their alcohol-inflated puffery fuels their pipe-dream exaggerations. What is at stake in the play is both illusion and reality, inculcated in the choice of the façade masking reality or cold-blooded nihilism. More than any playwright, O'Neill places squarely the choice whether it is better to live with a lie that sustains dignity and self-respect – however false – or face reality head-on, requiring the abandonment of hope. Hickey chooses the latter, stripping the barroom blarney from his friends and establishing the painful "truth." Like Ibsen's protagonist in *The Wild*

Duck who inveighs against the "life-lie," Hickey believes that an icy acceptance of "truth," however brittle, will liberate his comrades. Hickey pays for the liquor, food, and party necessities; he is not adverse to their pleasures. What he opposes is the pretense.

> HICKEY: If anyone wants to get drunk, if that's the only way they can be happy, and feel at peace with themselves, why the hell shouldn't they? [. . .] The only reason I've quit is – Well, I had the guts to face myself and throw overboard the damned lying pipe dream that'd been making me miserable, and do what I had to do for the happiness of all concerned – and then all at once I found I was at peace with myself and I didn't need booze anymore. That's all there was to it.[11]

Underlying Hickey's new-found sense of truth is an ethos of born-again redemption and a desire to share this discovery. He singles out each character's "dream," exposing the particular fraudulency to it. He rouses them from stupor and complacency, and, like a good salesman (and good actor), he achieves his goal through persuasion. His aim is that they find their way back to middle-class respectability. He is well schooled for this role. As a salesman, Hickey is a maestro, brandishing a unique charisma. But he comes with a hidden agenda.

Hickey has murdered his wife out of guilt. His intention is to make redeeming overtures evidence of insanity. Through his efforts to sober up the drunks, he hopes to demonstrate his own madness. O'Neill calls attention to an irony underlying Hickey's actions; on the one hand he is trying to expose the lies of his friends, but on the other he is creating his own. Hickey orchestrates a wholesale act of redemption, lurching each bar patron before his own symbolic mirror to unmask that person's illusions. Hickey knows that even if the patrons are induced to venture out into the world, it is unlikely they will find themselves or their past. As a result of Hickey's persistence, the liquor fails to attain its purpose; the patrons complain that the booze has lost its "kick," and that Hickey has doused their "high." In doing so, Hickey has also denied them their sense of dignity. The illusion, as it turns out, *is all they own.* It is only after the police catch up to Hickey and take him away that the patrons retrieve their boozy self-satisfaction. There are two exceptions: Larry Slade and Don Parritt. They are convinced by Hickey's eye-opening "truths." Slade abandons his life as the uncommitted sideliner, and Parritt confronts his guilty past (he turned in his radical mother to the police). In the end, Parritt commits suicide with Slade's blessings.

Throughout his career O'Neill was under the influence of Freudian psychology, Nietzschean philosophy, and Christian ethics, but he was also concerned with something more. In Hickey he creates a character that is an "actor" in a role. Hickey is both feigning madness and going mad. In this way Hickey is similar to Shakespeare's Hamlet, who also feigns madness and is likely bereft of his senses. Hamlet "acts" mad in order to discover certainty about his father's murderer; but he is simultaneously losing his mind. Hickey, too, dons an "act" of madness and is losing his bearings. Like a good actor (and good salesman), he must convince the bar patrons to "buy into" his madness so that they might testify on his behalf. This is his ploy to avoid execution, as well as his "role" to play as an actor. This yields two levels of development: realism, with its symbolic nuances and psychological detail, and theatricality, with its self-awareness of actors "being in the theatre."

The theme of the outsider is at the heart of the writings of O'Neill. Like O'Neill's real-life older brother, Hickey is a character uncomfortable in the world. He oscillates between respectability and debauchery, finding pleasure neither in the predictability of middle-class life nor in the highs and lows of bohemia. He is caught in a cycle of sin, guilt, and forgiveness; every time he returns from his bacchanal, he confesses to Evelyn and she forgives. In turn, every time he picks up his salesman life, he rediscovers its mandatory conformity. Yet, the notion of living life as a prolonged drunk has its own brand of unappealing status quo. In his effort to break free of the treadmill, he kills his wife in her sleep. He endeavors to "act" mad, coming to the bar in a futile effort to reform others. But he has also become "mad," killing his wife. Hickey murders the one person he loves in order to free himself from guilt. O'Neill challenges our assumption that the truth can triumph over self-deception. As the philosopher Larry says at the beginning of the play: "To hell with the truth! As the history of the world proves, the truth has no bearing on anything. It's irrelevant and immaterial, as the lawyers say. The lie of the pipe dream is what gives life to the whole misbegotten mad lot of us, drunk or sober" (9–10).

Serious dramas were not the only plays to examine the outsider trying to enter the mainstream. Comedies made use of the outsider as well. Thomas Heggen and Joshua Logan's 1948 play *Mister Roberts* enjoyed over one thousand performances on Broadway. The central character, Lieutenant Roberts (played by Henry Fonda), is the frustrated protagonist stranded on a Navy cargo ship during the final days of World War II. The ship is safely stationed away from the hot zones of military engagement. Roberts is tormented by the thought that he will remain on the periphery, missing his one chance to participate in a great world event. The play depicts his comic struggles with the Captain. Roberts wants the necessary transfer papers to a combat zone. He hopes to test his mettle in the crucible of combat. Inspired by patriotism and a sense of justice, he prods the Captain for the required transfer. He is finally granted his wish, earns his dream, and perishes in combat. Garson Kanin's *Born Yesterday* (1946) also enjoyed a significant run on Broadway, with 1,642 performances. The play depicts the romance of Harry Brock, an overbearing lug who made his fortune as a junkman, and his wife, Billie Dawn. Successful, he now wants to enter respectable society. But his wife's loud, working-class manners create problems (he, too, is not without boorish behavior). The play was mostly remembered for the hilarious performance of Judy Holliday, who brought a raspy, nasal twang and comic verve to the role of Dawn. Brock employs a liberal writer to teach his wife manners. Billie's wiseacre attitude was part of the period's "tough-talking dames" made popular in movies (Dawn's famous line in the play is when she tells Brock to "drop dead"). Other popular romantic comedies of the period include Moss Hart's frothy *Light Up the Sky* (1948), which pokes fun at the highs and lows of the backstage life of theatre people, and George Axelrod's *The Seven Year Itch* (1952), a teasing play about a man's "itch" for infidelity. N. Richard Nash's *The Rainmaker* (1954) and William Gibson's *Two for the Seesaw* (1958) examine female characters lacking self-confidence but who are persuaded by men to live up to their potential. However, the men prove insincere. The plays brought attention to two great American actresses, Geraldine Page and Anne Bancroft.

The theme of the outsider attempting to enter the mainstream is well represented by Arthur Miller's first successful play, *All My Sons* (1947). It portrays the Keller family and their role in manufacturing spare parts for the military during World War II. Joe Keller, the protagonist, is, in his words, "The beast! . . . the guy who sold cracked cylinder heads to the Army Air Force; the guy who made twenty-one P-40s crash in Australia."[12] Joe avoids prison by letting his partner, Steve Deever, take the fall for the faulty cylinder heads. Steve found the cracked cylinders during the night shift. He called his partner Joe at home for advice. Joe tells him to cover up the damage, and then denies having the conversation and sidesteps blame. He feigns illness as the reason why he avoided the shop that night. Joe, it turns out, refuses to accept responsibility. Speaking to his son Chris and Steve's daughter, Ann, he rationalizes: "It was a madhouse. Every half hour the Major callin' for cylinder heads, they were whippin' us with the telephone. The trucks were hauling them hot, damn near. I mean just try to see it human, see it human. All of a sudden a batch comes out with a crack. That happens, that's the business." He then lies; he in fact encouraged his partner to cover the cracked cylinders, but he says: "If I could have gone in that day I'd a told him – junk 'em, Steve, we can afford it. But alone he was afraid. But I know he meant no harm. He believed they'd hold up a hundred percent. That's a mistake, but it ain't murder. You mustn't feel that way about him. You understand me? It ain't right" (629).

Miller raises the stakes of the play by having one of Joe's sons missing in action. Joe's wife hopes that the son, Larry, will turn up. Chris, Joe's other son, loves Ann (Steve's daughter). Ann was supposed to marry Larry. By announcing their intentions to wed, Chris and Ann would ostensibly ring a death knell for Chris's brother – the marriage would admit to the mother that waiting for Larry is hopeless. Steve's son George, a lawyer, threatens to reopen the case against Joe to exonerate his father. Although Chris's mother protests the marriage, she will no longer shield her husband. Even though her son Larry never flew a P-40 (the specific planes damaged by the faulty cylinders), his likely death is equivalent to the death of all pilots. She says: "Your brother's alive, darling, because if he's dead, your father killed him" (646). Pressed by George and his own son Chris, Keller confesses at the end of Act II that he is a businessman who understands that if "you don't know how to operate, your stuff is no good; they close you up, they tear your contracts, what the hell's it to them? You lay forty years into a business and they knock you out in five minutes, what could I do, let them take forty years, let them take away my life? (*His voice cracking.*) I never thought they'd install them. I swear to God. I thought they'd stop 'em before anybody took off" (646–7). In a split second, Keller chooses to protect his family, but in doing so he sacrifices the lives of others. At the end of the play his son Chris says: "Once and for all you can know there's a universe of people outside and you're responsible to it, and unless you know that, you throw away your son because that's why he died" (653).

Miller brought to the forefront the conflict of individual greed and social responsibility. Pressing home the point of social responsibility as a supreme value, Miller shows what happens to society when this responsibility is ignored or forgotten. *New York Times* drama critic Charles Isherwood describes the upshot of Miller's play: "to sell your brother is to sell yourself."[13] Miller's entire work reaches out to the values of humanism, and more than any other modern playwright in America, Miller championed social realism rooted in Ibsen. Miller's realism exposes the manner in which capitalism rewards selfishness over altruism. His plays took firm hold because they objectively clarified social relationships against the reality of institutionalized avarice. By his own testimony, Miller was concerned with the "common man." Influenced by Henry Wallace's 1942 "century of the common man" speech quoted earlier, the "common man," Miller wrote in 1949, "is as apt a subject for tragedy in its highest sense as kings were."[14] His unrelenting advocacy of social responsibility was done in such a way as to reveal the plight of ordinary people facing moral choices. The point of realism, as Miller and others would have it, is to emphasize value judgment and ideological conflict. Miller's plays represent what the Hungarian Marxist Georg Lukács called the "new drama," in which "not merely passions are in conflict, but ideologies" as well. In this "modern" drama, Lukács contended, subjects are acted upon by the forces of history and antagonisms of individual and society are revealed through moral choices. The intention became one of showing that "History is meant as a substitute for mythology, creating artificial distance, producing monumentality, clearing away trivia and injecting a new pathos."[15] Even more than Soviet Socialist Realism, which Lukács had in mind, Miller's plays probe the essence of subjects who bear the consequences of history and resultant moral choice.

Tennessee Williams's *A Streetcar Named Desire* (1947) is likely his greatest play and one of the twentieth century's finest. Blanche, Williams's prototypical southern aristocrat fallen from grace, appears at her sister Stella's home in the French Quarter of New Orleans. She is broke, destitute, and at the end of the line. Ravaged by drink, she nonetheless exudes charm and appeal. She is on the verge of becoming what Amanda had warned of in *The Glass Menagerie* – the marginalized spinster – living on "crust of bread" handouts from unappreciative relatives. Unbeknownst to Stella, Blanche has lost their plantation home, used up the family inheritance (what little there was), and squandered her reputation as a high school English teacher by encouraging peccadilloes with teenage boys. Blanche arrives driven mad by guilt. Despite her sullied past, she is not without redemption; like Laura, she possesses poetic sensibility. She is the outsider, literally; her romantic sensitivity and distaste for crudity alienate her from the rough-and-tumble working class of New Orleans, and her brother-in-law in particular.

The narrative unfolds around the struggles between Blanche and Stella's husband, Stanley Kowalski, for Stella's "soul." Each fights to gain Stella's sympathy. Stanley epitomizes virility, masculine prowess, and boorish sensibility (made famous by Marlon Brando's visceral performance). For Stanley, sexual conquests grant him the right of ownership; his wife Stella represents a challenge to his ability to tame a social superior sexually. He has, as he says, removed Stella from her "columns" symbolic of her aristocratic upbringing (and evokes the replacement of one obvious phallic symbol for another). The play's opening tells all: Stanley brings home red meat for dinner and tosses it to Stella for cooking. Stanley is the hunter domesticating his clan (Stella is pregnant with his first child). He grows resentful of his intrusive sister-in-law, not merely because she is in his view a meddling in-law, but because she represents a much deeper threat. Blanche reminds Stella of their prior refinement and sophistication; Stanley's uncouth, slovenly manner and beer-drinking, poker-and-bowling nights – what Blanche calls a "party of apes" – offend (or should offend) Stella's past delicate sensibility. What Blanche cannot abide is Stella's voracious lust; Stella is lured by Stanley's red-hot sexuality. Blanche disapproves of the marriage and Stella's acceptance of Stanley's animal behavior, though she, too, is hardly unblemished.

The play conveys Blanche's inner world, while simultaneously depicting the struggle between Blanche and Stanley. Blanche is no saint, and herein lies the tragedy. She is aware of her transgressions, deceptions, and betrayals, especially that of her first husband. It is, in fact, this awareness that causes feelings of guilt. We admire her while accepting her imperfections. At first it appears that her condescension toward Stanley creates sympathy for him (and Brando's compelling performance has often been accused of tilting the scales too far to his side). The complexity of the conflict between Stanley and Blanche is testimony to Williams's craft. In this play, what is moral is, as in the case of Chekhov, ambiguous. It is only after Stanley crosses the line by raping that Blanche becomes recognizable as victim. All along, Blanche and Stanley's sexual chemistry and differing social backgrounds create an absorbing balancing act and subtext of both desire and loathing between them.

Blanche's past transgression, which occurred during her first marriage at the age of 16, is the basis of her anguish. She describes her young husband's suicide to Mitch. During the play Blanche woos Stanley's poker-night cohort and workplace colleague Mitch, whom she feels, despite his carousing, is "superior to the others." As their romance appears to grow, Blanche reveals her marriage: "There was something different about the boy, a nervousness, a softness and tenderness which wasn't like a man's, although he wasn't the least bit effeminate looking – still that thing was there."[16] The "thing" Blanche refers to is homosexuality. Blanche discovers her husband with an older man. At first she pretends ignorance; the three drive together to the "Moon Lake Casino, very drunk and laughing all the way." But her husband eventually leaves the dance floor and commits suicide (the sound of his gun shot repeats throughout the play). Blanche, dancing with her husband at the Casino, explains: "He'd stuck a revolver into his mouth, and fired – so that the back of his head had been – blown away. (*She sways and covers her face.*) It was because – on the dance floor – unable to stop myself – I'd suddenly said – 'I saw, I know! You disgust me . . .' And then the searchlight which had been turned on the world was turned off again and never for one moment since has there been any light that's stronger than this – kitchen – candle" (115). Blanche not only betrays the person she loved, she also betrays her ideals, succumbing to the crude homophobia and philistine insensitivity she detests.

Williams's self-consciously gritty and poetic language adheres to realism's certainty of time and space; Mitch and Blanche are at a specific place and it is evening in New Orleans. But the language is rich with symbolism. The candle Blanche describes, for example, epitomizes the beauty and delicacy she shares with Laura in *The Glass Menagerie*. Tom recalls Laura blowing out her candles; Blanche, too, remembers the dying flame. In both, a delicate light is extinguished, leaving only darkness and the roughness it conceals. Tom, Blanche, and Brick in *Cat on a Hot Tin Roof* (discussed below) have all betrayed someone who depended on them, and now must bear their guilty burden.

Blanche despises her own hypocrisy, and this honest self-awareness is what sets her apart. A Varsouviana and then a gunshot are heard in the background every time Blanche recalls the suicide, symbolizing her failure to live up to her moral creed. The background sound and poetic language elevate the melodramatic style of American drama to heretofore unexperienced levels. Arthur Miller summed it up best when he said that Williams "had pushed language and character to the front of the stage." *A Streetcar Named Desire*, he says, "was the fullest bloom of the vanished Group Theatre's intense, decade-long investigation into the Stanislavski Method; it was a form of realism so deeply felt as to emerge as a stylization."[17] Even Stanley's speeches, blunt and crude, are poetic. Stanley tries to convince Stella that Blanche should leave their home permanently. Stella, pregnant, runs from the house. Stanley grabs her: "When we first met, me and you, you thought I was common. How right you was, baby, I was common as dirt. You showed me the snapshot of the place with the columns. I pulled you down off them columns and how you loved it, having them colored lights going! And wasn't we happy together, wasn't it all okay till she showed up here?" (137). Williams's "colored lights" adds to the rich texture of language and symbols.

In the end Blanche feels her desperation tightening. Her betrayal and past transgressions come at a great cost: loss of job, reputation, home, and husband. She is an alcoholic and a liar; she leads Mitch on with notions of respectability when in fact she has been a prostitute. Yet Williams elicits our sympathy, because she does not deserve the anguish she undergoes. Like other great tragic figures – King Lear, for instance – Blanche is more sinned against than sinning. She misjudged, erred, and lied; but these very things make her all too human. When Stanley tells Mitch that Blanche is not the refined woman she pretends to be, Mitch is enraged. Blanche tries to explain: she was the caretaker for her Belle Reve home, sat at the bedside watching her mother, father, and other family members die, and watched as the estate went bankrupt. The cost of the plantation was too great, given, as she says, her "pitiful teacher's salary." Loneliness, the pain of watching progressive and prolonged illnesses, and the onset of poverty take their toll. As she speaks to Mitch, a street peddler selling flowers for the dead passes. The symbol of death is not merely in Blanche's mind, but brought to the fore by the cadence of the Spanish-speaking peddler. It brings Blanche to the brink.

BLANCHE: Death – I used to sit here and she used to sit over there and death was as close as you are . . . We didn't dare even admit we had ever heard of it!

MEXICAN WOMAN: *Flores para los muertos, flores – flores* . . .

BLANCHE: The opposite of desire. So do you wonder? How could you possibly wonder! (148–9)

Blanche conjures the Freudian conflict of desire (Eros) and death (Thanatos). She tries unsuccessfully to explain to Mitch how her self-indulgence kept death at bay. She prostitutes herself to affirm life over death. Her hedonism is not that of Stanley – his is born from machismo and self-assurance, hers from pain and guilt; his sexuality is overt, hers hides in darkness. They understand each other on the common ground of lust, but their desires come from very different places. In the end, Stanley uses brute force and rapes her on the night Stella gives birth to his child. His physical violence against Blanche tips the scales and leaves no doubt as to where the sympathy lies.

Beginning with *The Glass Menagerie* in 1945 throughout the 1950s, Williams enjoyed his greatest success. He was known for his lyrical dialogue, a mixture of Southern rhythms and poetic metaphors, and for his empathy for the underdog. In his major plays of this period, *Summer and Smoke* (1948), *The Rose Tattoo* (1950), *Cat on a Hot Tin Roof* (1955, perhaps his third greatest play), *Orpheus Descending* (1957), *Suddenly Last Summer* (1958), *Sweet Bird of Youth* (1959), *Period of Adjustment* (1960), *The Night of the Iguana* (1961), and *The Milk Train Doesn't Stop Here Anymore* (1963), Williams wrote about the derelict and forgotten, the over-the-hill movie star, the frustrations of life in a small town, and people's descent into madness. He challenged the bland moral certainty of the Eisenhower era, portraying characters risking ostracization to express their nonconformity. His dreamers and overly sensitive characters challenged American materialism, McCarthyism, and homophobia.

Williams's narrative can be described in terms of what David Savran calls the "guilty secret." For Savran, the homosexuality in *Cat on a Hot Tin Roof* or Blanche's culpability in the suicide of her gay husband reveals "the impossibility of its revelation during the 1940s and 1950s as anything other than the 'ugly truth.'" Williams was often gainsaid by public opinion to obscure his meaning, disrupting the logic coherence between what happened in the past and how it is described. As Savran says, the ambiguity of the past as told by the characters "seems to deny the primacy and intelligibility of that traumatic memory, both emphasizing and calling into question the determination of the present by a moment in the past." By disrupting the relationship between past (memory) and present (description), Williams's plays "tend to undermine the purely linear and irreversible temporal progression on which [Arthur] Miller's plays, and American realism in general, depends."[18] While correct up to a point, Savran makes far too much of a difference between Miller and Williams. Williams's plays hardly undermine "irreversible temporal progression" (Stanley's last line to Blanche occurring just before he rapes her, "We had this date from the beginning," underscores the temporal progression). Miller's characters share in guilty secrets (Joe Keller's culpability in the broken spare parts is his "dirty secret," and Willy's infidelity is his), and even their emotional releases, like the characters in Williams's plays, are hardly simplifying.

Arthur Miller's *Death of a Salesman* (1949) is one of America's defining dramas. In the play (originally titled *The Inside of His Head*), Willy Loman is an aging traveling salesman unable to keep pace. Like Blanche, he is facing old age in a culture that celebrates youth, and like Blanche he is failing financially. His sales are nil, becoming a burden rather than an asset to his company. His adult sons, Biff and Hap, have also failed to achieve the American Dream; though both showed promise in their youth, they are in their mid-thirties and adrift. Hap, known by his teenage name "Happy," is a ne'er-do-well, working as a shipping clerk, a philanderer with women, and living off assistance from his father. Biff, a former high school football star, is now a drifter, living in the West from ranch to ranch, and from jail to jail for his perpetual shoplifting. Both brothers are adolescents in perpetuity. Linda Loman, Willy's wife, tries desperately to hold the family together.

What sets the play apart is the emotional tug of the family, the social background, and the play's structure, which is anything but linear. Miller arranges the sequence of the dramatic action in three accompanying parts: present, flashback, and fantasy. In the present, the narrative occurs during Willy's premature return from a New England sales tour owing to exhaustion and suicidal thoughts. Biff visits at the behest of Linda, who fears for Willy's life. Willy is unable to endure the rigors of travel; his eyes are deteriorating and his stamina is dissipating. Interspersed are Willy's flashbacks, in which Biff, Happy, Linda, and other characters appear. Life then held hope. Like *The Glass Menagerie*, *Death of a Salesman* is a "memory" play. As Willy recalls, Biff was the football hero, Hap was the irresponsible younger brother (who carries a resentment for being the "second" son), while Linda was doting and dutiful. Willy bolsters his claims to success, but even in the flashbacks the Lomans live on what O'Neill would call "pipe dreams." Willy hardly earns as much as he says, and the future they envision is more illusion than reality. The third part of the narrative depicts Willy's fantasies. Willy conjures up his brother Ben, who left the family when Willy was a child. Ben went to Alaska and earned a fortune (whether this is true or not is deliberately uncertain). Ben epitomizes the American Dream: fortune through adventure, success follows initiative, and entrepreneurialism and audacity are required. Willy's imagination feeds on this illusion of the pioneering spirit; failure to attain it encourages his self-effacement and demise.

The designer Jo Mielziner did for *Death of a Salesman* what he did for *The Glass Menagerie*, creating a one-unit set that enabled the reality, flashback, and fantasy to coexist theatrically. Mielziner jettisoned the idea of an interior kitchen typified by "fourth-wall realism" (three actual walls and an imaginary "fourth wall" downstage, allowing the audience the sense of eavesdropping on the performers). Instead, he limned merely the frames of the house without walls. Specifically, the brick wall of the alley in *The Glass Menagerie* and the leaves of the backyard in *Death of a Salesman* were projected rather than built, creating a unique sense of onstage spatiality. In *Death of a Salesman* especially, Mielziner employed a skeletal design. With merely implied walls, actors could move through the kitchen and bedroom smoothly, playing scenes in different stage areas representing different states of Willy's mind. This suggested movement not merely in space but in time as well. Time and space become fluid rather than fixed in static sequence. Harry Smith remarks that the original text of Miller's play lacked the skeletal setting; only after Mielziner's designs did Miller adjust his descriptions to incorporate the set designer's influence. Using similar "forestage, scrim transparencies" to those employed in *The Glass Menagerie*, Mielziner added projections for the flashback sequences. As a result, Smith writes, the "performance pace would not be impeded by traditional scene-change methods, and the stodgy stage structure of beginning-middle-end, in that order, would not strain the intricate and fragile dramatic texture."[19]

Mielziner facilitated the experience of disconnection. Like Amanda and Laura in *The Glass Menagerie*, and Blanche in *Streetcar*, Willy's retreat from reality exposes his deteriorating inner life. Mielziner's contribution allowed future playwrights to write dialogue and scenes with the possibility in mind of theatrically represented interiority. Williams and Miller were able not only to move scenes in the narrative from one locale to another, but also to effect psychological shifts from perception to recollection. The plays depict lower-middle-class life in physical and mental manifestation. Miller's stage directions note the "towering, angular shapes" in the backdrop, with "only a blue light of the sky" falling on the house at center stage. An "angry glow of orange" surrounds the area. As the lights come up, "An air of the dream clings to the place, a dream rising out of reality." Miller emphasizes that the entire set "is wholly, or in some places, partially transparent" (11). When the actors perform in the present, they honor the imaginary boundaries of the house; but when they enact Willy's thoughts, such details are ignored.

Willy begins the play defeated. His crestfallen and stooped appearance is ghostlike. His career is nil, his sons are loafers, and his future is bleak. Yet he fights on relentlessly, believing in the American Dream and that somehow, with ingenuity and fortitude, he or his sons will prevail. Yet he bickers endlessly with his son Biff. Biff has been privy to Willy's dark secret, the reason why Biff threw away his life. As a senior in high school, Biff has several college football scholarships. He is, however, failing math. Biff, who loves his father beyond measure, takes a train to Boston to find him on the road and seek his advice. He believes in his father's powers of persuasion; indeed, Willy, when he is at his best, has, like Hickey, the convincing persona and charm of a good salesman. Biff is counting on his father to convince the math teacher to pass him. Biff's arrival at the hotel unfortunately catches Willy in an affair with one of the secretaries he uses to get in good with his clients (one of the many symbolic motifs running through the play is "stockings" – Willy gives the women a pair, and throughout the play guiltily urges Linda to cease darning stockings that she cannot afford to replace). Witnessing this Biff self-destructs, throwing away his sports scholarships (even though he could have recovered the math class in summer school) and ceasing to engage in life.

Biff is a kleptomaniac, drawn to things and objects he cannot possess. Even when he was in high school and before the discovery of his father's infidelity, he walked off with footballs. Yet he accumulates things without reason; like his father, he is welded to an American

Dream of ownership. Biff is drawn to nature, and in this he mimics his father's love of gardening. Still, his alleged love of the outdoors is of little consolation; in the end he is as aimless as when he began. His brother also lacks ambition and acts out his frustrations by chasing one woman after another. Yet even his conquests are unsatisfying ("they're like bowling pins," he says). Both lead a joyless, purposeless life. The brothers concoct an idea of starting a sporting line business together, yet this proves to be bluster. Biff and Hap have learned from their father that being liked is essential to success. Willy is a blowhard, but it is the nature of a salesman to boast. In a flashback Willy describes how the mayor of Providence greeted him as his two sons gather before Willy's feet to listen. He compares himself to his neighbor, the self-employed Charley (the boys call him "Uncle Charley"), promising his sons that one day he will have his own business, too. But Willy will surpass Charley, because, as he says, "Charley is not – liked. He's liked, but he's not – well liked" (30). Charley's son, Bernard, is also "liked, but he's not well liked" (33), and thus Willy calculates that his sons will also surpass Bernard. But the façade of being "liked" is another of Willy's illusions. He stakes too much on "being liked" and is, at times, insufferable. In one of his many bouts of self-criticism, Willy realizes that he jokes too much, and says to his wife (in confidence and away from the boys): "I'm fat. I'm very – foolish to look at, Linda. I didn't tell you, but Christmas time I happened to be calling on F. H. Stewarts, and a salesman I know, as I was going in to see the buyer I heard him say something about – walrus. And I – I cracked him right across the face. I won't take that. I simply will not take that. But they do laugh at me. I know that" (37). Linda provides support, but even as she does we hear the laughter of Willy's mistress in the background. Miller uses the laughter in the way that Williams uses music and the gunshot in *Streetcar*, as a theatrical aurality underscoring guilty memories. The play's power is enhanced by the overlapping visual and oral manifestations of memory.

In contrast to Willy, Ben carries, in Miller's stage directions, "an authoritative air." Ben is "utterly certain of his destiny, and there is an aura of far places about him" (44). Ben is on the move; he is only passing through. Willy is the "traveling" salesman, but he is never more frozen in his ways. Ben is a man of destiny, representing the mover-and-shaker, the self-sufficient, triumphal individualist who has severed all ties to family in order to pave his fortune. Ben's story,

Willy fantasizes, is that of Horatio Alger, someone who rose from nothing to riches. Willy emulates Ben but lacks his killer instinct. For all his bluster, Willy fails to grasp the ruthlessness of business. It is uncertain if Willy ever had the attributes to even survive in business, let alone thrive. Willy is borrowing money from Charley in order to pay the mortgage. In admonishing her sons for failing to care about their father, Linda describes Willy: "I don't say he's a great man. Willy Loman never made a lot of money. His name was never in the paper. He's not the finest character that ever lived. But he's a human being, and a terrible thing is happening to him. So attention must be paid. He's not to be allowed to fall into his grave like an old dog. Attention, attention must be finally paid to such a person" (56). In his important study of Miller, Christopher Bigsby notes that *Death of a Salesman* "is not an attack on American values." While he concedes that the play is "an exploration of the betrayal of those values and the cost of this in human terms," *Death of a Salesman* ultimately does not "attack" the "American dream of Thomas Jefferson and Benjamin Franklin."[20] If Bigsby's analysis is correct, how does America incorporate Willy? If we are to "pay attention" to Willy as Linda implores, how are we to consider a genuine failure like Willy (or Amanda, Laura, Blanche, and Hickey) in a world that has little use for losers? The play attacks the American Dream largely because it takes seriously the fact that some-one is worth more dead than alive. "Life is money," Walter Lee Younger says in *A Raisin in the Sun*, and in both plays death is money, too.

In the closing moments of the play, Willy has lost his job. Adding insult to injury, he is abandoned by his two sons in a restaurant while the boys pursue two women they picked up. Willy, feeling useless, looks for ways to make good for his boys. In his garden he talks to his imaginary brother Ben, saying: "A man can't go out the way he came in, Ben, a man has got to add up to something" (125). Ben tries to interrupt, but Willy continues. He considers suicide, with twenty thousand dollars life insurance going to his sons. Willy's death has become a commodity, defined in round figures ("on the barrelhead," he says). Raymond Williams put it best: "Willy Loman is a man who from selling things has passed to selling himself, and has become, in effect, a commodity which like other commodities will at a certain point be discarded by the laws of the economy." In this way, Willy "brings tragedy down on himself, not by opposing the lie, but by living it."[21] Willy visits his boss, Howard, in the hopes that Howard might take him off the road so he can sell closer to home. Howard, though much younger, condescendingly refers to Willy as "Kid." He impatiently dismisses Willy. Willy inveighs against Howard's treatment. Howard attempts to leave but Willy stops him, saying: "You mustn't tell me you've got people to see – I put thirty-four years into this firm, Howard, and now I can't pay my insurance! You can't eat the orange and throw away the peel – a man is not a piece of fruit!" (82). Miller remarked in his autobiography, *Timebends*, that during the opening night of *Death of a Salesman* an audience member approached him "outraged," calling the play a "time bomb under American capitalism." Miller said: "I hoped it was, or at least under the bullshit of capitalism, this pseudo life that thought to touch the clouds by standing on top of a refrigerator, waving a paid-up mortgage at the moon, victorious at last."[22]

As much as an indictment of capitalism, the play is also a deeply emotional drama about father–son relationships. In the final scene of Act II, Biff and Willy confront each other. Biff brings up the rubber tubing that Linda has discovered in the basement, evidence of Willy's intent to commit suicide. Willy turns the tables, confronting Biff for his despondency and wasted life, accusing him of throwing away his potential for "spite." The exchange between father and son is painful yet powerful.

> WILLY: (*With hatred, threateningly.*) The door to your life is wide open!
> BIFF: Pop! I'm a dime a dozen, and so are you!
> WILLY: (*Turning on him now in an uncontrolled outburst.*) I am not a dime
>   a dozen! I am Willy Loman, and you are Biff Loman! (132)

As they attack, Happy intercedes. But Biff continues, deflating the lies and exaggerations. This moving confrontation exposes both the truth and the love they share. Biff, in a moment of honest confession, says: "I am not a leader of men, Willy, and neither are you. You were never anything but a hard-working drummer who landed in the ash can like the rest of them! I'm one dollar an hour, Willy! I tried seven states and couldn't raise it. A buck an hour! Do you gather my meaning? I'm not bringing home any prizes any more, and you're going to stop waiting for me to bring them home" (132). In *Born Losers: A History of Failure in America*, Scott Sandage observes that Arthur Miller's *Death of a Salesman* "burned the contours of the doomed striver into our imagination." Sandage calls attention to the cover of the playbill and the original paperback edition of *Death of a Salesman*, both of which show Joseph Hirsch's portrait of Willy "from behind, a familiar silhouette, bent from years of lugging those heavy valises. He has no face because he has every face."[23] The crestfallen Willy carrying the weight of the world epitomizes the marginal figure in American life. In his biography of Miller, Martin Gottfried informs us that during rehearsals the director Elia Kazan and the actor playing Willy, Lee J. Cobb, remarked that Willy "was a *traveling* salesman," meaning "that he would be carrying a *second valise* packed with his clothes." Consequently, he carries two bags: "One heavy valise pulls a person down to the side. With two of them a bigger-than-life image was created, a man bent to the earth like a plow horse. . . . Backbreaking labor, carried out by an older salesman wearing a hat and suit, spoke for the working man in every man." The image of the burdened salesman's spine "loaded down with two valises would represent *Death of a Salesman* on its show cards (posters) and in advertisements, to be engraved on the consciousness of a generation of Americans forever."[24] (See figure 1.) His stooped spine and movement headed to the next appointment illustrates the American Sisyphus, eternally condemned to pushing a rock uphill.

If Willy's failing image is engraved in the American consciousness through his backbone, then James Tyrone in Eugene O'Neill's *Long Day's Journey into Night* (1956) and Big Daddy in Tennessee Williams's *Cat on a Hot Tin Roof* (1955) signify failure of the spirit. Both are rags-to-riches men, the former a Shakespearean actor turned matinee idol, the latter a plantation owner who owns some of the richest land along the Mississippi Delta. Superficially, both appear to be anything but failures. Still, Tyrone has failed as an actor, accepting stardom in a melodrama he repeated throughout his life rather than accepting more challenging roles. He tells his son, Edmund (representing O'Neill himself), what a great actor he once was. This after they observe Mary, Tyrone's wife, return to her dope addiction and Edmund's brother, Jamie, squander his life on booze. Tyrone is a character that reemerges throughout the Gilded Age: a self-made millionaire spiritually bankrupt. Big Daddy, too, rose from abject poverty to opulence. He managed the plantation owned by partners Jack Straw and Peter Ochello; when they died without an heir, they left him the land. Like Tyrone, Big Daddy worked and became rich, but, close to life's end, he wonders if it was worth it. He is dying of cancer (though at the start of the play

FIGURE 1   Arthur Miller's *Death of a Salesman* (Viking, 1949), drawing by
Joseph Hirsch. Reprinted by kind permission of the Joseph Hirsch Estate
and Penguin Books Ltd.

he is convinced he has been given a clean bill of health). Believing he will survive yet another ordeal, Big Daddy blusters and bullies his family assembled ostensibly to celebrate his sixty-fifth birthday. They have in fact gathered with his inheritance in mind. Like vultures, they descend for the pickings.

As the play begins, Brick suffers a broken leg and is drinking himself to death. A former football star, he broke his leg running hurdles while intoxicated. His self-destruction is motivated by the recent suicide of his closest friend and football soulmate, Skipper. Skipper, according to Brick's wife Maggie, had attempted a sexual liaison without success. Skipper then called Brick and let his homosexual desires be known. When Brick rebuffs his advance, Skipper commits suicide. Brick is traumatized; like Blanche in *Streetcar*, he has betrayed someone close. Like Blanche, he escapes guilt through alcohol (Blanche chooses promiscuity as well). Though Brick's feelings for Skipper are made deliberately ambiguous, Williams made it clear that their friendship was, in Brick's words, "pure." The relationship between Brick and his wife Maggie (referred to as the "cat") has been unsettled all along; Brick has always been closer to Skipper than to Maggie. Tension mounts because Brick's brother, Gooper, a lawyer and the father of five children Maggie calls "no-neck monsters," has his sights on Big Daddy's inheritance. Grandchildren mean a great deal to Big Daddy; Brick and Maggie have so far failed to produce them. Gooper (sometimes referred to as "Brother Man") and his wife Mae (called "Sister Woman"), despite being sycophants, are "good breeders." No one wants to tell Big Daddy that his death is imminent. They continue to deceive him. This deception is mocked by Brick, who throughout the play calls it "mendacity" – the lies we must live by. "Mendacity" is Tennessee Williams's rendering of O'Neill's "pipe dream."

Williams's play, loosely based on his 1952 short story *Three Players of a Summer Game*, is perhaps the finest example of American dramatic realism. It is tightly woven, performed in real place and time; it is set in one room, Brick and Maggie's bedroom, with action in real time. The two dramatic breaks for intermission are perfectly structured to coincide with the apex of dramatic conflict. It superbly choreographs a confrontational scene between Brick and Big Daddy in Act II, a scene in which each character peels away the "mendacity" and reveals the truths they hold: Big Daddy's mortality and Brick's alcoholism. Brick drinks till he hears the "click" in his mind, the moment when the booze subdues the mendaciousness and guilt. Brick blames Maggie for Skipper's death: "She took this time to work on poor dumb Skipper. He was a less than average student at Ole Miss, you know that, don't you?! – Poured in his mind the dirty, false idea that what we were, him and me, was a frustrated case of that ole pair of sisters that lived in this room, Jack Straw and Peter Ochello!"[25] Skipper, drunk, had called Brick, but Brick turned his back on his friend. Now Brick turns the spotlight on his father, knowing that Big Daddy is being charmed for his money while everyone continues the deception. When the truth emerges that he will die, Big Daddy is incredulous, but Brick reminds him: "Mendacity is the system that we live in. Liquor is the one way out an' death's the other" (694).

Maggie, like Williams's Amanda and Blanche, is a survivor. Unlike them, however, she is devoid of sentimentality. Born poor but strikingly attractive, Maggie uses her beauty to her advantage. Like Amanda and Blanche, she is also aware that beauty, in Blanche's words, "is a transitory thing." But unlike her predecessors, she is without illusion. Maggie's beauty will fade. She is a hardened realist who knows that time is against her. In her view, her husband is likely gay or at least so inclined. Brick denies this, but the denials are of little concern to Maggie. She makes this clear in her climactic speech at the end of Act I. Brick is enraged at Maggie for provoking Skipper. He tries to hit Maggie with his crutch but misses. Maggie explains she is unlike her husband; she cannot afford morality and admits to setting Skipper up for a purpose:

> MAGGIE: Missed me! – Sorry, – I'm not tryin' to whitewash my behavior, Christ, no! Brick, I'm not good. I don't know why people have to pretend to be good, nobody's good. The rich and the well-to-do can afford to respect moral patterns, conventional moral patterns, but I could never afford to, yeah, but – I'm honest! Give me credit for just that, will you *please*? – Born poor, raised poor, expect to die poor unless I can manage to get us something out of what Big Daddy leaves when he dies of cancer! But Brick?! – *Skipper is dead! I'm alive! Maggie the cat is –* (Brick hops awkwardly forward and strikes at her again with his crutch.) – alive! (674)

If Maggie can produce children she can rebut Gooper and Mae's claims to Big Daddy's fortune. She knows that Big Daddy loves Brick more than Gooper, and would prefer to offer the plantation to his favorite son over the smarmy pandering of Maggie's in-laws. But Big Daddy is unlikely to squander money to subsidize Brick's alcoholism. Big Daddy desires heirs, and unless Brick and Maggie can produce them, they are out of the loop. She tries seducing Brick, using every tactic she knows to keep the marriage afloat. Whether Brick is gay or not, she will do whatever it takes to avoid poverty in her old age.

Like Williams in *Cat on a Hot Tin Roof*, O'Neill examines the fraught relationships of family and the pressures to belong in a society regardless of its intolerance. In a 1940 letter to George Jean Nathan, O'Neill writes that his play *Long Day's Journey into Night* is the "story of one day, 8 A.M. to midnight, in the life of a family of four – father, mother, and two sons – back in 1912, – a day in which things occur which evoke the whole past of the family and reveal every aspect of its interrelationships." O'Neill adds that it is a "deeply tragic play, but without any violent tragic action. At the final curtain, there they still are, trapped within each other by the past, each guilty and at the same time innocent, scorning, loving, pitying each other, understanding and yet not understanding at all, forgiving but still doomed never to be able to forget."[26] Gerald Berkowitz considers *Long Day's Journey into Night* the likeliest candidate for "the single greatest American play" because "in this unflinchingly probing exploration of what it is like to be human, O'Neill exposes some of the most frightening truths about what we do to ourselves and each other, and then probes even deeper to find, in the horrors themselves, the means of surviving the horrors."[27] For raw power and emotional depth, few are its equal.

O'Neill's *Long Day's Journey into Night* (1956) and *A Moon for the Misbegotten* (1957) are plays joined by the author's own life experience: his actor father, trapped by success; his morphine-addicted mother; and his brother (the focus of *Moon for the Misbegotten*), who drowned his talents in alcohol. These plays are intimate quartets, not symphonies such as *The Iceman Cometh*. O'Neill examines the intimacies of, among other things, Irish Catholic fatalism and close family bonds that are both a blessing and a curse. O'Neill's universe is an unforgiving place in which the only protection is self-deception. The past is romanticized as a once loving world, where, if only the characters could return to it, they would find bliss. The "pipe dreams" of O'Neill's characters are severely tested by circumstances, and the masks people wear to conceal themselves are compensatory for personal shortcomings. The intimate details of each character's life reveal an unexpected largess; for O'Neill, each character represents something of a Greek tragedy. Their way of speaking unlocks the poetry of American vernacular; like Miller and Williams, O'Neill's language uncovers poetic idioms in American usage.

Arthur Miller's two plays *The Crucible* (1953) and *A View from the Bridge* (1955 as a one-act, 1956 as full length) attack the witch-hunting McCarthyism of the early 1950s. *The Crucible* examines the Salem witch-hunting trials of 1692 as a metaphor for the activities of Joseph McCarthy and the House UnAmerican Activities Committee (HUAC). John and Elizabeth Proctor dismiss Abigail Adams from their service for her promiscuity and love of John. In revenge she accuses Elizabeth of witchcraft (a metaphor for Communism). The hunt for Reds during the early 1950s is mirrored in the brutalization of Salem citizens of the late seventeenth century. John is ultimately tried for his refusal to confess. In the charged atmosphere of "naming names," Miller's *A View from the Bridge* focuses on the sexual desire of Eddie Carbone for his niece. When the family cousins arrive at their Brooklyn waterfront home as illegal immigrants, Eddie at first welcomes them. But when the younger of the two, Rodolpho, falls in love with his niece, Catherine, Eddie "drops a dime" on them (a metaphor derived from the pay phone, which cost a dime, to designate turning some-one in to the police). *A View from the Bridge* was Miller's response to the Bud Schulberg–Elia Kazan film *On the Waterfront* (1955), which endorsed naming names. Miller, however, made Eddie a sympathetic character, turning the protagonist's condition into a larger-than-life tragedy. Like O'Neill, Miller sought to inculcate Greek tragic themes into American drama.

William Inge has received less attention than his contemporaries. His plays, too, convey themes of an outsider trying to belong. His major works – *Come Back Little Sheba* (1950), *Picnic* (1953), *Bus Stop* (1955), and *The Dark at the Top of the Stairs* (1957) – concern such characters. Thomas Adler has rightly called Inge "the most significant dramatizer of the Midwest."[28] The Midwest is the setting for *Picnic*. Small-town life is interrupted by the entrance of Hal, a handsome drifter. He meets up with his old friend, Alan, who is engaged to Maggie. Alan is on the path toward a middle-class job. When he asks Hal what he wants to be, Hal says: "*(This is his favorite fantasy.)* Oh, something in a nice office where I can wear a tie and have a sweet little secretary and talk over the telephone about enterprises and things. *(As Alan walks away skeptically.)* I've always had the feeling, if I just had the chance, I could set the world on fire."[29] Alan's skepticism is justified; Hal is an irresponsible petty thief. He epitomizes a character who wants to belong but lacks the wherewithal. Perhaps more than any playwright of the period, Inge captures the meaning of people living "lives of quiet desperation." Although the term "quiet desperation" is now clichéd, at the time it had significance. In *Picnic* as in *Bus Stop* (his two best-known plays), Inge conveys the restless energy of people frustrated with the status quo. Just as Maggie eventually runs off with Hal, Cherie, a "chanteuse" portrayed by one of the great American actresses, Kim Stanley, eventually runs off with Bo Decker. Bo, a high-testosterone, bronco-busting cowboy, meets Cherie in a small-town roadside diner during a snowstorm. The play is also noteworthy for its underlying homoerotic relationship between Bo and his cowboy pal, Virgil.

Five plays from this period deserve mention for their delicate portrayal of the outsider. Carson McCullers's *The Member of the Wedding* (1950, based on her novel) looks at the three-way relationship of Berenice, a black woman caretaker (played by Ethel Waters) of two children, Frankie Adams (played by Julie Harris) and John Henry West. It takes place in rural Georgia, and is Frankie's coming-of-age story. Frankie, age 12, is a lonely girl whose only friendships are Berenice and John Henry. Robert Anderson's *Tea and Sympathy* (1953), like *Cat on a Hot Tin Roof* two years later, takes up the issue of homophobia. Tom Lee is ridiculed at boarding school for lack of aggressiveness. This treatment continues until Laura, wife of the headmaster, takes notice of him. Their relationship counters the accusations of homosexuality, and the play affirms the status quo of heterosexuality. *Inherit the Wind* (1955), written by Jerome Lawrence and Robert E. Lee, dramatizes the real-life Scopes trial of 1925. The story is one of a biology teacher, John T. Scopes, accused of promoting the anti-Biblical lessons of Darwin's theory of evolution. The highlight of this courtroom drama is the conflict between William Jennings Bryan, defender of creationism, and the nation's leading defense lawyer, Clarence Darrow, working on behalf of Scopes. The debate over teaching evolution versus creationism persists to this day. Archibald MacLeish's *J. B.* (1956) is a verse play depicting the surreal adventures of Job (J. B.), who loses everything in his search for God. Another subject of history, the life of Helen Keller is the theme of William Gibson's *The Miracle Worker* (1959), but the major character in this play is Annie Sullivan (played by Anne Bancroft), Keller's teacher.

In 1954 the Supreme Court declared racial segregation illegal, eliminating the "separate but equal" decree of *Plessy v. Ferguson* in 1896. However, the decision had only moderate effect at the outset. White resistance, in fact, hardened. Opportunity remained unavailable and racial discrimination produced widespread poverty. The ideals of the American Dream boomeranged; it became evident that the liberty and opportunity fought for in World War II were still denied. Lorraine Hansberry's *A Raisin in the Sun* (1959) conveys a powerful social message based on these realities. The play portrays a black family living in Chicago's South Side during the 1950s and seeking to improve their condition. One facet of the play is the desire to relocate to another neighborhood. After World War II there was no greater struggle in racial conflicts than that over urban space, particularly housing. This was true in virtually every city, but it was especially true of Chicago. In 1947 (twelve years before the play was produced), Chicago's South Deering Improvement Association helped enforce segregation. Blacks attempting to move into the predominantly white Trumbull Park neighborhood were met with violence. Arnold Hirsch reports in his book, *The Making of the Second Ghetto: Race and Housing in Chicago, 1940–1960,* that "the housing issue" continually disrupted the city's peace. In the years immediately following World War II, Hirsch notes: "Chicago endured a pattern of chronic urban guerrilla warfare." Racially motivated zoning laws during the 1940s, "carried out with government sanction and support," fueled a situation creating racial tension.[30]

Raisin takes up the desire of a family seeking to improve its lot through education (Beneatha), business (Walter Lee), and moving to a better neighborhood (Lena Younger). These concerns become interrelated by a single event: the anticipated arrival of ten thousand dollars. The death of Walter Younger, Sr., the family patriarch, is expected to provide the Younger family with life insurance money. Beneatha, the daughter, wants to use her share to become a doctor. Her brother, Walter Lee, frustrated by his dead-end chauffeur's job, dreams of owning a liquor store. Ruth, Walter's wife, is pregnant with another child and merely hopes to regain her husband's love. Lena Younger, mother of Beneatha and Walter Lee, wants to see the money invested in her grandson Travis. Lena describes herself as having "come from five generations of people who were slaves and sharecroppers" (396). She finally has the opportunity to purchase a new home in the Cylbourne Park neighborhood. But institutionalized segregation stands in the way.

When it comes time for the Youngers to move, a "friendly" white representative of the Cylbourne Park Improvement Association appears. The Association, representing the white community, sent the representative to the Youngers' apartment in hopes of buying back the home the Youngers are attempting to purchase. In this way the white neighborhood, as Walter Lee puts it, "won't have to live next to this bunch of stinking niggers!" (397).

The insurance check motivates the action of the play. The play itself belongs to a line of American dramas – *Awake and Sing!, Death of a Salesman* – that consider the value of life. Like *Death of a Salesman, A Raisin in the Sun* examines the role of money. The dreams of the children – Biff and Happy, Beneatha and Walter Lee – depend on the life insurance policy. Hansberry's social criticism is reflected in Walter Lee's comment: "This morning, I was lookin' in the mirror and thinking about it . . . I'm thirty-five years old; I've been married eleven years and I got a boy who sleeps in the living room – (*Very, very quietly.*) – and all I got to give him is stories about how rich white people live" (313). Walter Lee is thinking along the same lines as Maggie in *Cat on a Hot Tin Roof*: what must one do to escape poverty? Walter Lee's obsession with money and improving his family blinds him to a swindle he is about to undertake in acquiring the liquor store. He persuades his mother to hand over most of the money as down payment, but it turns out the plan is a hoax perpetrated by two "partners" who abscond with the cash.

A Raisin in the Sun takes up the issues of "participation" raised by Ralph Ellison's essay "The Negro and the Second World War" in the 1943 edition of *Negro Quarterly*. Ellison challenges the objectives of the war, described as a fight for democracy, at a time when blacks were afforded minimal recognition in their own country. Calling for "critical participation," Ellison writes that the "historical role of the Negro" is "integrating the larger American nation," thereby "compelling it untiringly toward true freedom."[31] Hansberry's observations on housing, class divisions within the black community, the generational conflicts, the struggle for economic empowerment, and the desire for human dignity while living in a money-driven society shape the play's social message of critical participation. This concept of "participation" runs through the plays of this era. With few modifications, Walter Lee's following speech could come from Tom in *Glass Menagerie*, Biff in *Salesman*, or Tennessee Williams's Amanda, Blanche, and Maggie:

WALTER: (*Quietly.*) Sometimes it's like I can see the future stretched out
in front of me – just plain as day. The future, Mama. Hanging over
there at the edge of my days. Just waiting for me. (*Pause.*) Mama –
sometimes when I'm downtown and I pass them cool, quiet-looking
restaurants where them white boys are sitting back and talking 'bout
things . . . sitting there turning deals worth millions of dollars . . . sometimes I see guys don't look much older than me –   (345)

While Walter Lee's concerns for his manhood, economic demands,
and race are crucial to the play, Beneatha's goals are of no less importance. She is wooed by a businessman, George Murchison, and an
African, Joseph Asagai. Murchison represents themes of the middle
class that are attractive to Beneatha, but Asagai represents her interest
in her heritage. George stands for the "facts" of life: money, career,
success. Asagai invokes Beneatha's spiritual values. At the play's conclusion it is important that Beneatha chooses neither, preferring to
keep open life's possibilities.

The centrality in *Raisin* of family relationships and topical social issues
typifies the American dramatic tradition of the 1930s, 1940s, and
1950s. The setting of the play projects the thrown-together quality of
a family living on the edge in the tenements of Chicago. The "kitchen-
sink" atmosphere so necessary in plays of this genre appears quite
genuine: dripping tap water, furniture that does not match, and walls
in need of repainting. The strength of *A Raisin in the Sun* relies as well
on performance depth and nuances. Walter Lee (portrayed by Sidney
Poitier) and his sister, Beneatha (played by Diana Sands), believe talent
and hard work ought to be rewarded. Though Walter Lee's interests
are professional and Beneatha's are related to education and spiritual
matters, both seek upward mobility. If America as an ideal represented
the possibility of such mobility – becoming wealthier, more spiritual,
happier, and feeling youthful – then the Younger family supplies this
ideal. This optimism helps create a family possessing vitality combined
with restlessness.

A Raisin in the Sun closes a chapter of great American plays dealing
with social justice. The yearning to bridge the economic divide is per-
sistently explored. The end of the war provided Americans with the
sense that their way of life had triumphed and the enjoyment of liberty
was sacrosanct. Playwrights examined in this chapter took it upon
themselves to show that this "triumph" was disingenuous unless all

could participate. Amanda, Laura, and Blanche, as well as the Loman, Tyrone, and Younger families, are willing and able to pitch into the new American triumphalist experience. They know that "money is life," but their efforts to obtain it are thwarted. Bruce McConachie observes that "Like Odets and other socialist playwrights from the 1930s, Hansberry used the specific language, cultural habits, and social situations of a particular ethnic group to suggest the dilemma of many groups at a similar stage of history. From her Popular Front perspective, the African American experience of the Younger family could be both particular and universal."[32] The same can be said of Williams, O'Neill, Miller, and Inge; each made the economic life of his characters a significantly motivating force. The playwright Tony Kushner, in his eulogy for Arthur Miller, said of him that he "created in his greatest play [*Death of a Salesman*] a drama in which it is impossible to avoid thinking about economics – money – in any attempt to render coherent the human tragedy unfolding before you." Miller's "great personal courage," Kushner adds, "allowed him to retain his sympathy, his affinity for the disinherited, the marginal and the powerless. He never wanted us to forget that without economic justice, the concept of social justice is an absurdity and, worse, a lie."[33] The same can be said of Hansberry; as Walter Lee puts it in *Raisin* (quoted at the beginning of this chapter): "it was always money, Mama. We just didn't know about it" (346). We now take up a new paradigm, making way for the rebellion that marked the 1960s and first half of the 1970s. Christopher Bigsby put it well when he said that in "1959 something was coming to an end."[34] That "something" was playwrights with a social conscience giving way to new sensibilities of drama.

CHAPTER 3

Reality and Illusion: American Drama, 1960–1975

MARTHA: *Truth and illusion, George; you don't know the difference.*
GEORGE: *No; but we must carry on as though we did.*
Edward Albee, Who's Afraid of Virginia Woolf? (1962)[1]

LULA: *And we'll pretend the people cannot see you. That is, the citizens. And that you are free of your history. And I am free of my history. We'll pretend that we are both anonymous beauties smashing along through the city's entrails.* (She yells as loud as she can.) *GROOVE!*
Amiri Baraka, Dutchman (1964)[2]

DONALD: *He could have been telling the truth – Justin could have lied.*
MICHAEL: *Who knows?*
Mart Crowley, Boys in the Band (1968)[3]

BILLY: *On no, Artie. If I ever thought you and Bananas weren't here in Sunnyside, seeing my work, loving my work, I could never work again. You're my touch with reality.*
John Guare, The House of Blue Leaves (1971)[4]

TAM: *Born? No! Crashed! Not born. Stamped! Not born! Created! Not born. No more born than the heaven and earth. No more born than nylon and acrylic. For I am a Chinaman! A miracle synthetic! Drip dry and machine washable.*
Frank Chin, The Chickencoop Chinaman (1972)[5]

JUAN: *Cupcake, you went past the money and blew it . . . yah, that's right, this is cop and blow . . . and you blew it becuz you placed yourself above understanding.*
Miguel Piñero, Short Eyes (1974)[6]

I've got one word for you, Benjamin . . . plastics.

Calder Willingham and Buck Henry,
The Graduate (Embassy Pictures, 1967)

Our attention now turns to American drama 1960 to 1975. Unlike characters examined in the previous chapter who longed to participate in the mainstream, the dramatists of this period wrote characters who challenged mainstream presumptions. The challenge was not merely supplemental to this period of American drama; it was its defining feature. The "consumer society," a common phrase of the 1960s, described a material abundance many dramatists regarded as spiritually bankrupt. Throughout the late 1940s and 1950s, consumer sovereignty obviated challenges to market-based economies; for dramatists it was a matter of bringing everyone to the table of affluence. Playwrights of the 1960s and early 1970s turned against a world of excessive consumption. The message typifying the rebellious 1960s and early 1970s was summed up by the one word from the film *The Graduate*: "plastics." Pillorying the "plastic" world of commercialization, a new insouciance arose. Although mainstream Broadway flourished, disaffected playwrights looked to nonprofit regional theatres and alternative Off- and Off-Off-Broadway. Jack Poggi reports that the Ford Foundation granted under half a million dollars to regional theatre in 1959, but in a mere three years Ford's donations increased to over six million.[7] Led by a number of theatres including the Arena Stage in Washington, DC, the Cleveland Playhouse, Houston's Alley Theatre, the Seattle Rep, Baltimore's Center Stage, and Minneapolis's Guthrie Theatre (appearing in 1963), innovative productions began to surface. Alternative groups such as Joe Cino's Caffé Cino, Ellen Stewart's La Mama, Al Carmines's Judson Memorial Church Theatre, Judith Malina and Julian Beck's Living Theatre, Woodie King's New Federal Theatre, Theatre Genesis, Negro Ensemble Company, Joe Chaikin's Open Theatre, Barbara Ann Teer's National Black Theatre, and the Robert MacBeth's New Lafayette Theatre in Harlem thrived in New York, created a theatre scene the likes of which had not been witnessed in New York since Greenwich Village's Provincetown Players of the 1910s. The San Francisco Mime Troupe contributed radically alternative work on the West Coast. The new movements sought change, yet goals were hardly homogeneous. Mathew Roudané asserts that "There was no one single, unifying troupe, movement, or playwright responsible for launching *the* American theater circa 1960." Rather, the "volcanic confluence of public issues and private tensions" yielded a "particular ambivalence and intensity."[8] Despite the diversity, dramatists possessed a common iconoclasm summed up in the popular phrase "polymorphously perverse." Beat poetry, rock 'n' roll, Motown, pop art, abstract expressionism, experimental drugs, disability rights, feminism, Civil Rights movements, anti-Vietnam War protests, and the deep social fissures of American politics were watershed events. Ruby Cohn comments that during the 1960s, "Revolt seethed Off-Off-Broadway."[9]

Many of the dramatists were influenced by the European "absurd." Martin Esslin described this post-World War II movement which "strives to express its sense of the senselessness of the human condition and the inadequacy of the rational approach by the open abandonment of rational devices and discursive thought." Its operating assumption was that "what *happens* on the stage transcends, and often contradicts, the *words* spoken by the characters."[10] Although each playwright was unique, many stressed incomprehensibility, irrationality, and oblique patterns onstage. Incorporating the playfulness of many European absurdist playwrights such as Samuel Beckett, Jean Genet, Friedrich Dürrenmatt, and Eugène Ionesco, American dramatists turned the absurd into political statements. This was particularly true of plays such as *The Zoo Story, Dutchman, Who's Afraid of Virginia Woolf?, House of Blue Leaves, Funnyhouse of a Negro, Luv,* and *Short Eyes.* These dramas and playwrights tended to downplay purposelessness in favor of social activism. For example, in his brief one-act play *FAM and YAM* (1960), Edward Albee, arguably the era's most influential playwright, presents two characters: YAM, which stands for "Young American Playwright," who wants to meet FAM, "Famous American Playwright." YAM visits FAM's home in order to convince FAM to help compile a list of "enemies," people determined to maintain the theatre's status quo. YAM wants change. FAM feels that he, too, might be on this list. FAM gets drunk, saying at the end: "The new generation's knocking at the door. . . . You youngsters are going to push us out of the way."[11] The playwrights altered the direction of American drama by embracing absurdism and *théâtre engagé* – dramas undertaken for social purpose.

Three plays – Edward Albee's *The Zoo Story* (1959, premiering in America in 1960), Jack Gelber's *The Connection* (1959), and Arthur Kopit's *Oh Dad, Poor Dad, Mamma's Hung You in the Closet and I'm Feelin'*

So Sad (1962, sarcastically subtitled "A Pseudoclassical Tragifarce in a Bastard French Tradition") – are the acknowledged trendsetters. Gelber's *The Connection* was inspired by the Beat poets of the 1950s by incorporating jazz and the avant-garde through a realistic setting. The play concerns drug addicts awaiting their dealer, Cowboy, while at the same time a filmmaker is making a documentary (creating a "play within a play" scenario). Directed by Judith Malina and designed by her husband, Julian Beck, both of whom emerged as leaders of the influential Living Theatre, the play's inaction – drug addicts waiting for their fix – is linked conceptually to the inertia of the European absurdists. Kopit's play is farcical. Madame Rosepettle carries her husband's dead body to a resort in Havana and hangs him in the closet. Reminiscent of Christopher Marlowe's English Renaissance two-part play *Tamberlane* (a king who keeps his dead queen incased wherever he goes), Rosepettle crates her husband's corpse wherever she goes. The play trades on the grotesquery of familial relationships. In the spirit of the absurd, it features Venus flytraps eating humans and one character that eats cats. The belligerent Rosepettle harasses hotel clerks as well as her stammering son, Jonathan. In a "bedroom farce" scene, the Commodore tries to seduce Rosepettle. He asks about her late husband. Rosepettle asks if he would like to see him. The Commodore takes this to mean a photograph. Rosepettle: "No, my husband. He's inside the closet. I had him stuffed. Wonderful taxidermist I know. H'm? What do you say Commodore? Wanna peek? He's my favorite trophy. I take him wherever I go."[12] Along with Albee's *Zoo Story*, three additional plays – Amiri Baraka's *Dutchman*, Adrienne Kennedy's *Funnyhouse of a Negro*, and Murray Schisgal's *Luv* – represent a turning point in American drama.

Albee's plays address, among other things, bourgeois values and societal connections. His first play, *Zoo Story*, premiered in Germany in 1959 along with Samuel Beckett's one-act *Krapp's Last Tape*. The doubling with Beckett is hardly serendipitous; Albee's *Zoo Story*, along with his other early plays *The Sandbox* and *The American Dream*, are conceptually linked to Beckett and the absurd. However, the link is not a comfortable one. Christopher Bigsby provides three reasons why American theatre is "ill-suited" to the absurd: "its actor training was committed to psychological veracity, its theatrical tradition at odds with the absurd's denial of social conflict," and "more fundamentally," absurdism "was in radical conflict with basic American myths having to do with the integral self and the inevitability of progress."[13] Apart from an overemphasis on actor training (actors rarely spearhead cultural movements), Bigsby pinpoints American theatre's discomfort with the surreal because Americans retain a sense of possibility and they consider drama a guide to understanding. Europeans experience limitations resulting from the fixity of social classes. Hence, European dramas reflect the futility of resistance and the limits of action. By contrast, the quintessential American iconoclast of the 1950s and 1960s, the writer Jack Kerouac, personifies the "get-up-and-go" exhilaration of being on the road. No matter how absurd reality can be, Kerouac and other Beats assert the power to change things. Society is flexible, and dramas are meant to reflect this adaptability. American dramas also emphasize the social because audiences consider drama socially symbolic; disassociating drama from the world violates perceived objectives of drama. W. T. Lhamon remarks on this, saying that American artists rely on social connections just as they absorb mid-twentieth-century abstract art. "In painting and fiction, jazz and rock 'n' roll, drama and film, poetry and photography," Lhamon contends, the artistic movement in America was inclined "to extend formal sophistication achieved under modernism, but also to regain social connection."[14] Despite the success of Jackson Pollock, Barnet Newman, Mark Rothko, Adolph Gottlieb, Willem De Kooning, and other abstract expressionist painters, American art and drama maintain adherence to social relevancy. Albee's *Zoo Story* is one good example.

The Zoo Story takes place in Central Park during a summer afternoon. At the opening is Peter, a middle-aged, upper-middle-class publisher of textbooks. He sits on a bench reading. He takes seriously his Sunday stroll through Central Park, anchoring himself to the same bench. Peter's goals are success, happiness, children, wife, pets, status, and most of all the certainty of routine. Jerry follows, and for an hour he harasses Peter. The hyperactive Jerry is everything Peter is not: derelict, profligate, transient, itinerant, beatnik, and orphan. Jerry seems irrational, prone to freewheeling tirades along with inchoate descriptions. His actions express his desperation. Jerry seeks Peter's companionship, but Peter is suspicious. Jerry's condition is epitomized by his description of two empty picture frames in his squalid apartment. Peter's sanitized world contrasts starkly against Jerry's emptiness. Whereas Peter visits the bench for privacy, Jerry goes to the zoo seeking companionship. Jerry's opening line, "I've been to the zoo," is meant to startle Peter;

Jerry repeats the line and finally shouts it. He becomes antagonistic, challenging Peter's right to sit on the bench. Jerry finally becomes violent. Amidst the struggle, Jerry impales himself on the knife Peter holds.

Characteristic of the play is its use of the "extended monologue" (Kopit's play also uses an extended monologue, a "bedtime story" in which Madame Rosepettle describes why she did away with her husband). Albee breaks from the traditional use of conversation, introducing a diatribe. The extended monologue is inspired in part by jazz "riffing." Characters in the dramas of this period often shatter conventional conversation by launching into solos. Jerry's extended monologue, which he himself calls "THE STORY OF JERRY AND THE DOG," highlights his volatile and aimless life. The dog threatens Jerry on the stairwell whenever he passes his landlady's apartment. For revenge, Jerry inserts rat poison in the dog's hamburger. The dog becomes ill but survives. Following the ordeal the dog acknowledges grudging respect. Jerry describes his new-found relationship: "I have learned that neither kindness nor cruelty by themselves, independent of each other, creates any effect beyond themselves; and I have learned that the two combined, together, at the same time, are the teaching emotion. And what is gained is lost. And what has been the result: the dog and I have attained a compromise; more of a bargain, really. We neither love nor hurt because we do not try to reach each other."[15] At the close of the play, Jerry usurps Peter's sole right to occupy the bench. The struggle over the bench symbolizes ownership and authority. For Peter, the bench signifies his collectables; along with his wife, two daughters, two birds (two of everything, like Noah and his ark), the park and bench are his possessions. Albee's message is that any evaluation of authority must include the dynamic of power and how it comes to be. Albee accents the political through Peter's faith in his world and Jerry's threat. Peter's precarious sense of security is made evident by Jerry's confrontation to his moral authority.

Evident in Amiri Baraka's 1964 play is a critique of the middle class. *Dutchman* shared its opening in a double bill with Albee's *American Dream* (see figure 2). The play unfolds as a subway ride in which Lula, a white woman, meets Clay, a black man. The bodacious Lula targets Clay for his bourgeois appearance. Clay is, in many ways, a hybrid resembling both Walter Lee and Beneatha of Lorraine Hansberry's *A Raisin in the Sun*: Beneatha typifies intellectual striving and Walter Lee

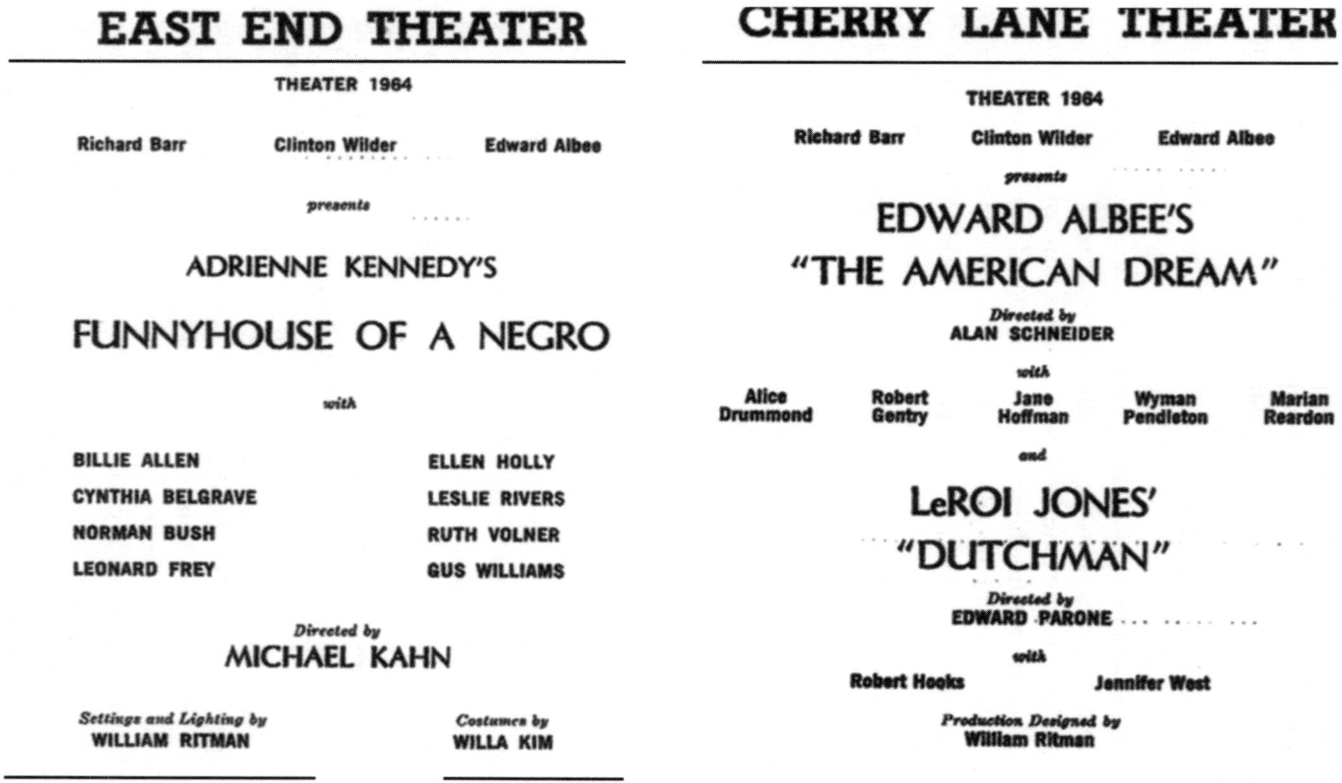

CHERRY LANE THEATER

THEATER 1964

Richard Barr   Clinton Wilder   Edward Albee

presents

EDWARD ALBEE'S
"THE AMERICAN DREAM"

Directed by
ALAN SCHNEIDER

with

Jane Hoffman   Wyman Pendleton   Marian Reardon

and

LeROI JONES'
"DUTCHMAN"

Directed by
EDWARD PARONE

with

Alice Drummond   Robert Gentry   Robert Hooks   Jennifer West

Production Designed by
William Ritman

EAST END THEATER

THEATER 1964

Richard Barr   Clinton Wilder   Edward Albee

presents

ADRIENNE KENNEDY'S
FUNNYHOUSE OF A NEGRO

with

BILLIE ALLEN   ELLEN HOLLY
CYNTHIA BELGRAVE   LESLIE RIVERS
NORMAN BUSH   RUTH VOLNER
LEONARD FREY   GUS WILLIAMS

Directed by
MICHAEL KAHN

Settings and Lighting by   *Costumes by*
WILLIAM RITMAN   **WILLA KIM**

FIGURE 2 Playbills, author's collection, courtesy of the Hatch-Billops Collection.

business ambition. Clay personifies both attributes as well as assimilation. Like Peter in *Zoo Story*, he conceals himself behind his conformity, with a significant difference: Clay's bourgeois behavior does not obscure his blackness. Lula exposes his façade through shrill but effective confrontation. She makes use of her sexuality and audacity to penetrate Clay's defenses. She inveighs against Clay's need for acceptance, using epithets and even racial slurs. What Jerry does to Peter, Lula does to Clay: they both challenge the comfortable life.

Dutchman takes up what it means to be black in a culture that holds out the promise of success at a cost. The play also follows the patterns of the theatre of the absurd, calling attention to theatricality and artifice. Lula orchestrates Clay's behavior, instructing him on what to say and how to say it much like a director does with an actor. She is choreographing his "blackness," illustrating, in existential fashion, how his put-on whiteness is mere embellishment. She illuminates Clay's bourgeois surface appearance (mocking his Ivy League suit and tie, close-cropped haircut, and way of speaking), while simultaneously instigating him. She forces out his hidden "self," the underlying reality of his blackness. Clay's identity buried behind layers of middle-class accoutrement is exposed as a façade by Lula's facetious and lubricious confrontation. She compels Clay to observe the price he pays for his appetite to devour the symbol of white civilization: sex with a white woman, which represents the ultimate inculcation of mainstream success. The play, Baraka says, "is not just a tale about being seduced by a white woman; it's a tale about the kind of seduction the black middle class, particularly black intellectuals, experience."[16] Baraka critiques middle-class African Americans all too willing to abandon their heritage and cater to liberals. When Lula provokes Clay to the breaking point, he explodes into an extended monologue, revealing just how little Lula knows about him. She understands the surface appearance, but cannot comprehend what he calls "the pumping black heart." Baraka frames Clay's monologue in a way consistent with saxophonist John Coltrane's rendition of *My Favorite Things* recorded in 1960. Coltrane's version of this popular tune begins by following the conventional melody. He then departs from convention with an improvisatory "riff." Baraka describes Coltrane's artistry as diverging from the funky, "hard bopper" aesthetics of Miles Davis while moving in the direction of "bebop." Players like Coltrane, Thelonious Monk, and Sonny Rollins, Baraka says, "literally scream and rant in imitation of the human voice, many times like the unfettered primitive shouters." During his solo, Coltrane in particular "attacks each chord and seems to almost want to separate each note of the chord (and its overtones) into separate entities and suck out even the most minute musical potential."[17] Similarly, Clay's splintering melody and volatile screed mark his own auditory breakout. Clay wishes to destroy the very convention of dialogue: "I'll rip your lousy breasts off!" Clay shouts. He defends his complacency: "Let me be who I feel like being. Uncle Tom. Thomas. Whatever. It's none of your business" (34). Clay's extended monologue swings from invective to defensive; like Coltrane, he attacks and retreats. Clay evokes familiar associations with another jazz icon:

> CLAY: Charlie Parker? Charlie Parker. All the hip white boys scream for Bird. Bird saying, "Up your ass, feeble-minded ofay. Up your ass." And they sit there talking about the tortured genius of Charlie Parker. Bird would've played not a note of music if he just walked up to East Sixty-Seventh Street and killed the first ten white people he saw. Not a note! And I'm the great would-be poet. Yes. That's right. Poet. Some kind of bastard literature. (35)

Clay tries to hide behind his smile. He nods obsequiously and writes poetry. The poet Paul Laurence Dunbar wrote in 1895: "We wear the mask that grins and lies," symbolizing the disguise required for survival. In 1935 Zora Neale Hurston described something similar, what she called "feather bed" resistance: "the Negro, in spite of his open faced laughter, his seeming acquiescence, is particularly evasive. . . . We smile and tell him or her something that satisfies the white person because, knowing so little about us, he doesn't know what he is missing."[18] Clay, too, wishes the same. Like Peter, he masks his feelings and seeks a reputation as an intellectual above the fray. But Baraka will not let him off the hook. Clay pays with his life – in the end Lula calls on all the train passengers to kill Clay using knives. Clay's body is tossed from the train; the unexpected murder is in keeping with the absurdist notion of the improbable. Once Clay is disposed of, another middle-class black enters. Like Clay, he seeks acceptance and acquiescence. He steps onto the train, Lula saunters to him, and the play ends. The cycle, Baraka is suggesting, will repeat until African Americans cease "riding the train."

Albee and Baraka seek to outrage the bourgeoisie by demonstrating that their protective insularity and precious interiority are a shell. They pit shock against complacency, using violence to shatter the illusion of middle-class security. Not only do Albee and Baraka strip off the bourgeois façade, they attempt to create theatre as a place for reevaluating norms. Their plays are set in New York locations that appear ordinary; a Central Park bench and the New York subway hardly deviate from the commonplace. Yet Albee and Baraka challenge the ordinary through extended monologues, surprise violence, and irrational behavior. They elucidate the entrapment entailed by middle-class experiences. *Dutchman* accentuates motion; the train represents Clay's fateful journey. Peter and Clay have buried their undeveloped talents and sacrificed their inner selves in routine and appearances. They have swallowed pride in order to secure a place in the food chain. Jerry and Lula, who begin as strangers to Peter and Clay, become provocateurs. Pushed to the edge, Clay warns Lula that her instigation may unleash more than she bargained for. He draws from another jazz icon, Bessie Smith, who, according to Clay, would have killed every white person she could if she merely tossed aside her façade: "If Bessie Smith had killed some white people she wouldn't have needed the music. She could have talked very straight and plain about the world. No metaphors. No grunts. No wiggle in the dark of her soul. Just straight two and two are four. Money. Power. Luxury. Like that. All of them. Crazy niggers turning their backs on sanity. Murder. Just murder! Would make us all sane" (35).

Adrienne Kennedy's *Funnyhouse of a Negro* (1964), produced by Edward Albee (see figure 2), radically departs from dramaturgical tradition. It avoids the certainty of plot in order to experiment with language, mask, and theatricality. Kennedy's main character, Negro Sarah, appears in four locations: Queen Victoria's bedchamber, the Duchess of Hapsburg's chamber, a Harlem hotel, and the jungle. Sarah may or may not have killed her father; the deliberate illogical quality of the play makes this difficult to ascertain. Like August Strindberg's *A Dream Play* (1901), *Funnyhouse* occurs in Negro Sarah's dream-state framed by an amusement park "Funnyhouse." Sarah's world is disorienting and fragmentary. Characters wear wigs, whiteface masks, and move about in a ghostly vacuity. The play is simultaneously a dream, an expressionist drama, and theatre of the absurd. The plot can be described as follows: Sarah is a student living with her Jewish boyfriend, Raymond, in a Harlem hotel room. Her mother is a light-skinned African American with straight hair, and her father is dark. Her parents' violent relationship has led to assault and rape. Along the way Patrice Lumumba, Jesus Christ, and Queen Victoria appear.

The "plot," however, is told to us in ways that leave everything open to question. Sarah lets it be known that events are suspect: "Mother loved my father before her hair fell out. A loving relationship exists between myself and Queen Victoria, a love between myself and Jesus but they are lies."[19] In the dream-like quality of the play, as with many of Kennedy's dramas such as *The Owl Answers* (1965) or *A Movie Star Has to Star in Black and White* (1976), the central characters are black women who struggle to unite their fragmentary identity. Kennedy's dramas follow a tradition set by Harlem Renaissance playwright Marita Bonner, whose plays *The Purple Flower* (1927) and *Exit: An Illusion* (1927) depict race relations as if in a fragmented dream. Characters are often in conflict with themselves, fighting internally their sense of belonging and not belonging, being a part of a racial minority but attracted to the majority. For Kennedy and Bonner, it is as if W. E. B. Du Bois's famous observation on "double consciousness" has provoked traumatic recollection. In *Funnyhouse* events are recalled in disturbingly violent flashbacks accompanied by amnesia; Negro Sarah sometimes remembers too much, sometimes not enough. The splintering memory is theatrically realized as characters in *Funnyhouse* move from role to role, repeat phrases said by others, and experience difficulty recognizing who and where they are. Bonner and Kennedy, as well as Suzan-Lori Parks during the 1990s, create dramas rejecting formulaic structures in favor of collage, cryptograms, and repetitive symbols. For Kennedy, madness, death, violence, and the negation of the self result from an insane world. Rationality in the face of frightful events – assassinations, deception, rape, war – often breaks down. Sarah tries to decipher the signs and symbols of violence. She speaks in extended monologues that try but fail to make sense of her volatile condition. *Funnyhouse*, Marc Robinson contends, "moves in spasms, exhaling long passages of confession then subsiding into a low rumble, as the characters consider and work over everything that has just been said, and test out images about to come forward in the next spasm of language."[20] One symbol appearing in spasm-like fashion throughout *Funnyhouse* is "hair." It is referred to by most of the characters as straight, kinky, flowing, or falling out. Negro Sarah lives on the border of two worlds – black and white – with hair texture expressive of her divided identity. Hair is institutive of most standards of beauty paraded throughout the media, and Sarah knows this.

If *Funnyhouse* considers Negro Sarah's angst over issues of race, Murray Schisgal's *Luv* (1964) examines the agony of Harry Berlin, who at the play's opening is seen contemplating leaping off a bridge. Like Sarah, the world, as the poet Wordsworth might say, is too much with him. Harry has lost the meaning of life; he drifts aimlessly; and he meets his old friend Milt, who graduated with him fifteen years ago.

> MILT: Well, how's it been going, Harry? Let's hear.
> HARRY: (*Mournfully.*) Awful, Milt; awful. It couldn't be worse. I'm at the end of the line. Everything's falling apart.
> MILT: (*Still perplexed.*) I don't get it.
> HARRY: The world, Milt. People. Life. Death. The old questions. I'm choked with them.[21]

Harry has tried everything to subdue his existential anguish. Milt tries to bring his old friend back from the brink. Love, Milt claims, is salvation, but not with his wife. Milt encourages Harry to take his wife Ellen. Ellen enters, holding a graph of their marriage with all the arrows pointing downwards. Eventually Harry and Ellen bond, but the relationship is short-lived. Ellen returns to her husband, and each returns to his or her neurosis. Referring to the title, Schisgal says: "The emotion of love has been perverted and misused to such an extent that it can only be defined by using another word [*Luv*] which comes closer to what we experience, to what we think, and how we behave." Love, he adds, "has become a commodity rather than an emotion."[22]

Schisgal's exploration of neurotic self-obsession is the bread and butter of modern American Jewish comedy. Jewish comedy is born of tragedy; if Miller's *Death of a Salesman* is the quintessential American Jewish tragedy – what Tony Kushner calls Miller's "lonely path" toward writing tragedy that is "Jewish in its demanding interiority" and possessing "faith that words have an awesome, almost sacred, power, force, weight"[23] – then Schisgal's *Luv* represents Jewish comedy (African American comedies do something similar: for example, George C. Wolfe's *The Colored Museum*, discussed in the next chapter). Self-obsession and intense analysis of the 1950s are satirized in 1960s

Jewish comedy, and the sanctity of the word – in Schisgal's case, "love" – is rendered absurd. Freudian psychoanalysis permeated American popular culture during the 1950s. Jewish playwrights of the period represented most prominently by Miller discovered in Freud and sometimes Marx a possible remedy for oppression. Schisgal turns this remedy upside-down, ridiculing Harry's self-indulgent breakdown. If Willy Loman's suicide is tragic, Harry Berlin's thoughts of suicide are absurd. Schisgal turns the sublime into the ridiculous. Influenced by the iconoclastic tummler Lenny Bruce, Schisgal opened the way for Jewish self-reflection by numerous playwrights such as Neil Simon, Wendy Wasserstein, Woody Allen, Israel Horovitz, Elaine May, Bruce Jay Friedman, and even Mel Brooks movies, television's *Seinfeld* of the 1990s, and Larry David's twenty-first-century HBO series *Curb Your Enthusiasm*.

Schisgal set the tone of Jewish existential comedy, but he was not alone in this. More conventional Jewish humorists Herb Gardner and Neil Simon also presented Broadway with acceptably rebellious Jewish characters. Gardner's *A Thousand Clowns* (1962) concerns a nonconformist, Murray Burns, forced to confront his bohemian lifestyle. Burns is a TV writer for a children's show called "Chuckles the Chipmunk" but quits. He adopts his precocious nephew, Nick, but in so doing must tidy up his "act." Much like Gardner's later *I'm Not Rappaport* (1985) and *Conversations with My Father* (1991), this play makes Jewish nonconformity the centerpiece. Neil Simon, too, makes nonconformity palatable to Broadway audiences, but unlike most authors, his success has dominated Broadway. His plays demonstrate well-shaped, tightly ordered narratives, with superb comic timing and concise plot developments. His TV experiences assisted him in shaping the length of a scene, as well as framing comic misunderstandings. He possesses an alert ear for common vernacular, especially for the wicked sarcasm of Jewish humor. Like the stylized English Restoration comic wits of the late seventeenth century (with whom Simon deserves comparison), he understands the importance of comic timing and the occasional bumptiousness required for slapstick. Wit and physical humor combine to stir up a comedic stew, a Jewish version of Oscar Wilde's pithiness and George Feydeau's farce. Among his many hits, *The Odd Couple* (1965) is a model of comedic situation, clever dialogue, and slapstick – for example, the tossing of linguini on the wall. However, Simon's mayhem never oversteps decorum exemplified by Marx Brothers-type anarchy. By comparison, his physical humor is tame. In the *Odd Couple*, two newly minted divorced men move in together. They are, as the title suggests, an odd couple: Oscar Madison is a sports writer and slob, Felix Unger is an obsessive-compulsive tidier. Like oil and water, their comic shenanigans are marked by scenes of cooking, cleaning, arguing, and seducing the "Pigeon Sisters," Gwendolyn and Cecily. Simon dominated Broadway with *Barefoot in the Park* (1964), *The Star-Spangled Girl* (1966), *Plaza Suite* (1968), *Last of the Red Hot Lovers* (1969), and other plays throughout the second half of the twentieth century.

Bruce Jay Friedman's *Scuba Duba* (1967) and *Steambath* (1970) pick up the thread of American Jewish absurdism. *Scuba Duba* takes place at a French resort château, where the protagonist, Harold Wonder, lost his wife to an African American scuba diver named "Frogman." His wife has since taken up with a black intellectual. Wonder is beset by numerous woes. His mother and psychiatrist nag. A bikini-clad nymphomaniac seductively prances around his abode. Wonder, however, is unable to consummate a relationship because he remains upset over his wife. The play is a Jewish nightmare, with Wonder confronting all the clichés: unobtainable sex, overbearing mother, anti-Semitic environment, guilt-inducing psychiatrist, and his liberalism challenged by African Americans having relations with his wife. *Steambath* examines narcissistic self-effacement among Jews in a steambath confronting God in the guise of a Puerto Rican attendant. Tandy, the protagonist, is a former policeman researching Charlemagne. This satire takes up the concept of Jews' ability to talk directly to God. The Puerto Rican "God" behaves more Jewish than the others (his name is Morty, his dialogue is spotted with Yiddish, and he obsesses over good lox).

A mixture of absurdity and reality, illusion and truth, farce and tragedy is condensed in Edward Albee's first full-length play, *Who's Afraid of Virginia Woolf?* (1962). It takes place during a late Saturday evening following a faculty party. George and Martha, husband and wife, return drunk and argumentative. George is an Associate Professor of the History Department at New Carthage, a small New England college. Martha is the daughter of the college President. Older than George, she considers her husband a failure who has not lived up to his potential. The play begins with her braying "What a dump!" Their marital problems are complicated by a list of factors stemming from childlessness and dissatisfaction. Martha and George are expecting a young visiting couple, Nick and Honey. Nick is a new faculty member for whom the party was held. Despite the late hour, an invitation to the home of the President's daughter is "required." Although it is obvious on their arrival that George and Martha (a pun on George and Martha Washington) are engaged in an argument, Nick and Honey nevertheless proceed to make themselves comfortable. Like O'Neill in *Long Day's Journey into Night*, Albee compacts a long evening into an intense exchange between drunks who show no restraint in ranting about each other's failures and disappointments.

The play is a story of childlessness, games, and illusions. Honey convinced Nick to marry her based on what he calls her "hysterical pregnancy." George and Martha's relationship is fixated on the illusion of having a "son." Martha informs Honey of their "son's birthday" tomorrow, forcing George's compliancy with her make-believe "game." Deciphering what is real from what is illusion is integral to the play. Honey asks when their "son" will return. At first Martha is reluctant to discuss the child, but George persists, calling him the "little bugger." Martha accuses George of having "problems" and suggests that he might not be the father (a similar suggestion is made in August Strindberg's play, *The Father*).

MARTHA: George's biggest problem about the little . . . ha, ha, ha, HA! . . . about our son, about our great big son, is that deep down in the private-most pit of his gut, he's not completely sure it's his own kid.
GEORGE: (*Deeply serious.*) My God, you're a wicked woman.
MARTHA: And I've told him a million times, baby . . . I wouldn't conceive with anyone but you . . . you know that, baby.
GEORGE: A deeply wicked person. (202)

Act I ends with Honey puking in the bathroom. Act II (subtitled "Walpurgisnacht" – German for Halloween) finds Nick and George drinking more. George relates a traumatic event in his life. Although the story is described as another boy's accidental killing of his parents, it is later discovered that the event was likely caused by George. One night a 16-year-old George and his boarding school chums go to a New York illegal gambling house. The boy, who had killed his mother accidentally, attempts sophistication. He asks for a drink: "bergan, bergan and water." George and the others laugh at the mispronunciation, and the evening turns out to be "the grandest day of my . . .

youth" (217). The boy later kills his father accidentally in a driving accident. Nick shares his past. His father-in-law was a traveling preacher who had amassed a small fortune. Never one to miss an opportunity, Nick marries for advancement. George fleshes Nick out, discovering his true intent at the College.

> NICK: Nyaah ... what I thought I'd do is ... I'd sort of insinuate myself generally, play around for a while, find all the weak spots, shore 'em up, but with my own name plate on 'em ... become sort of a fact, and then turn into a ... a what ... ?
> GEORGE: An inevitability.
> NICK: Exactly. ... An inevitability. You know. ... Take over a few courses from the older men, start some special groups for myself ... plow a few pertinent wives ...
> GEORGE: Now that's it! You can take over all the courses you want to, and get as much of the young elite together in the gymnasium as you like, but until you start plowing pertinent wives, you really aren't working. The way to a man's heart is through his wife's belly, and don't you forget it. (329)

In Act II the "games" become increasingly vicious. Martha reveals that George attempted to write a novel about a boy who had accidentally killed his parents. Her father put an end to the book, finding it pointless. But Martha let it be known that the book was taken from George's life. George tries to strangle Martha, who has been dancing (actually grinding) with Nick (see figure 3). George exacts his revenge on Nick by telling the story that Nick shared about his father-in-law and the marriage. The act ends with George and Martha declaring "total war." Martha's bellicosity takes the form of bringing Nick upstairs for sex.

Act III (subtitled "The Exorcism") begins with Martha descending from the bedroom. Drinking has apparently inhibited Nick's "performance." However, Albee is deliberately unclear on this; when George enters seeking revenge for Martha's betrayal, Martha informs George that Nick failed to "perform," prompting her to call him the "houseboy." George asks Nick to perform a menial task, noting that if he is the house "stud" he need not "perform" the task, but if he failed to "perform" in the bedroom he is then indeed the "houseboy." Nick defensively replies, "I am not a houseboy."

FIGURE 3 *Who's Afraid of Virginia Woolf?*, by Edward Albee, 1976. Michael
LaGue (Nick) and Lynn Cohen (Martha). Reprinted courtesy of Kansas City
Repertory Theatre (formerly Missouri Repertory Theatre).

GEORGE: No? Well then, you must have made it in the sack. Yes? (*He is breathing a little heavy; behaving a little manic.*) Yes? Someone's lying around here; somebody isn't playing the game straight. Yes? Come on; come on; who's lying? Martha? Come on!

NICK: Tell him I'm not a houseboy.

MARTHA: No; you're not a houseboy.

GEORGE: So be it.

MARTHA: Truth and illusion, George; you don't know the difference.

GEORGE: No; but we must carry on as though we did.

MARTHA: Amen. (285)

This dialogue conveys most of the play's meaning; the ability to decipher appearances is complicated by changing statements. Nick is and is not a "houseboy," depending on the "part" he plays. The concept of role-playing is endemic to the theatre, where identity is informed by costume, mask, action, and description. The role of parent, which emerges as the central "part" George and Martha play, is a lie, but it is also a "role." George plays a final game, "Bringing Up Baby," which begins with their son returning home for his birthday. George baits Martha until she describes her childbirth "experience" and the "raising" of her son. A telegram, George says, has arrived while Nick and Martha were upstairs. George informs Martha that the telegram says their son has been killed while driving on a country road (in much the same fashion that George accidentally killed his father, or so he says). Martha vents that George "cannot do that," meaning he cannot fictionalize killing the boy. Nick fails to understand that this is merely another of their many games. "He hasn't decided anything, lady," Nick says: "It's not his doing. He doesn't have the power" (305). On the contrary, George indeed has the power by virtue of description. Descriptive power fuses theatrical impetus. George's "game" is exposed as soon as Martha demands to see the telegram. George replies he "ate it." Nick now understands. He and Honey leave. George and Martha sit alone as the sunlight emerges, and a long night of games, illusions, and deception concludes.

Martha is a termagant and virago spewing emasculating invectives at any target within range. But her life has been suppressed. Anita Maria Stenz makes this point clear when she says that Martha is "a potentially powerful human being" who is "discouraged by family, education and society from having personal goals." Martha is the "victim not only of her lack of self-esteem but also of thwarted aggressiveness."[24]

Martha resembles Henrik Ibsen's protagonist in *Hedda Gabler* (1891). Martha and Hedda live vicariously through the men in their lives, and both were raised by domineering fathers: Hedda's father was "General Gabler," and Martha's the president of the university. Both men – general and president – are "commanders." Their husbands pale by comparison. George is an "associate" professor, which means he is not a "full" professor. Nor is he, as Martha mockingly points out, the Chair of the History Department. Hedda's husband, also named George, falls short of expectations as well. Martha's sarcasm, like Hedda's frustration, is a manifestation of suppressed ambition, not merely spousal disappointment. But with their expectations thwarted, Martha and Hedda expect the men in their lives to resemble their fathers in order that their husbands may surrogate their unrealized ambitions. Martha's ambition is to create a child; instead she creates a fantasy. Hedda, too, has such fantasies, but of a different sort. Although pregnant, Hedda focuses on the manuscript by Lovborg and Thea, a manuscript referred to as their "child." Hedda and Martha share the need to create fantasies because reality is unsatisfying. The games played by Martha and Hedda exercise their intelligence and provide challenges in what is otherwise a dull life. Hedda plans for her husband's success, Martha does the same for George, and both must come to grips with husbands unable to make the grade.

To see George as a failure, however, is to miss the point. He comes up short because from his perspective success is a matter of labels and reality is permeated with death. George has learned, through games, fantasy, and child-like dialogue with Martha, to live with disappointment and death. Like Hickey in *Iceman*, he is a carrier of death; he causes the death not only of his parents, but also of his "son." The theme of death by the mere act of description is one of Albee's major themes. Death by description operates effectively in the *theatrum mundi*. Unless an actor "fakes" death, death by description is the only way it can occur onstage. The death of George's parents, his novel about their death, and finally the telegram reporting the death of his son, are all "death by language." Death in the theatre is a language game.

George and Martha's counterattacks are often cruel. Their puerile dialogue, even going so far as flattening their "w" sounds like children, and their engaging in echolalia, repeating each other's words, are not meant to elicit sympathy. Nor is their cryptic cynicism intended to awaken our compassion. Yet they are honest about themselves and their place in society. Nick and Honey, by contrast, pretend to be sincere but remain disingenuous throughout. Nick is willing to sleep with other faculty wives for advancement and Honey oscillates between having and not having children depending on the social benefits of childrearing at any given moment. They are, in a word, "phonies," as J. D. Salinger's Holden Caulfield in *The Catcher in the Rye* would say. George and Martha mock Nick's pretensions by deliberately confusing his "department." They care little which department he is in; they know they can throw Nick off balance by mocking his place in the pecking order. They tease their guests because they know as social climbers they will say and do almost anything to boost their status. Walter Davis observes that Nick and Honey "are the same in public and in private because for them there is no difference." Their marriage is based on a lie, hence there is little reason to cease lying for convenience. George and Martha, Davis contends, "are uneasy in public, given to acting out behaviors, because they see social space (academic evenings, etc.) as a vast theatre of lies."[25]

We are meant to empathize with George and Martha. From their point of view, reality has left them broken. For Nick and Honey, children are merely a single piece of a larger social puzzle designed for success. But for George and Martha, childlessness has led them to compensate and climbing the social ladder is a compromise of integrity. They regress to the level of children they do not have, but this is understandable. Real-world traumas – lack of children, professional failures, bitter marriage, and the killing of parents – are made bearable only in the imaginary. For them the imaginary and the real often crisscross because the imaginary assuages their disappointment. They construct memories not only to ameliorate life's painful reality, but also in the way actors create roles. For George and Martha, the mingling of truth and illusion structures their awareness. Despite cynicism and boorishness, they earn our respect for their unwillingness to play the social climbing game. They delude themselves, but compared to Nick and Honey, they are refreshingly honest. In a 1981 interview, Albee said that his concerns as a playwright "are the facts that we are too short-sighted, that we will not live on the precipice, that too many people prefer to go through this brief thing called life only half-alive, [and] that too many people are going to end up with regret and bitterness at not having participated fully in their lives."[26] For all their vituperative language and social impropriety, George and Martha care little for the life of debasement and pandering one finds in Nick and Honey.

One of Albee's riskiest and at the same time most opaque plays is *Tiny Alice* (1964). It is poetic, turgid, and recondite. Here Albee uses the drama to attack conformity, religion, wealth, power, and pretense. Julian, a lay priest, is assigned to help Tiny Alice distribute wealth she has promised to the Church. Manipulated by her agents the cardinal, Tiny Alice's lawyer, the butler, and Tiny Alice herself, Julian enters Alice's home and is drawn into deception and eventual death. He is exposed to wealth beyond his dreams. Julian represents innocence, unable to resist the temptations of the flesh. He is seduced by Tiny Alice, soon leaves the priesthood to become her lover, and is finally betrayed. Onstage is a replica of Alice's home in miniature. When Julian peers into its windows, it is alleged that he can see figures moving about, suggesting a box within a box. Things are not what they appear: Tiny Alice first appears onstage as elderly, only to remove her wig and reveal a comely woman. The butler's name is "Butler" (a pun on people's identity and names), and the cardinal and lawyer may have had a relationship. The play was poorly received, but it remains a complex study in self-deception.

In *A Delicate Balance* (1966), Albee returns to a more conventional setting. The play concerns the blankness of upper-middle-class existence. Despite the opulence of the Tobias family, they are dysfunctional and their friends neurotic. The characters include an alcoholic sister, a daughter unable to hold a marriage, and two friends terrified of the unknown. We discover that the friendship is vacuous, held together by social clubs and shopping. Albee creates a conflict of expected protocols and feelings lurking beneath the surface. The play builds on a "delicate balance" of human bonds relying on tenuous threads; all of the characters avoid the truth until it is forced upon them. Tobias's friends Harry and Edna arrive terrified, but the cause of their fear is ambiguous. They seek refuge in the Tobias home, manipulating their way into the daughter Julia's bedroom. When Julia challenges this encroachment of "intruders" she is rebuffed by Tobias, who tries to support his friends in need. Agnes, Tobias's wife, sides with her daughter. She considers the invasion a "plague." However, Tobias defends the visitation: "Oh, for God's sake, Agnes! It's our friends! What am I supposed to do? Say: 'Look, you can't stay here, you two, you've got troubles. You're friends, and all, but you come in here clean.' Well, I can't do that. No. Agnes, for God's sake, if . . . if that's all Harry and Edna mean to us, then . . . then what about us?"[27]

In pointillist fashion, Albee dots his dialogue with symbols. Death, relationships of people to animals (recall Jerry and his dog), and references to time and space are alluded to throughout *A Delicate Balance*. Time and space, in particular, are underscored as characters inform us of the many years they have known each other and speak often of "filling space." The metaphor of space is recurrent in Albee's plays, structured on an inside–outside framework: characters "inside" usually own the turf while "outside" characters invade it. In *Zoo Story*, Peter holds the bench, Jerry takes it. In *Virginia Woolf*, George and Martha live in their home filled with illusions. They are invaded by Nick and Honey. In *Tiny Alice*, the model of the home vulnerably occupies center stage. During the play it catches fire, symbolizing its precariousness. In *A Delicate Balance*, Tobias and Agnes host the invading Harry and Edna. In the climax of Act III, Harry asks Tobias what he "wants." Tobias explains to Harry, in what Albee describes as an "aria," his trepidation: "You come in here, you come in here with your . . . wife, and with your . . . terror! And you ask me if I want you here! (*Great breathing sounds.*) YES! OF COURSE! I WANT YOU HERE! THIS IS MY HOUSE! I WANT YOU IN IT! I WANT YOUR PLAGUE! YOU'VE GOT SOME TERROR WITH YOU? BRING IT IN!" (115).

For Albee plague and death arrive invasively from the outside. This is evident in his *All Over* (1971), which takes place entirely in the bedroom of a dying patriarch hidden behind an upstage curtain. Friends and family have been summoned to participate in a deathwatch. The characters are named by their relationship to the dying man: Wife, Mistress, Daughter, Son, Friend, Doctor, and Nurse. Otherwise, they have neither name nor identity. Inside and onstage are comfort and security; roles are clearly defined; and everything and everyone have a place. When death enters, security is obliterated. *All Over* explores the discomfort of a deathwatch, presided over by wasted lives. The characters have lived only as appendages vicarious to the patriarch. The play incorporates music in an important way. The dialogue is written rhythmically; while the Doctor and the Nurse speak harmoniously, the others are dissonant. They speak disjointedly, their thoughts moving in staccato fashion from one idea to another. *All Over* is Albee's most trenchant study of women preceding his *Three Tall Women* (1992). The female characters dominate. The men are ineffectual. The Mistress cannot anchor herself; like Tobias's sister Clair in *A Delicate Balance*, she is adrift. In her final speech, she describes what she will do when her lover dies. She intends to travel, but we discover that traveling is merely her continuation of avoiding commitment. The Wife plays "roles" (wife, mother, widow, rock, and little girl) related to the dying man. She, like the Mistress, has squandered her life in the service of her husband. The Wife and Mistress observe the rising women's lib movement in which they are too old to participate.

Middle-class ennui has been a recurrent American theme during the second half of the twentieth century, aided in part by the novels of Ann Beattie, John Cheever, and John Updike, and films like *The Graduate* and *American Beauty*. Albee, too, has helped enshrine suburban boredom in the American cultural lexicon. In *All Over*, the Wife's family lives an illusion of happiness but suffers stifling emptiness. The Son is spineless and the Daughter, like Julia in *A Delicate Balance*, flits from one unhappy marriage to the next. Albee examines mother–daughter relationships, beginning in *A Delicate Balance*, taking root in *All Over*, and continuing in *Three Tall Women*. The Daughter in *All Over* and Julia in *A Delicate Balance* are spoiled, shrewish, vulnerable, and at odds with their mothers. The Daughter endures a physically abusive relationship. In *All Over*, the Wife, Mistress, Friend (who had an affair with the Wife), Son, and Daughter interject truths about each other, especially when they attack. However, their self-awareness consists merely of narrow, half-perceived observations. They project upon the world their sense of reality, but in fact nothing they say about the world or themselves can be confirmed. The only certainty is that they are identified by their relationship to a man approaching death. In the death of the patriarch, they must come to terms with their roles – their names – which now no longer have meaning. They are pathetic and vulnerable. Albee endows them with poignancy, but he is critical of their self-indulgences and hypocrisy. Their adherence to the establishment and its codes of conduct has crippled their imagination and stifled their potential.

Dramas attacking the "establishment" are common during this period. Some examples are Tom Eyen's *The White Whore and the Bit Player* (1964), Rochelle Owens's *Futz* (1967), Megan Terry's *Calm Down Mother* (1965), *Keep Tightly Closed in a Cool Dry Place* (1965), and *Viet Rock* (1966), Barbara Garson's *MacBird* (1967), Michael McClure's *The Beard* (1965), Arthur Kopit's *Indians* (1968), and Jean-Claude van

Itallie's three one-acts titled *America Hurrah* (1966). More conventional in form, but no less critical of the status quo, are Leonard Melfi's *Birdbath* (1965), Israel Horovitz's *The Indians Want the Bronx* (1968), and Jason Miller's *That Championship Season* (1972). These plays were influenced by the anti-war movement and the rise of "happenings," a term coined by Allan Kaprow in 1958 related to Jackson Pollock and abstract art. Like Marcel Duchamp's notion of the "ready-made" – art found in everyday objects – happenings, notes Arnold Aronson in his book *American Avant-Garde Theatre*, yield performances "independent of logical analysis." Happenings convey random depictions and characters without "psychological or motivational basis for their behavior," and "no information was passed from one scene to the next."[28] Eyen's *The White Whore and the Bit Player* is a two-character play exploring media image-making. The "White Whore" is a Marilyn Monroe prototype while the "Bit Player" is a Nun. The conflict of sexuality and repression are explored as the characters assume roles. Owens's *Futz* is a satire of pastoral life. Characters partake in bestiality, intended to shock and offend. Megan Terry, according to Helene Keyssar, is the "mother of American feminist drama";[29] she, along with Owens, Maria Irene Fornes, Rosalyn Drexler, Adrienne Kennedy, and actress-director Julie Bovasso, formed the Women's Theatre Council in 1972. Terry, in particular, worked closely with Joseph Chaikin's Open Theatre. Her anti-war play, *Viet Rock*, is a fast-paced drama shedding light on the propaganda machine that led to Vietnam. Most of Terry's plays are developed by ensemble, with actors playing multiple roles. *Keep Tightly Closed in a Cool Dry Place* examines three men – Jasper, Michaels, and Gregory – incarcerated for the murder of Jasper's wife. The play is deliberately vague regarding the murder, but it is evident that the three share culpability. Garson's *MacBird* is written in verse, imitates Shakespeare (mostly *Macbeth* but makes use of other plots), and attempts social satire. The play revolves around Lyndon Johnson's "assassination" of John Kennedy, with Johnson paralleling Macbeth and "Lady Bird" Johnson as Lady MacBird. Robert Kennedy is Shakespeare's Malcolm who kills the assassin. McClure's poetic drama, *The Beard*, scandalized during its run in San Francisco, its performances being shut down by the police. While its language is tame by today's standards, the play was revolutionary for its time. Like *White Whore*, it depicts media creations Jean Harlow and Billy the Kid. Symbols of sex-stardom and outlaw-cowboy are demythologized. The play engages in fantasy and reality, building on the idea that fantasy might be merely another function of reality. Kopit's *Indians* also examines Western legends, in this case Buffalo Bill Cody and his exploitation of American Indians. The relationship between what is "show" and what is "real" is accentuated, as well as the Pirandello-style sense of role-playing. Van Itallie is most closely associated with the Open Theatre (1963–1973), an experimental group that produced a number of controversial dramas. His *America Hurrah* sheds light on the omnipresent media and consumerism, particularly television. For example in *Motel*, one act of the three acts that comprise *America Hurrah*, there are three grotesque dolls that hover in the background. Only the disembodied voice of the hotelkeeper permeates the dialogue. The dolls are frozen images of blindness, sterility, and incapacity resulting from media bombardment. Melfi's *Birdbath* takes place in a realistic setting. A lonely writer, Frankie, takes an interest in a co-worker, Thelma, a waitress at a restaurant where he is the cashier. Inviting her back to his apartment on Valentine's Day, Frankie learns of Thelma's abuse and subsequent retaliation. Horovitz's one-act play, *The Indians Want the Bronx*, starred Al Pacino as the violence-prone Murph who intimidates Gupta, played by John Cazale. Miller's *That Championship Season* displays the hypocrisy of five former basketball players and their coach. They take pride in a championship won by false pretenses.

Four other playwrights – Maria Irene Fornes, Terrence McNally, Sam Shepard, and Lanford Wilson – began their careers among this iconoclastic group, eventually becoming widely produced and critically acclaimed American dramatists. Although more will be said in the next chapters, several of their early works deserve attention. Fornes adumbrates an interest in games and role-playing. *Tango Palace* (1963), originally titled *There! You Died*, was produced at the San Francisco Actors Workshop. Two characters, Isidore and Leopold, live in a surreal world of assorted props and relate to each other through violence. Andrew Sofer compares the two principals to Beckett's Pozzo and Lucky in *Waiting for Godot*. The Hegelian "master–slave" relationship of Isidore and Leopold, Sofer remarks, creates a "symbiotic relationship with no exit. Despite the antic zest of Isidore's routines, *Tango Palace* is a claustrophobic nightmare from which the callow Leopold, doomed to seek Isidore's love for eternity, can never escape."[30] *Tango Palace* anticipates Fornes's *Mud* (1983), which explores the entrapment of a vibrant woman by two immature men. Terrence McNally's *Bad*

Habits (1974), two one-acts, takes place in two separate hospitals. McNally is interested in the relationships of power and control.

One of the most prolific playwrights of alternative theatre, Sam Shepard set a standard for brazenness and imagination. Two of his early plays, *Cowboy Mouth* (1971) and *Action* (1975), deal with characters torn between loyalty and fear. The plays are influenced by rock 'n' roll, country-western, and sexual intensity. *Cowboy Mouth* takes place in a room with a "fucked-up bed center stage. Raymond, a dead crow, [is] on the floor."[31] Slim and Cavale, the principal characters, are embattled lovers standing amidst the detritus of old tires, hubcaps, and photos of country-western singers. This lovers' duet and trailer park ambiance will resurface in Shepard's *Fool for Love* (1983). *Cowboy Mouth* was co-written by the rock singer Patti Smith (Shepard and Smith allegedly pushed a typewriter back and forth as each contributed his or her lines). The play takes the form of a psychedelic dream, with characters like the Lobster man onstage and the protagonist claiming to be the "rock 'n' roll" savior. Food is a persistent icon in this and other Shepard plays. Slim and Cavale swing wildly from hostility to affection, rehearsing a love–hate relationship that will recur in his mature plays. *Action* is set on Thanksgiving Day, with food preparation at the centerpiece of the action. Pilgrims are alluded to, and characters express the feeling of imprisonment. Shepard's plays are a sensual panorama; smells and aromas are suggested. He is attracted to narratives of visceral intensity. His characters are helpless to communicate, lashing out in frustration and subsiding into despair. Love, family, and the desire to escape commitment pervade Shepard's work. *Action* examines the dysfunctional family and patriarchical bonds that become the quintessential themes in Shepard's *Curse of the Starving Class* (1978) and *Buried Child* (1978), and underlie the sibling rivalry in *True West* (1982).

Shepard is considered the dramatist of the Old West. Ross Wetzsteon has commented on this, noting: "to say that Shepard's major theme is a lament for the Old West is to overlook the fact that his plays imaginatively link the nineteenth-century obsession with the frontier spirit and the twentieth-century obsession with the alienated self." The combination of rugged Western individualism and alienated outsider marks Shepard as the "existential cowboy."[32] In addition to themes of the Old West and the existential outsider, Shepard's *Forensic & the Navigator* (1967), *The Unseen Hand* (1969), *Geography of a Horse Dreamer*

(1974), *Suicide in B Flat* (1976), and other plays explore music, relationships, the individual versus society, and the concept of theatrical presentation. In Shepard's plays the theatre itself becomes a self-contained space from which characters attempt to free themselves. This conflict of escape and return is a result of his love–hate relationship with the theatre; the space inside the theatre is too contained and narcissistic, yet the outside overwhelms. Like the expansive "West," the freedom of the wide open range compels but its vastness frightens. The theatrical space is metaphorical for Shepard's relationship to his father. In many of Shepard's plays, a father figure lurks either in the background or onstage from which characters seek to escape.

If Shepard is the "existential cowboy," Lanford Wilson inherits from William Inge the mantle of the Midwest. Wilson's *The Rimers of Eldrich* (1966) was not his first play, but it established his presence as a dramatist examining the prejudices of Midwestern life. Skelly Mannor is the town "outsider," a character deemed "weird" by the inhabitants but who is a kind of "fool-on-the-hill." He lives alone in a shack witnessing the follies of the town from a distant vantage point. Although a voyeur of sorts, he is the only character with a moral perspective. His kindness will prove to be his undoing. Wilson's *Hot L Baltimore* (1973), like *Rimers*, depicts a large ensemble cast in a realistic setting, in this case a run-down hotel. Wilson's misfits and losers evoke sympathetic underdogs, the sort of thing he returns to throughout his œuvre.

If Shepard and Wilson examine regional locales, David Rabe takes up the Vietnam War. His trilogy, *The Basic Training of Pavlo Hummel* (1971), *Sticks and Bones* (1971), and *Streamers* (1976), exposes war's brutality. The early 1970s and even into the 1980s observed the rise of ant-war books and films, such as Ron Kovic's *Born on the Fourth of July*, inspired by Dalton Trumbo's 1939 novel *Johnny Got His Gun*, as well as *The Deer Hunter, Apocalypse Now, Coming Home, Platoon, Casualties of War*, and *Full Metal Jacket*. Rabe covers most of the themes explored in these books and movies: the consequences of soldiers coming home from an unpopular war; the impact of war on those unprepared for it; and the circumstances faced by people from different walks of life forced to fight together in a war they barely comprehend. Rabe focuses on innocence and madness. His characters typically resemble either the naïveté of Charlie Sheen at the beginning of *Platoon*, or the cryptic cynical father, Martin Sheen, in *Apocalypse Now*. Rabe also shares with *Full Metal Jacket* the depiction of chaos in recruiting soldiers and the spontaneous violence that erupts during war. He sets his first two Vietnam War plays in locations where past and present commingle. Pavlo Hummel is a model of "Sad Sack," the unsophisticated GI thrust into war without the required tools of survival. Rabe creates a sympathetic character who, albeit naïve, struggles to make sense of a senseless situation. His death by a grenade tossed into a brothel depicts one of several scenes exploring his wasted life. *Sticks and Bones* is more satirical but no less bizarre. David, blinded during the war, returns home to pristine surroundings. The cheery good nature of his parents, named Ozzie and Harriet, is contrasted by David's depression. His inability to tolerate the family's hyper-happiness – they live as if in a TV sit-com – ends in suicide. His parents assist David in the grotesque slashing of his wrists. *Streamers* is set in an army barracks where recruits await deployment to Vietnam. Two veterans come and go from the barracks drunk and oblivious to the rising tension among the recruits. The drama examines class and racial conflicts. The primary relationship is between Billy and Roger, but two other members of the barracks, Richie, a gay man, and Carlyle, complete a foursome. Carlyle, from the ghetto, is alienated from the others. Roger is black, but feels comfortable among the white recruits. The claustrophobic space of the barracks and the fear of going to Vietnam result in short tempers. The play explores characters unprepared for the violence to come. As in *Full Metal Jacket*, Rabe condemns the righteousness of America, which took innocent Americans and made them killers.

This volatile period witnessed not only the conflicts of the Vietnam War, but also a rising demand for racial justice. From Civil Rights and Black Power movements emerged the Black Arts Movement. Along with the Harlem Renaissance, the Black Arts Movement inspired African American art, literature, music, and drama. Playwrights and theatre companies surfaced, some working in white neighborhoods (such as the Negro Ensemble Company), and others creating theatres in black communities (the New Lafayette Theatre of Harlem). These theatres contributed to a "black aesthetic" pertinent to black life. Playwright Ronald Milner, author of the morality play *What the Wine-Sellers Buy* (1968), wrote "Black Theater – Go Home!" in 1968. The essay enjoined black dramatists, actors, and directors to put down roots in the black community. A new theatre, he said, "must be housed in, sustained and judged by, and be a useable projection of, and to, a black community!" In the communities "are materials, your situations and conflicts – relevant and powerful."[33] Inspired by Hansberry, Baraka, and Kennedy, the dramas of the Black Arts Movement centered on militancy, social justice, and black life without the approval of white audiences and critics.

African American dramatists sought an affirmative message capable of promoting black culture. For black dramatists, it was less a question of confronting stereotypes than inspiring change. Harlem, for instance, became more than a "ghetto"; in black dramas, it was a thriving community possessing a unique economy and dynamic. Harlem is the backdrop for Charles Gordone's *No Place to Be Somebody* (1969), subtitled a "Black-black Comedy." Gabe Gabriel, a writer, serves as the play's narrator, and the action takes place in a bar. Gabe is a light-skinned African American actor, a fact that allows him to examine what "skin tone" means (he is too light to play black characters, and too dark to play white ones). This slice-of-life play concerns hustlers, musicians, and poets who long to escape their limitations. Like O'Neill's *Iceman Cometh*, the bar setting explores conflictual situations. At the conclusion Gabe kills Johnny Williams, the bar owner who challenges the white mob's control. Johnny seeks to enlist Gabe in his rage against whites: "It's your war too, Nigger. Why can't you see that? You wanna go on believin' in the lie? We at war, Gabe! Black ag'inst white." Gabe resists, saying, "You're wrong, John. You're so goddam wrong."[34] Johnny instigates and Gabe retaliates, leading to a violent conclusion. Gordone's melodrama complicates the usual moral issues; neither is Gabe ethically pure nor is Johnny just an angry hustler. Gabe ends the play as he began it, directly addressing the audience. When Gabe appears in his extended monologue, he recites poetry (a kind of precursor to rap), and in the end enters "dressed as a woman in mourning." The play attempts to encourage social activism. The playwright Ed Bullins put it best when he said that "conditions must be created for sweeping social and cultural change. It is the Black artist's creative duty to plant, nurture and spread the seeds of change."[35]

The dramatists' efforts "to dynamically interweave organizational development, political activism, and racially exclusive cultural production" through revolutionary separatism were justified, writes Mike Sell, "by a philosophical project that aimed to create a critical metaphysics that would help redefine and revive" African American culture.[36] Separateness, redefinition, and revival are all exemplified by Lonne Elder's *Ceremonies and Dark Old Men* (1969). The play takes place in a Harlem barber shop. The Parker family tries to eke out a living legally or illegally. The oldest son, Theo, is the entrepreneur of illegal booze with a "still" placed in the back of the shop. The youngest son is involved in gang life. The daughter, Adele, tries to keep the family together, while the patriarch, Russell Parker, is a dreamer unaware of his children's plotting. Joseph Walker's *The River Niger* (1972), like *Ceremonies*, takes place in Harlem. John Williams (played by Douglas Turner Ward) is a poet who drinks himself to death. His son Jeff is a former air force officer who resists its racism. Like Russell Parker in *Ceremonies*, John Williams is a middle-aged man who sees opportunities squandered. Alice Childress's early play *Wedding Band* (1966, later produced in New York in 1972) is about an interracial relationship occurring in South Carolina during the summer of 1918. Her best-known work, *Wine in the Wilderness* (1969), takes place in Harlem and criticizes the black bourgeoisie for its condescending attitudes toward the working class. The protagonist, Tomorrow Marie, is "used" as a model for an artist, but she is also used as a "case study" by the bourgeois characters. Sonia Sanchez's plays also use Harlem as background, exploring militant themes in *The Bronx is Next* (1968) and *Sister Son/ja* (1969). Philip Hayes Dean's *The Sty of the Blind Pig* (1971) and Leslie Lee's *The First Breeze of Summer* (1975) overlap in several important themes: the power of the matriarch in the African American family; the significance of black spirituality; the effect of migration in African American life; and racial self-effacement. *The Sty of the Blind Pig* takes place in Chicago just before the Civil Rights Movement and concerns a mother and daughter's struggle for independence. *The First Breeze of Summer* takes place in the South, examining the final days of a mother as she recalls her failed relationships.

Ed Bullins must be mentioned for having established the concept of the "twentieth-century cycle plays" (picked up by August Wilson), for his unflinching observations of life amidst the underclass, and for his experimentation. Amiri Baraka's description of Ron Milner as an "activist cultural worker" applies to Bullins as well.[37] Bullins's *Clara's Ole Man* (1965) is set in the black neighborhood of South Philadelphia and deals with a lesbian relationship that is both loving and abusive. This mixture of rage and compassion can be found in his "cycle dramas" *In the Wine Time* (1968), *The Duplex* (1970), *It Bees Dat Way* (1970), *In New England Winter* (1971), *The Fabulous Miss Marie* (1971), and *Home Boy* (1976). The bleak landscape that reveals few moments of tenderness is illuminated in Bullins's *Goin' a Buffalo* (1968). One of his best plays, *Goin' a Buffalo* is set in Los Angeles. Like most of his works (and Gordone's *No Place to Be Somebody*), it features a collage of characters. The opening stage direction sets the tone: "This play is about some black people." The rootlessness of the characters is evident in the play's fits and starts. Violence erupts suddenly, only to subside quickly. Motifs of chess, music, and enclosed spaces (cramped apartments, small honky-tonks) underscore routine and claustrophobia. While the drama is panoramic, the principal relationship is between Curt and Art. Curt is a pimp saved by Art in jail. Brutality is the norm, yet there is compassion, exemplified by this passage:

> CURT: When I saw you in action, Art, I said to myself I could really use this kid. Man, you're like a little brother to me now, man. I watch the way you act around people. You think on your feet and study them like a good gambler does. You're like me in a lot of ways. Man, we're the new breed, ya know. Renegades. Rebels. There's no rules for us . . . we make them as we break them.
> ART: Sounds kind'a romantic, Curt.
> CURT: And why shouldn't it? Man, this ain't a world we built, so why should we try and fit in it. We have to make it over the best we can . . . and we are the ones to do it. We are, man, we are![38]

Bullins never judges his characters. Brutality and compassion are part of the landscape, and characters act on their desires and frustrations. Bullins's brand of melodrama concerns the quotidian; he absorbs the realistic tradition and shapes it into what he sees as the rhythms of life. Kimberly Benston refers to his dramas as a "physicalized *blues lament*." Bullins, says Benston, "initiated the modern black drama movement by taking the 'well-made play' as his basic form but subjected it to social and symbolic pressures that exposed its conceptual underpinnings (especially, the congruency of familial reintegration and theatrical mimesis) and opened it to a fresh realization."[39] Bullins is associated with Harlem's New Lafayette Theatre. Hired as writer-in-residence, Bullins had been an important influence. James Edward Smethurst remarks that becoming writer-in-residence "transformed Bullins from an essentially regional playwright in the Bay Area to perhaps the most important national Black Arts dramatist." Because of this theatre's high visibility, Smethurst contends, "the New Lafayette became a lightning rod for many of the intense debates over aesthetics, subject matter, and what might be considered territorial disputes over ideological and institutional turf between groups that characterized the Black Arts Movement in New York."[40] Most of Bullins's plays are realistic, but his methodology was not limited by this tendency. His experimental dramas eschew plot and simplistic causal relations, bringing instead the "experience" of blackness to the stage. Douglas Turner Ward's *Day of Absence* (1965), Baraka's *Slave Ship* (1968), Paul Carter Harrison's *The Great MacDaddy* (1974), and Bullins's *The Theme Is Blackness* (1966) are among a number of innovative dramas attempting to express life's significance rather than merely observing its passing. Bullins sought to bring out what Mance Williams calls the "Black Experience or Black Consciousness" and what Paul Carter Harrison calls *"feeling*, rather than strict adherence to form."[41]

The Black Arts Movement inspired others. One of the foremost plays dealing with gay rights was Mart Crowley's *Boys in the Band* (1968). Crowley's drama examines the deformation of personality wrought by life in the closet, with its accompanying fear of opprobrium and career-ending disgrace. In retrospect, the play's message appears clichéd – characters suffering guilty feelings for their alleged transgression – but the play's importance is difficult to overstate. Within a year of its first presentation the Stonewall Uprising would render the message of *Boys in the Band* somewhat archaic. Yet it remains important because of its place within an unfolding social phenomenon. The play takes place in the home of Michael and Donald who throw a birthday party for Harold. The party guests include Bernard, an African American; Emory, a flamboyant wiseacre; Cowboy, Harold's birthday "present"; a couple, Hank and Larry; and an unexpected old "straight" friend of Michael's, Allen. The play's conflict centers on Allen, who may or may not be gay. During a party game in which the guests must call someone they secretly love, Michael attempts to draw Allen out. He bullies him into phoning. While the guests try to dissuade Michael, he is relentless. Allen eventually makes the call, but it is to his wife. In the end, Harold confronts Michael's self-effacement, saying: "Now it is my turn. And ready or not, Michael, here goes. (*A beat.*) You are a sad and pathetic man. You're a homosexual and you don't want to be. But there is nothing you can do to change it. Not all your prayers to God, not all the analysis you can buy in all the years you've got left to live. [. . .] Always, Michael. Always. Until the day you die" (390–1).

John Guare's *House of Blue Leaves* (1971) examines a "movement" of another sort. It portrays the absurd extremes people will go to in order to achieve fame. Guare's plays, including *Rich and Famous* (1976), *Landscape of the Body* (1977), and *Bosoms and Neglect* (1979), consider the way society and especially pop culture warp perceptions. The dream of one big "break" – here the chance to crack into the music industry – is the action of *Blue Leaves*. Underlying the plot is Guare's examination of the waning American Dream. The devotion to fame is condemned as corrosive. But the play is more than satire; it is an exercise in Guare's ability to blend absurdism and realism. The play takes place in what he describes as a "cold apartment in Sunnyside, Queens, New York City," on October 4, 1965 (3). The time is important because on that day the Pope visited New York City. Setting the play in Queens is also significant to Guare because it was never "a borough with its own sense of identity." Just as Brooklyn was to the film *Saturday Night Fever*, Queens "was either a stepping stone to something greater or the place where hopes stalled and the whole web of ambition unwound."[42] Along with its realism, absurdist elements surface: characters speak directly to the audience and the dialogue is often illogical and humorous. While the play might be considered a farce, it is beyond the merely zany. The music, as in the case of Artie's song, is out of tune (the term absurd means "inharmonious, tasteless, out of tune"). Artie's music is trite; his song "Where is the devil in Evelyn?" opens the play and lets us know that his quest for fame is hopeless.

This wacky drama centers around three main characters. Artie Shaughnessy is a 45-year-old musician working as a zookeeper. That it is a zoo is suggestive of Albee's *The Zoo Story*; like Jerry, Artie is frustrated with his life with animals. He stakes his hopes on his childhood friend, a successful producer, Billy Einhorn. Artie believes Billy will discover his music and make Artie his composer. Artie's wife, Bananas, is, as her name suggests, loopy. She is in the "fool-on-the-hill" tradition, never getting out of her pajamas, but often something of a prophet. She is the only character who realizes the hopelessness of Artie's music. Disappointed in her lack of faith, Artie turns to Bunny Flingus. Bunny's claim to fame is her cooking; she openly admits to being a flop in bed, but she succeeds in enticing men with her culinary talents. Among the other inhabitants in this bizarre play are Artie and Bananas's son Ronnie (who plans to assassinate the Pope), a hearing-impaired movie starlet, Corrinna Stroller, three Nuns, and the movie producer.

The characters of *Blue Leaves* barely cling to sanity. Bananas wanders on snowy rooftops in her bare feet, and she dreams of Green Buicks driving along Broadway, meeting Cardinal Spellman, Jackie Kennedy, Bob Hope, Johnny Carson, and President Johnson. These are icons she sees on TV. Bunny, too, daydreams of the Pope's blessings; "the Pope is flying through that star-filled sky, bumping planets out of the way, and he's asleep dreaming of the mobs waiting for him. When famous people go to sleep at night, it's us they dream of, Artie" (10). Artie's desperation leads him to abandon Bananas: "I feel I only got about this much life left in me, Bananas" (24). Artie clings to his music as his ticket out of Queens. Like Willy Loman, Artie is a poor judge of reality, and we witness how his erroneous judgment leads to irrational behavior. However, unlike in *Death of a Salesman* or *Raisin in the Sun*, the American Dream in *Blue Leaves* is warped. It is hardly characterized in terms of money. For Artie and Bunny, success is symbolic of a psychological hold on reality that is slipping rapidly into madness. Reality is a "blessing" (to be blessed by the Pope); it is off the charts (Artie's music is dreadful); and it is absurd (Ronnie dreams of achieving fame by blowing up the Pope). As soon as Billy Einhorn eats Bunny's food, he falls in love with her and she abandons Artie. Like Artie, her goal is to leave Queens. Feeling lost and trapped, Artie strangles Bananas. Like other plays of this period, the American Dream is presented as a fickle deity.

The rebelliousness of the 1960s took on many forms, not the least of which was demonstrated by the rise of minority movements. What many Native American, Asian American, and Chicano/Latino playwrights learned from the Black Arts Movement was that theatre and drama could play a critical role in the development of ethnic identity. The 1965 Immigration Act eliminating the quota system and the 1968 Bilingual Education Act bolstering Spanish in schools inspired self-awareness and a creative outpouring. Hanay Geiogamah's *Body Indian* (1972), Frank Chin's *The Chickencoop Chinaman* (1972), and Miguel Piñero's *Short Eyes* (1974) became exemplary dramas of their time. Geiogamah's play, premiering at the Native American Theatre Ensemble, opened next at Ellen Stewart's La Mama Theatre in New York. Like Maxim Gorky's *Lower Depths*, the play portrays poverty-stricken characters. The plot involves Native Americans near Oklahoma

City. Howard's one-room crash pad is a way-station for his nephews and relatives who are intent on raising money for their next booze-fest. Geiogamah makes it clear that these people have talent, but their lack of education and social conditions are confining. Howard's language evokes poetic images, yet is disturbingly violent and nihilistic. The drunken affects of the characters are countered by a sense of group solidarity. They may not hesitate to steal, but they are aware of their shared bonds and communal relationships.

The underlying need for connections is at the root of Chin's *Chickencoop Chinaman*. Tam Lum is trying to film a documentary about the father of a former prizefighter, Ovatine Jack Dancer. Tam visits his Japanese friend, Blackjap Kenji, and a Eurasian woman, Lee. The play examines masculinity, fatherhood, and familial bonding. Interspersed with realistic situations are dream sequences. Tam dreams of the Lone Ranger and Tonto, as well as Hong Kong Dream Girl, the fantasy Asian woman. Such caricatures of the docile Asian man and the exotic Asian woman are illuminated, anticipating David Henry Hwang's *M. Butterfly* (discussed in the next chapter). Like *Body Indian*, *Chickencoop Chinaman* is about heritage and how people of color examine their own "double consciousness." Chin situates his play in Pittsburgh's black neighborhood. The characters shift their language from what might be characterized as hip-black, Asian cliché (stereotypes of "Charlie Chan" dialect), and affectatious whiteness. The sense of rootlessness exposed in the language is the central theme as characters partake in "accents" for larger purposes. Dorinne Kondo describes this "shifting identity" when she remarks that "Asian American playwrights problematize notions of a singular home and of a singular identity. Dislocation, contradiction, unforeseen cultural possibilities, multiple geographies of identity exceeding the boundaries of nation-states emerge as motifs."[43] Ways of speaking are a way of accentuating this rootlessness. Tam explains: "I mean, we grow up bustin our asses to be white anyway . . . 'Don't wear green because it makes you look yellow, son.' Now there's Confucius in American for you. 'Don't be seen with no blacks, get good grades, lay low, apple for the teacher, be good, suck up, talk proper, and be civilized'" (26).

Chin's dream sequence incorporates the Lone Ranger and Tonto. Listening to the radio as a child, Tam believed that the Lone Ranger was Asian. In the play, the Lone Ranger is an aged cowboy barely able to walk. He is a geriatric hero assisted by Tonto, whose "Indian" dialect often slips from proper English to a "Kemo Sabe" accent. The Lone Ranger, partly blind, thinks Tonto has disappeared when he abandons the caricature accent and speaks "properly." The Lone Ranger is reassured of his friend's presence when he hears the stereotypical accent. For many raised in the 1950s and 1960s, the Lone Ranger and Tonto symbolized the white conqueror who tamed the "noble savage." Like the *Mad Magazine Bedside Reader* of 1959, with its satiric "The Lone Stranger Rides Again" (and its famous phrase "what you mean we, white man"),[44] Chin is satirizing the history of a white hero and his "colored sidekick" who saves his life and teaches him to navigate the wilderness. Nattie Bumpo in James Fenimore Cooper's *Leatherstocking Tales* of the nineteenth century, or Tarzan of the 1930s, represent themes picked up by the Lone Ranger, the eponymous rugged individual who turns to a non-white ally ("Kemo Sabe" means "faithful friend" in Pottawatomie) for aid and camaraderie through the frontier. For Chin these notions reify an existing hierarchy of white dominance.

The West Coast Chicano Movement – *La Causa* – began in 1962 with César Chávez establishing the National Farm Workers Association, eventually becoming the United Farm Workers (UFW). The UFW sponsored El Teatro Campesino. Let by Luis Valdez, this bilingual theatre company was formed in 1965 to unionize farm workers. The result of El Teatro Campesino was the establishment of a Chicano theatrical movement. The East Coast Hispanic Movement followed along similar lines. The barrios of East Spanish Harlem (El Barrio), the South Bronx, and the Lower East Side (Losaida) formed a triangular locale for the Nuyorican literary movement. Nuyorican style consisted in a street figure (usually biographically drawn) who takes on the role of oracle. The protagonist is often a participant, moving fluidly from inside events to narrator. The events are reported as personal history rather than from the perspective of detached observer. The barrio is described as a congeries of family, violence, and love. The Chicano Movement shares certain similarities with the Nuyorican, such as using its backdrop of Los Angeles or rural hamlets of Southern California and Texas. In the Chicano literature, the male protagonist is sometimes the Pachuco, an Aztec warrior and *vato loco* (literally, a brave and crazy man), displaying machismo in the face of his oppressors. The Nuyorican authors provide a somewhat different view than *La Causa*, having a proclivity to cynicism. For instance, in his Puerto Rican coming-of-age autobiography taking place in Spanish Harlem during the 1960s, Piri

Thomas began his *Bildungsroman, Down These Mean Streets,* with a pro-
logue honoring but also deromanticizing his neighborhood: "Man!
How many times have I stood on the rooftop of my broken-down
building at night and watched the bulb-lit world below. Like somehow it's different at night, this my Harlem."[45] Along similar lines,
Nuyorican poet Miguel Piñero's play *Short Eyes* (1974) is set in New
York's Riker's Island prison. The anger and hopelessness of the long-
time prisoners are revealed in raw account. Piñero wrote the play as
part of a prison theatre workshop. It is set in the dayroom where
black, white, and Puerto Rican prisoners await trial. A middle-class
white prisoner enters. He is welcomed at first, particularly by Charlie
"Longshoe" Murphy, the "Don-Gee" (head) of the whites. But things
change when it is discovered that he is a "short eye," prison argot for
child molester. In prison hierarchy the least regarded are snitches and
sexual predators. Antipathy toward the "short eye" gathers momentum,
eventuating in his murder. In "Deviancy in a Deviant Society," I
noted that throughout the play, "Piñero challenges the audience not
to become complicit bystanders, but rather observers of a morality
play designed to confront our penchant for labeling deviancy."[46] Prison
life, as Piñero sees it, creates a heightened sense of status but it also
dehumanizes. Juan, the play's protagonist and moral center, resists
joining the others. This puts Juan at risk. Piñero builds on the metaphysical outlook of the cynical observer and participant in Nuyorican
literary style; where stigmatization leaves an indelible mark, cynicism
provides a way out. Juan serves as the play's moral compass, warning
his protégé Cupcake: "Oye, espera, no corra – just one thing, brother,
your fear of this place stole your spirit. . . . And this ain't no pawnshop" (121). Once gone, the spirit departs forever.

Not every playwright during this period sought to expose the darker
side of America. Frederick Knott's *Wait Until Dark* (1966) is a potboiler
thriller; Robert Anderson's *I Never Sang for My Father* (1968) looks
closely at a father–son relationship; Bill Manhoff's *The Owl and the
Pussycat* (1964) is a titillating comedy; and Leonard Gershe's *Butterflies
are Free* (1969) examines sexual liberation with a young man from
Scarsdale and his neighbor. Michael Weller's *Moonchildren* (1972) also
takes up the issue of sexual liberation. The play is a comedy about
college students during a period of "free love." Paul Zindel's *The Effects of
Gamma Rays on Man-in-the-Moon Marigolds* (1970) concerns a family's
struggling amidst a shrill mother, two teenage daughters, and an aging

grandmother. Arthur Miller's contributions during this period consist of *After the Fall* (1964), a study of his marriage to Marilyn Monroe with the Holocaust as backdrop; *Incident at Vichy* (1964), which examines moral choices in the wake of Nazi horrors; and *The Price* (1968), an intimate study of three siblings sifting through their past in the parents' attic.

It is appropriate to close this chapter with Robert Patrick's *Kennedy's Children* (1975). The period's spiritual "decedents" are taken up in this play, essentially as an "extended monologue." Five characters reminisce about the loss of idealism. They sit at a bar and talk to the audience. Though they do not address each other, they share disillusionment. Spangler is a gay actor who helped make the Off-Off-Broadway scene. Now he curses the commercialization of downtown theatre. Wanda speaks about John Kennedy's age of Camelot. Mark is a Vietnam veteran who picked up drugs and now seeks solace in Buddhism. Rona is a radical washout who conjures a picture of liberalism's betrayal. Carla is a Marilyn Monroe groupie, longing to emulate her idol's career. Rona, at the conclusion of the play, offers up a monologue about the corruption of the 1960s: "The last big march was against the mining of the harbor at Hanoi, and besides the old chant of 'one-two-three-four, we don't want your fucking war,' my friends were muttering, 'Why are we here? We've been marching since we were babies and all we did was make Jane Fonda famous.'"[47] Patrick's play marks the conclusion of an era. The cynicism that remained was left for subsequent generations. In the next period, playwrights picked this up and railed against both sides of the ideological spectrum.

CHAPTER 4

Mad as Hell: American Drama, 1976–1989

Teach: Fuckin' Ruthie, fuckin' Ruthie, fuckin' Ruthie, fuckin' Ruthie, fuckin' Ruthie.

David Mamet, *American Buffalo* (1976)[1]

Kitty: Lil, you're not being reasonable.
Lil: Fuck reasonable! This is my body, my life. I'll decide what's going to happen to me.

Jane Chambers, *Last Summer at Bluefish Cove* (1980)[2]

May: I'm gonna' kill her and then I'm gonna' kill you. Systematically. With sharp knives. Two separate knives. One for her and one for you. (She slams wall with her elbow. Wall resonates.)

Sam Shepard, *Fool for Love* (1983)[3]

Lloyd: Don't talk back to me. I'll kick your ass.
Mae: Fuck you, Lloyd.

Maria Irene Fornes, *Mud* (1983)[4]

Eddie: Somethin' terrible is goin' on, Mickey. It's a dark time.

David Rabe, *Hurlyburly* (1984)[5]

Pale: Goddamn this fuckin' place, how can anybody live this shit city?

Lanford Wilson, *Burn This* (1987)[6]

Bradley: You're acting like a Chinese Stepinfetchit. That's what you're acting like. Jesus fucking Christ, Vincent. A Chinese Stepinfetchit.

Philip Kan Gotanda, *Yankee Dawg You Die* (1989)[7]

Go to your windows and shout: I'm mad as hell and I'm not going to take it anymore!

Paddy Chayefsky, *Network* (MGM/UA 1976)

This chapter interprets American drama from 1976 to 1989 as an expression of rage. This interpretation is based on two central claims. The first derives from the rage growing out of social conditions of the second half of the 1970s. The United States exited Vietnam in 1973; Saigon collapsed the following year. Nixon's resignation amidst scandal diminished trust in government. The oil embargo of 1973 contributed to economic instability. Rising "stagflation" – a term coined by economists of the time describing a combination of inflation and recession – marked the end of America's post-World War II boom. From the end of World War II to the mid-1970s, America witnessed an increase in low-cost housing, rising wages, reserve currency backed by gold, technological supremacy, motivated workforce, trade surplus, and a rising stock market. Following the economic turnaround, large sections of the nation experienced moribund incomes. Despite a sharp increase of women in the workplace and a bump in the economy during the early 1980s, the middle-class suffered. Unlike the crash of 1929, this decline was gradual; however, the nation's psyche was still affected. Christopher Capozzola contends that "as the Great Society liberalism of the postwar era collapsed under the burdens of a troubled economy and a hostile public," the situation turned grim, leading to "taxpayer revolts, antiwelfare agitation, and bitter fights over subsidies for the nation's troubled cities."[8] The second consequence concerns the 1980s, which saw the AIDS epidemic, the Reagan administration, and continuing obstacles to minority participation in the economy. The anarchy and liberation of the 1960s gave way to rampant individualism and acquisitiveness even within the most liberal segments of society.

The representative play of this era is David Mamet's *American Buffalo* (1976). The entrance of Walt Cole, called "Teach," into Don Dubrow's "Resale Shop," a "junk" or pawnshop, is a watershed moment in American drama.

TEACH: (*Appears in the doorway and enters the store.*) Good morning.
DON: Morning, Teach.
TEACH: (*Walks around the store a bit in silence.*) Fuckin' Ruthie, fuckin' Ruthie, fuckin' Ruthie, fuckin' Ruthie, fuckin' Ruthie.

DON: What?
TEACH: Fuckin' *Ruthie* . . . (9)

Mamet's play sets a tone similar to what John Osborne's *Look Back in Anger* did for post-World War II British theatre in the 1950s. Teach is angry at Ruthie for specific reasons, but he is enraged for more general reasons as well. He lashes out at the dissatisfaction of his life and the absence of compelling values. A late 1970s poll reported that "almost two-thirds of Americans felt that the nation was in very serious trouble."[9] In July 1979, President Carter delivered his "Energy and the Crisis of Confidence" address that came to be known as the "Malaise" speech. Adding to this was the rise of the cultural wars. The sexual revolution, rebellion against authority, and the repudiation of conventional morality of the 1960s and early 1970s led to a backlash. Ronald Reagan's 1984 "Morning in America" speech was for many a welcome relief from pessimism and decline of moral certainty. Reagan's patriotism inspired the public just as Franklin Roosevelt's "You have nothing to fear but fear itself" speech did for the 1930s. In his book *Morning in America*, Gil Troy remarks that "Reagan's combination of visionary rigidity and tactical fluidity reinvigorated the presidency. His Hollywood-slick, small-town faith in America as a shining 'city upon a hill' restored many Americans' confidence in themselves and their country."[10] Reagan's followers and his opponents laid the ground for the culture war; *American Buffalo* played a significant role in determining the borders of this battlefield. Teach, like Travis Bickle (played by Robert De Niro) in Martin Scorsese's 1975 film *Taxi Driver*, rages not merely against specific people, but also against the status quo. Bickle's intimidating refrain, "You talkin' to me," while looking in the mirror – and directly at the camera – epitomized the period's frustration. Paddy Chayefsky's protagonist in *Network* (1976) commanding everyone to open their windows and shout "I'm mad as hell" (quoted in the chapter's epigraph) exposed the rage taking hold of America's psyche. Mick Jagger put it best in 1978 when he sang: "What a mess / this town's in tatters / I've been shattered / My brain's been battered!"[11]

Before Teach enters, Don and Bobby have been discussing business. Don, the owner of the junk shop, berates his protégé, Bobby, for failing to follow through. Bobby was supposed to "case" a perspective "mark." But Bobby's heroin addiction makes him unreliable. Don uses their associate, Fletch, to make his point. For Don, Fletch is the quintessential businessman which Bobby is not: "You take him [Fletch] and you put him down in some strange town with just a nickel in his pocket, and by nightfall he'll have that town by the balls. This is not talk, Bob, this is action" (4). Action, as the play makes clear, is the sine qua non of manhood and business. However, in Mamet's world, talk frequently trumps action. Bluster and puffery is the essence of Mamet's dialogue, artfully disguising ineffectuality.

Teach enters. He circles the junk shop. He observes the remnants of a poker game (cards, drinks, etc.) on the table – a game in which he lost heavily. Teach (his nickname is an important symbol) begins to recite rhythmically: "Fuckin' Ruthie." Ruthie, another associate of Don, was the previous night's poker winner. Teach's rage stems from the fact that at a diner over breakfast Teach (who had been awake all night) entered, ran into lovers Grace and Ruthie, sat down with them, and helped himself to a piece of toast from Grace's plate. According to Teach, Grace said, "Help yourself." This infuriates Teach, who feels that his past generosity to Grace and Ruthie entitles him willy-nilly to her toast. Teach suppresses his anger, but once inside the shop he unleashes his vitriol: "from the mouth of a Southern bulldyke asshole of a vicious nowhere cunt can this trash come" (10–11). Teach feels the sting of injustice; people who win at poker should remain humble. There ought to be honor among thieves.

Mamet's plays focus on the "con." Characters bluff, feint, pretend, and analyze others in search of weaknesses. The con artist as salesman (established by O'Neill's Hickey in *The Iceman Cometh*) provides Mamet the opportunity to create a language of the mountebank. In Mamet one finds spiel interspersed with imaginatively phrased explicatives and duplicity. This legerdemain appears first in Mamet's *Sexual Perversity in Chicago* (1974). In this play two men and two women jockey for positions of authority in their sexual warfare. The *homo ludens* (irresponsibly sportive men) hyperbolize their sexual conquests while disguising their insecurities. Their bonding ritual is exposed as mere bluff against insecurity and rejection. In *American Buffalo*, the junk shop setting serves as a safe haven for the three characters. The play explores the male bonding of small-time hoodlums who huddle together for protection. Inside (onstage) there is safety; outside (offstage), danger. Inveterate losers, they form an extended family. Their ineptitude – their scheme to steal a buffalo nickel goes awry – is likely one of several missed opportunities. They symbolize the dog-eat-dog system that is the basis of American business. Here is where business loyalty shifts precariously depending on who "holds the cards."

The language of *American Buffalo* comprises the syncopated rhythms of ragtime. When, for example, Teach says, "fuckin' Ruthie," the four syllables are 4/4 time accentuating the second, or off-beat ("in" and "ie"). The off-beat is the signature that marks ragtime. Like Harold Pinter, Mamet makes use of pauses and circumlocution in his dialogue, transferring them to an American vernacular. This allows for the particular spontaneity and improvisation of people who think on their feet. When, for instance, Donny presses Teach to explain how he will break in and why no one else should command the operation, Teach makes his case up on the fly. His language circles the subject, using metaphors of place ("Fort Knox") and time ("Middle Ages"): "What the fuck they live in Fort Knox? (Get in.) (*Snorts.*) You break a *window*, worse comes to worse you kick the fucking *back door* in. (What do you think this is, the Middle Ages?)" (77). Mamet carefully controls the rhythm by inserting parentheses. The comments in parentheses intend sarcasm mitigating overt hostility. Teach is angered by the skepticism directed his way. Yet for all his machismo, there is humor in the fact that he is no better prepared for breaking and entering than Bobby. His breaking a window or kicking in a back door hardly qualifies as superior know-how. Not action but Teach's language persuades Donny. Expletives are not intended merely to shock; they emphasize and sustain conviction. Yet action rarely takes place. Unlike J. L. Austin's speech act theory, in which we "do things" with words and an utterance is "performative" when it consists of an act "that is being performed,"[12] Mamet's characters speak of doing but rarely do anything. They use transitive verbs to instigate, provoke, and alter the environment, yet reality rarely changes.

Mamet's language maximally employs metaphor as a tool of persuasion. For instance, Teach finds out that Donny, Bobby, and Fletch plan to steal the coin from the "mark." Donny and Bobby assume the nickel to be a valuable collector's item because the mark paid dearly for it. Teach, sussing out the plan, attempts to assert his presence in the scheme. He makes the case that Bobby is failing to keep "clean," and that he, rather than Fletch or Bobby, possesses the necessary skills for the crime. Donny, however, maintains his loyalty. Teach admires Donny for the "things" he has done for Bobby. Don says, "I don't do anything for him," but Teach insists he does. Still, Teach warns: "I mean, the guy's got you taking his high-speed blender and a Magnavox, you send the kid in. You're talking about a real *job*." He adds: "We both know what we're saying here. We both know we're talking about some job needs more than the kid's gonna skin-pop go in there with a *crowbar*" (34). Metaphor implies comparison and is necessarily non-literal. Teach is using the metaphor of blenders, tape players, and crowbars to suggest that Bobby's inexperience and addiction will cause him to botch the job and avoid "real" items of value. The essence of metaphor, write George Lakoff and Mark Johnson, "*is understanding and experiencing one kind of thing in terms of another.*"[13] Metaphor is well illustrated by Teach's references to "skin-popping" or "crowbar." This figure of speech utilizes descriptives; it alludes to one thing through the imaginative terms of another. Mamet's plays are more akin to radio than film – more descriptive than visual – because they are orchestrated orally. In his best works there are one or two sets at most – a junk shop, a Chinese restaurant and an office, a teacher's office, a producer's office, and a home. Mamet experiments with "filmic" depictions in his plays (*Edmond* and *Sexual Perversity*, for instance) incorporating different locales, yet his emphasis on language remains a defining feature of his technique.

If Mamet's plays depend on aural rhythms, Ntozake Shange accentuates physical expression. During the 1960s and early 1970s, social justice informed the Black Arts Movement. It emphasized primarily a male struggle. This situation was emended with Shange's *for colored girls who have considered suicide when the rainbow is enuf* (1977). In this play seven female characters are brought together through the medium of dance. Motion in this play is as important as words. The characters sometimes express inner conflict, other times commiserate together, but primarily they move individually and in unison. Shange creates an interactive world of ideas. Her play is not so much about conflict as interaction. This is accomplished through storytelling, dance, and poetry, what Shange calls a "choreopoem." Seven storytellers dress in the colors of the rainbow: yellow, red, green, purple, blue, and orange, with the addition of one color outside the rainbow, brown. The rainbow signifies shared experience as women of color. Their stories include abuse by men, historical figures, friendship, loss, and recovery. As the Lady in Orange says: "ever since I realized there waz someone callt / a colored girl an evil woman a bitch or a nag / I been tryin not to be that & leave bitterness / in somebody else's cup / come to somebody to love me."[14]

Black women are not depicted as a monolithic group with uniform aims, but rather the play celebrates their differences. For Shange, the rainbow represents "a fabulous symbol," because "If you see only one color, it's not beautiful. If you see them all, it is. A colored girl, by my definition, is a girl of many colors. But she can only see her overall beauty if she has to look deep within her."[15] Movement here is meaningful; it allows for complexities beyond words. Shange explains that the "freedom to move in space, to demand of my own sweat a perfection that could continually be approached, though never known, waz poem to me, my body & mind eclipsing, probably for the first time in my life" (xv). Along with movement, Shange introduces a lexicon for women of color. She calls the play "the words of a young black girl's growing up, her triumphs and errors, our struggle to become all that is forbidden by our environment, all that is forfeited by our gender, all that we have forgotten."[16] The word "stuff," for instance, reveals complexity. The Lady in Green says: "somebody almost walked off wid alla my stuff" (52). *Stuff* is saturated with meaning, referring to belongings and objects, but also identity and self-respect. It is, as I have remarked elsewhere, "a *living word* with a surplus of inferences, rich in nuance."[17] *Stuff* comes alive when spoken by the actress; its meaning is carried by inflection. The more it is repeated, the more contexts it accumulates. The final words praise black women evolving: "& this is for colored girls who have considered suicide / but are movin to the ends of their own rainbows" (67). Its communal emphasis notwithstanding, Shange's *for colored girls* carries its own brand of rage. Its climax occurs when the Lady in Red describes life with Beau Willie Brown, a drunken, abusive veteran who dangles her children out of the window: "he kicked the screen outa the window / & held the kids offa the sill / you gonna marry me / yeh, I'll marry ya / anything / but bring the children back in the house." But her entreaties are to no avail: "I stood by beau in the window / with Naomi reaching for me / & Kwame screamin mommy mommy from the fifth story / but I cd only whisper / & he dropped em" (63). The cold-blooded defenestration reverberates in one's memory.

Gesture is emphasized stylistically in Luis Valdez's *Zoot Suit* (1978). The plot concerns the racial violence that erupted in Los Angeles in 1943, when white soldiers attacked Chicanos who wore zoot suits. Zoot suits were designer coats extending down to the knees, loose-fitting pants called "Punjab," and long watch-chains that draped from the pocket to the waist-belt and dangled close to the ground. The outfits were colorful and flamboyant. The term "zoot" means something performed in exaggerated style. The zoot suit symbolizes the "Pachuco." It defines machismo, defiance, and what Stuart Cosgrove calls "a subcultural gesture that refused to concede to the manners of subservience."[18] World War II meant shortages of gas and other essentials, especially fabrics needed for uniforms. By wearing the heavily layered zoot suit, Chicanos asserted their opposition to the war they believed had little to do with their lives. The Pachuco attitude, writes Valdez, is the "recalcitrant rebel who refuses to give in, who refuses to bend, refuses to admit that he is wrong. He is incorrigible." Theatrically, Valdez describes the posture of the Pachuco character: "The stance is almost ideological, even cultural; it's mythical."[19] *Zoot Suit*'s protagonist Henry Reyna is falsely accused of what was known at the time as the Sleepy Lagoon Murders. The plot moves from Reyna's life prior to the murder and trial, to his relationship with a Jewish social worker who falls in love with him. The play makes use of screens flashing news reports of the war and the trial. Henry is shadowed by El Pachuco (played with choreographic grace by Edward James Olmos), who serves as alter ego and narrator. Jorge Huerta describes El Pachuco as representing "the Aztec concept of the '*nahual*,' or other self as he comes to Henry's support during the solitary scene in prison."[20] Reyna's internal struggle consists in emulating Pachuco and attempting to break free of his influence at the same time. The play itself incorporates dance, flashback scenes, and music.

Theatricality is a concern of Sam Shepard, whose plays unleash restless destructiveness conveyed with born-again passion. His *Curse of the Starving Class* (1978) and *Buried Child* (1978) explore homecoming, memory, familial bonds, food, time, and space. In *Buried Child*, Dodge is the patriarch of a farming family. He always sits in the same chair and sneaks sips of whiskey. His wife Halie carries on an affair with Father Dewis. The family's two sons, Tilden, the oldest, and Bradley, an amputee, work the farm. The action centers on the return of Vince, Tilden's son, and his girlfriend, Shelly. Shelly serves as a sounding board for the other characters; she, along with the audience, views the bizarre goings on with incredulity. The return of the prodigal son, Vince, to the Illinois farm is meant to be temporary, or so he thinks.

The play's hidden secret is a buried child, the family's incestuous offspring. Vince's return complicates things. In the end Shelly leaves and Vince remains.

Shepard's *Buried Child* is about fate and free will. Vince has left home. But once he returns he is powerless to leave. His homecoming is cyclical – a recurrence similar to dreams or rituals – what Nietzsche calls eternal recurrence: "the idea that whatever there is will return again, and that whatever there is, is a return of itself, that it has all happened before, and will happen again, exactly the same way each time, forever. Nothing happens that has not happened an infinite number of times and which will not happen again, for all eternity, in exact iteration of itself."[21] For Shepard, characters return both figuratively and literally to the stage in "exact iteration." Their actions are ritualistic and theatrical. Vince's experience of leaving and returning is repeated exactly with each performance. During the play Vince agrees to buy his grandfather a two-dollar bottle of whiskey. The simple trip to the liquor store becomes eye-opening. When he returns Shelly asks, "What happened to you Vince? You just disappeared." Vince replies: "(*Pauses, delivers speech front.*) I was gonna run last night. I was gonna run and keep right on running. I drove all night. Clear to the Iowa border. The old man's two bucks sitting seat beside me." He attempts to assert his free will, but the hold of family and fear of the outside determine otherwise. While driving he observes his reflection in the windshield, noting that his "face became his father's face. Same bones. Same nose. Same breath. And his father's face changed to his Grandfather's face. And it went on like that. Changing."[22] Vince is transfixed as he observes unfolding imbrications of his ancestry. The face Vince sees in the mirror is not merely his lineage, but a doppelgänger along the order of Grant Wood's *American Gothic* (1930). Wood's classic painting of two lean, elderly Iowan farmers, husband and wife, with pitchfork in hand and barn in the backdrop, is an American classic. Similarly, Vince is caught in the grip of images he sees as his fate which thwart his effort to escape. The stage itself is the center of gravity gripping Shepard's characters. They are drawn back only to reenact the ritual of escape. Shepard shares with Eugene O'Neill the notion that no matter how dysfunctional the family, it retains a hold on consciousness. What is illustrated by the theatrical ritual is the limitation of freedom.

Two themes are prominent in Shepard's plays: the division of appearance and reality, and the conflict between freedom and the determining influence of the past. In Shelly's first impression of the home she invites comparison with a Norman Rockwell painting. For her the family she sees at first is frozen in time, its pristine ambience unsullied by modern life. But this appearance is deceptive. Thomas Adler reminds us that Shepard "steadily undercuts such mythicizations of the American nuclear family as it appears in popular culture by showing the disparity between the real and the imagined." In *Buried Child*, the family is in denial, "inhabiting a fetid atmosphere."[23] Dodge denies the past even as he admits to his past deeds – he drowned the baby and buried it in the yard. However, not all the characters are in denial, nor does the play allow the denials to endure. The corn Tilden brings onstage represents earthly fecundity and serves as a reminder of the buried baby. Vince tries to deny his past, yet accepts its full weight by staying on the farm. While *Buried Child* owes much to Harold Pinter's *The Homecoming*, it follows an American literary tradition. S. J. Bottoms observes that *Buried Child* "suggests the probable influence not only of O'Neill but of rural-gothic novelists such as Carson McCullers, Truman Capote, and Flannery O'Conner." The play's "rustic-creepiness" typifies the genre. The mood of "death and decay," says Bottoms, "haunts the remotely situated farmhouse; some unspoken damnation hangs over the family, like a Damoclean sword, blighting their land and relationships alike."[24]

Dodge is the source of the play's comedy. His ribald dirty-old-man remarks to Shelly and his demand for his "bottle" of whiskey, also symbolizing his nursing bottle, are reminiscent of Ham in Beckett's *Endgame*. Dodge, sitting in the same chair center stage, resembles Ham on his throne. Ham is blind and thus dependent on Clov. Dodge's blindness is spiritual. He is locked in his chair drinking while the TV's blue reflection stares at him. The theme of food in the form of corn is recurrent throughout *Buried Child*. Like Shepard's *Curse of the Starving Class*, food symbolizes spiritual hunger amidst material abundance: fertility runs amok while values go awry.

Shepard's next major play, *True West*, premiered at San Francisco's Magic Theatre in 1980. Its heralded transfer to New York bode well. Opening at the New York Public Theatre, it had all the ingredients of success: written by a well-established dramatist, directed by Joseph Papp, and starring well-known actors Tommy Lee Jones and Peter Boyle. Yet the play was dismissed by the critics. It was not until 1982, when it reopened with a fledgling Chicago theatre company, Steppenwolf, starring John Malkovich and Gary Sinise (who also directed), that Shepard's drama became highly acclaimed. *True West* is the story of Austin, an Ivy League Hollywood screenwriter in his late thirties, and Lee, his older brother, a drifter living in the desert. Lee and Austin are like Neil Simon's *Odd Couple*, two entirely different people forced into a testosterone-driven rivalry. The backdrop is their mother's California home. She has departed for Alaska. Austin, suffering writer's block, sequesters himself to complete his screenplay. Lee arrives unannounced, with the objective of stealing household appliances from the neighbors. Austin was commissioned to write a Western, but cannot gain a handle on the subject. Lee jealously pesters his brother. Saul, a Hollywood producer, arrives and is intrigued by Lee's "authenticity." Lee appears the essence of the frontier, the individualist who gets around the system and faces down the drones. For Saul, Lee is plucky, clever, and inventive – like Huck Finn, he finds a way to prevail. His rugged individualism makes him, not Austin, the "real" cowboy of the "true West." Saul consigns Lee to write the screenplay, causing a jealous Austin to take up robbery. Appalled that Lee is now doing his job, Austin turns the tables: drunk and challenged, he rampages through the neighborhood stealing toasters. Like *American Buffalo*, robbery provides the action. However, the unlikely thief in this case is Ivy Leaguer Austin. While Lee toils at the typewriter hitting the keys with a golf club, Austin parades proudly around the house with hundreds of toasters, testing their "merits" ceremoniously. Annoyed at his brother's drunken shenanigans, Lee threatens Austin (see figure 4).

This sibling rivalry symbolizes two American icons: corporate success and the lone cowboy. The term "icon" refers to venerated monuments of cultural or religious beliefs. Austin and Lee represent America's twin paradigms of wealth and individualism. Austin has a wife, family, car, profession, business, and money – all ingredients required for his civilized and yet, as the play unfolds, mundane life. Lee is the reckless gambler and cowpoke who banks on luck, the next turn of the card, and faith that providence will deliver the goods. Lee refers to his time spent in the desert as a place where cash is made or lost quickly, and where life is as hostile as the environment. Austin the screenwriter and dream-maker, and Lee the inveterate gambler, share a characteristically American optimism; for them, success is always within reach. One stakes his faith in the Puritan work ethic, the other takes the Las Vegas attitude that his number will emerge if he rolls the dice long

FIGURE 4   *True West*, by Sam Shepard, 1984. Jim Birdsall (Lee, left) and
Mark Robbins (Austin, right). Photograph by Keith Flannery. Reprinted
courtesy of Kansas City Repertory Theatre (formerly Missouri Repertory
Theatre).

enough. Both willingly trade their past for the chance at the big lotto
– the wholesale, top-to-bottom overhaul of their lives. The action of
the play is provided by Austin's transformation; his successful thievery
emboldens him. He undertakes to convince Lee to take him to the
desert in exchange for ghost-writing the screenplay. Austin's rebirth
is synonymous with a "Great Awakening"; when asked by Lee why
he is so obsessed with "toast" as if it is his "salvation," he says:

> AUSTIN: Well it is like salvation sort of. I mean the smell. I love the smell
> of toast. And the sun's coming up. It makes me feel like anything's
> possible. Ya' know?
> LEE: (*Back to Austin, facing window upstage.*) So go to Church why don't ya'?
> AUSTIN: Like a beginning. I love beginnings.
> LEE: Oh yeah. I've always been kinda' partial to endings myself.[25]

Lee would like an "ending" befitting the completion of the screenplay. Austin is euphoric, convinced that his successful thievery unequivocally proves his worth for Austin's desert "paradise."

Their sibling rivalry endures through the play. Each seeks to break free of his predictable condition, each wanting to be "born again" by becoming the other. In the penultimate scene, Austin begs Lee to take him to the desert. Lee is shocked: how can his little brother abandon Hollywood success for scrounging and hustling? Austin, however, believes he might discover the "true West" rather than his make-believe tinsel town. Austin sees his brother as the cosmic optimist holding to the belief of manifest destiny – the upbeat, can-do spirit of "Morning in America." Lee's arrival brings the lucky chance required to remake Austin's drab existence. For Lee, the screenplay is his shot on the wheel of fortune. Their competing tension to beat the other at the other's game reveals their deteriorating psychological state. Their wrestling match at the play's end, in which the enraged brothers try to kill each other in front of their mother, is evidence of their breakdown. Shepard's stage represents psychological and physical corrosion: the mother's well-kept kitchen at the beginning disintegrates during the course of the play, manifested by the death of the plants, the littered beer and liquor bottles, and the empty pages of an unwritten screenplay. Like Mamet's junk shop in *American Buffalo*, the ravages of conflict leave fragments of a once flourishing household. The visual cues – the stage mess and the brothers' donnybrook – define the deepening decay. By the end the aim of creating a "cowboy story" is destroyed, symbolizing the collapse of Western mythology.

The Western frontier is one of America's most enduring myths. In his book *Gunfighter Nation*, Richard Slotkin observes that the reality of the West meant "the conquest of the wilderness and the subjugation or displacement of the Native Americans." The mythic component, says Slotkin, establishes "our achievement of a national identity, a democratic polity in an ever-expanding economy, and a phenomenally dynamic and 'progressive' civilization."[26] Frederick Jackson Turner's 1893 "Frontier Thesis" speech portrays the "frontier" as "productive of individualism" and "democracy."[27] However, Turner alleges that western expansion was terminated by the Pacific Ocean; only the notion of expansion remains. The next century transformed the frontier from reality into myth. Buffalo Bill shows, for example, flourished during the late 1890s and early 1900s as the "true West" merged into folklore.

Hollywood soon capitalized on this idea, one that would extend through the century. Reagan in the 1980s is often seen in cowboy attire, personifying the "John Wayne" symbol of rugged individualism. For Shepard, the frontier imagined gloriously turns out to be either dull or terrifying. Lee's "true West" is hardly the glamour Saul, Austin, or the media imagined. Lee knows that life in the Western desert is "not something you get out a boy scout handbook" (48). Yet Austin and Saul are convinced Lee has what it takes. Austin at first objects to Lee's concept of the West, saying it is "too much like real life" (23). But Saul's rebuttal argues that Lee's idea "has the ring of truth" in it, capturing "something about the real West" (53). Austin's skepticism changes into belief. He is enamored by his brother's freewheeling attitude and reckless disregard for rules. He comes to realize that what Lee has – even if he is only staring at a cactus in the desert – is freedom.

But freedom in *True West* is merely vastness; the Alaskan frontier, which the mother ran off to, is cold and dissolute. The brothers' toothless father, who lives in the Arizona desert, has only his dentures lost in a bag of chop suey to show for his independence. The Western freedom Austin longs to experience exists only in his mind. As the play makes clear, appearance and reality clash. Lee trumps his brother because he has what Americans value: real-life experiences. Lee, skeptical at first, claims that Austin's "pitch" for the film is a "phony," nothing more than a retread of a "Hopalong Cassidy" TV story that was prevalent during their childhood. But Saul buys it, believing Lee has the goods. "Something about the real West," he says.

AUSTIN: Why? Because it's got horses? Because it's got grown men acting like little boys?
SAUL: Something about the land. Your brother is speaking from experience. (35)

Austin tries to persuade Saul otherwise, saying: "He's been camped out for three months. Talking to cactus. What's he know about what people wanna see on the screen!" (35). However, he cannot undermine Lee's "experience." In America, experience carries cachet. Martin Jay reminds us that even before the Revolution, "Americans frequently drew on the rhetoric of experience as a source of legitimation against rational abstraction or the deadweight of unexamined authority. Experience meant here both novel experimentation and learning valuable lessons from the past to be imaginatively applied to the future. It meant profiting from bodily encounters with a new and often harsh environment and drawing lessons they produce in the ordinary, everyday lives of common men and women."[28] But for Shepard reliance on experience exaggerates its value. The value of the mythic West, the so-called individual struggling against the elements, is in *True West* kitsch – little more than someone talking to a cactus.

Austin and Lee, like Vince, are terrified of the outside world. Lee seeks the safety of their mother's home because he "can't make it out there." Austin, a Hollywood screenwriter, lives life in a cocoon. Lee repeatedly recounts "true-to-life stuff" (15), telling Saul that he can provide the "real Western" or "true-to-life Western" needed for a Hollywood film. Yet the "true West," like the outside, is hardly the stuff of dreams. The opening of *True West* confirms this point: the stage directions note that Austin is illuminated by candlelight, while Lee in the kitchen is lit by moonlight. Lee's is the lighting of the outdoor "real" light; Austin's is by manmade candle. In scene seven, after roles have reversed, the candlelight now shines on Lee, and Austin is in the kitchen staring out the window. But the "authentic" light from the window hardly casts a "glow" suggestive of adventure. Rather, the dull reality of the West is evidenced at the opening, where Shepard's stage directions refer to coyotes making background noises with "a dog-like bark," rather than the "long, mournful, solitary howl of the Hollywood stereotype" (4). Lee is the romanticization of the loner (epitomized by his reference to Kirk Douglas in the film *Lonely Are the Brave*). But in *True West* the loner is just a scared little man. Austin is the successful, materialistic screenwriter in search of "authenticity." His success is unsatisfying compared to his brother's exploits. Yet when he implores his brother to take him to the desert, Lee dethrones the myth:

> LEE: Do you actually think I choose to live out in the middle a' no-where? Do ya'? Ya' think it's some kinda' philosophical decision I took or somethin'? I'm livin' out there 'cause I can't make it here! And yer bitchin' to me about all your success! (49)

Shepard's next play, *Fool for Love* (1983), again focuses on siblings. Set in a motel at the edge of the Mojave desert, *Fool for Love* is about

May and Eddie, a couple enduring a 15-year-long love–hate relationship. Their hostile mating dance moves the plot forward; Eddie cannot live without May, but he cannot live with her either. The uninterrupted, intermission-less play explores the emotional whirlwind of a twisted yet passionate relationship, replete with slamming doors, scaling walls, and physical intensity. The angry May literally throws Eddie out of her life then begs him to stay. Eddie consoles May, offering her the overprocessed American staple, Ovaltine and potato chips. Like *Curse of the Starving Class*, food represents more than a communal routine; Eddie's purpose in feeding her is to negate rather than nourish. We discover they are half-siblings. Though they bonded before knowing of their relation, they cannot escape feelings of guilt. Their father, the "Old Man," remains a corrosive omnipresence onstage, sipping whiskey in the downstage left corner of the motel room. The "Old Man" in *Fool for Love* has much in common with Dodge in *Buried Child*, as well as the "old man" referred to in *True West*. In *Fool for Love* the Old Man is situated onstage in a chair viewing the play's action. Yet he is delegated to the side of the stage, whereas in *Buried Child* Dodge is center. This new placement signifies the father's waning influence. Only Eddie acknowledges him, but he is more a presence in May and Eddie's mind. The Old Man functions as an interactive narrator, moving in and out of the drama to comment on the action. Like Dodge, he never leaves the stage, rising from his rocking chair only at the end. Martin, May's "date," is the guinea pig on which Eddie and May test their respective tales of the past. He also provides much of the comedy. Through the play's two protagonists, Shepard explores themes of sexual connection by means of their on-again, off-again relationship. Eddie continually professes his love for May, telling farfetched stories. May is full of contradictions; she both loves and hates Eddie. While the other characters – Eddie, the Old Man, and Martin – are oblivious to aspects of her personality, the audience is privy to her innermost feelings. Her pre-packaged suitcase, emotional highs and lows, sexual desire, loneliness, and bursts of rage are pieces of her fragmented personality. May's sincere declarations of love for Eddie on the one hand, and her personal animus and physical assaults against him (she kicks him in the groin) on the other, are projected with satiric wit. May has been stranded by Eddie so often she has become wise to his entreaties. A violent slamming of doors, gunshots offstage, and the physical wrestling match between Eddie and Martin create a rollicking momentum. The interaction between Eddie and the Old Man is equally compelling. The Old Man's struggle to hold onto his fading influence is conveyed by his manipulation. But, like his presence on the sideline, his domination is slipping into the wings.

Eddie returns to May after repeatedly abandoning her. This action, she says, has infected her "like a disease" (30). Viewed as part of a larger patriarchal structure, Eddie is a binding force and his systematic return is a means of controlling May. Yet, for Shepard, the lines of demarcation are not so clearly drawn. While Eddie's continual comings and goings are a means toward maintaining gender roles of domination and subordination, Shepard creates a situation which, during this particular meeting, leaves the audience unsure of who has abandoned whom. May, not Eddie, has fled from their immobile trailer to a motel room on the edge of the Mojave desert. Eddie, as soon as he finds May there, remarks, "What'd you have to go and run off for anyway" (25). May agrees to "date" Martin in the hope of breaking the cycle. Like Vince, she tries to terminate the patterns of her life. The only way to free her weighty web is through renewal. Like Austin, she wants to recreate herself. May's departure at the end suggests that she might succeed. The Old Man seems to think the relationship of Eddie and May is inextricable, but May's exit creates uncertainty.

Shepard presents characters who, like Eddie, "dream things up" (27). Both May and Eddie seek to create a past apart from each other. Eddie and May are determined to define themselves independently: Eddie through his alcohol, stunts, rodeo, and womanizing, and May through her new job, home, and "date." Both use imagination to retool their lives. But their self-involvement is merely temporary. Eddie insists, "You know we're connected, May" (31). Attraction and abandonment constitute a fateful recurrence. Their love–hate ritual exudes an explosive quality, what Marc Robinson describes as Shepard's "centrifugal force, scattering [characters] to the margins of their stage-world, where they are marooned on their own self-interest."[29] Yet their self-interest is merely a pause from attraction too compelling to overcome. It is as if Shepard's characters are held by rubber bands; they can depart the stage for a determined distance before the elastic tension snaps them back. The outside beckons, but once there they realize they are no match for its magnitude. Though May and Eddie are trapped and want to exit, the outside is too threatening. The violent sounds and lights of offstage car horns, gunshots, and burning vehicles penetrate their motel room, menacing their existence and impelling them to cling together. The stage space itself – its conventions of proscenium, wings, audience, and limited exits – entraps Shepard's characters. This is made evident in *Fool for Love* when the characters bang on the walls for release.

True West and *Fool for Love* present a kaleidoscope of images and allegories related to memory and its theatrical representation. Recalling the past creates a "magic reality" wherein symbols surface and are made manifest in theatrical ways (the father in the rocker stage left, for instance). By contrast, Shepard's dialogue is realism in the raw – no-holes-barred sexual passion, father–son relationships, and sibling rivalry. Yet his plays pose questions about the theatre itself and there is an attempt to explore the two most important concerns of twentieth-century theatre – how to square the popular conceptions of reality with apprehensions, dreams, and memories, and how to present the struggle between free will and fate. Shepard's representation of consciousness, especially his love–hate relationship to his father, derives from present events and memory, often conflating fact and fiction in the process. His inner conflict depicted in *True West* is reconfigured in *Fool for Love*; loyalty and freedom, confinement and liberation, and literally being onstage and offstage are his concerns. The sibling connection allows Shepard to explore a mesh of crisscrossing desires. These two plays are Shepard's best, containing a farrago of paradoxes and contradictions. Characters seek to extract themselves from the inevitable, rage against what in fact attracts them, and use storytelling to gain control of their lives. These plays are comedies, with the twisting of truth taking on a palette of the unpredictable. Yet the plays also expose human fragility; Lee and Austin, and May and Eddie, are vulnerable wanderers amidst the debris of wrecked lives. The image of an adult-child wandering in the desert is evident in Shepard's 1984 screenplay, *Paris, Texas*. Wim Wenders's direction of the film accentuates Harry Dean Stanton's catatonic walk through a desert canvas suggesting the enormity of the landscape. The wide-angle shots portray a tiny figure, Stanton, barely visible in the vast Western terrain. As the film makes clear, he is overwhelmed by its size. He wanders zombie-like, eventually returning to his family for strength, even though they suffocate him emotionally. For Shepard's characters, the impulse is both one of self-affirmation and defiance: Vince seeks to escape to play his saxophone; Eddie leaves May to become a rodeo cowboy; May walks out of the motel to wander like Odysseus; Lee roams the desert; and Austin steals toasters to prove his self-sufficiency. Yet the ultimate outcome of self-reliance is loneliness that comes with freedom. Characters parade their independence, yet they return begging for shelter. These are themes Shepard continues to explore in *A Lie of the Mind* (1985), *Simpatico* (1994), and *The Late Henry Moss* (2000).

Feminist playwrights of the era shared a sense of rage with other dramatists but sought different ways of expressing it. During the 1970s and into the 1980s the women's movement, led by the National Organization for Women (NOW) and the movement for the passage of the Equal Rights Amendment, inspired playwrights to explore the objectification of their bodies and gender-based inequities. The plays of Marsha Norman and Maria Irene Fornes exemplify an awareness of women suffocated by glass-ceiling inertia. They also demonstrate an opposition to the optimism of their time. If Reagan's "Morning in America" became the narrative of the 1980s, these two dramatists provide an alternative story. Gil Troy notes that in 1983 "the great economic boom – the baby boom boom, the Reagan boom – began. It was the boom of service jobs, not manufacturing, of the Sun Belt and silicon chips, not the Rust Belt and smokestacks."[30] In the same year, Norman and Fornes produced plays that raised the stakes of opposition by portraying characters isolated from boom times. Their characters are women from Rust Belt Middle America who bear the double burden of economic alienation and second-class citizenship.

Comparing Norman and Fornes appears at first counterintuitive: the former deals in conventional realism while the latter experiments with form. Norman's early play *Getting Out* (1978) is a realistic drama depicting the life of a juvenile delinquent and her effort to reform. The play divides the single protagonist into two characters, Arlie and Arlene. The plot moves back and forth from the rebellious adolescent Arlie in jail to the adult Arlene trying to get her life straight. Norman uses two actresses to portray one character. Despite this device, the play is set in a specific time and place and uses standard narrative form. Fornes's early play, *Fefu and Her Friends* (1978), takes place in 1935 in the New England home of Fefu. The play experiments by having audiences move to different locales in the theatre as situations develop. Despite these formal dissimilarities, their finest works, Norman's *'night, Mother* (1983) and Fornes's *Mud* (1983), possess common objectives.

Norman's two-character play *'night, Mother* "takes place in a relatively new house built way out on a country road."[31] It focuses on the final ninety minutes of the life of Jessie Cates. She is preparing Mother for life after her suicide. The play takes place in "real time": there is an actual clock on the wall meant to be set according to the time of the performance. There is no intermission. Fornes's three-character play *Mud* takes place in "a wooden room which sits on an earth promontory." The earth in this promontory "is red and soft and so is the earth around it. There is no greenery. Behind the promontory there is a vast blue sky" (15). "Mud" means quicksand: the protagonist, Mae, is spirited and determined yet sinks beneath the demands of her lovers, Henry and Lloyd. Henry becomes disabled and Mae must help him relearn how to speak. Lloyd rarely speaks aside from a grunt. Mother in *'night, Mother* and Lloyd and Henry in *Mud* are helpless without Jessie and Mae; the men depend on Mae for sex and emotional support, and Mother depends on Jessie for companionship and emotional buttressing as well. Lloyd begins the play as Mae's lover, eventually replaced by Henry. Neither proves satisfactory to her. Norman and Fornes create isolated environments – the outside world is remote – and in both situations the women must cater to others. Unlike the uninterrupted momentum of *'night, Mother*, Fornes's *Mud* occurs in 17 scenes. This structural difference notwithstanding, both plays depict trapped protagonists. Death hovers and it is no coincidence that both Jessie and Mae die. Jessie takes her own life and Lloyd kills Mae, but these are merely surface facts belying deeper concerns.

Norman and Fornes explore the dissatisfaction and anger that incorporate a radical feminist sensibility. In her otherwise trenchant book *The Feminist Spectator as Critic*, Jill Dolan underestimates the politics of Norman's play. According to Dolan, "like most traditional American dramas, *'night, Mother*'s focus on individual suffering and the play's unwillingness to discuss Jessie's dilemma in terms of a wider social context make it weak as a political statement and inadequate from a materialist feminist perspective."[32] Norman's "wider social context" is implied rather than overt. *'night, Mother*, as well as *Mud*, countermands the optimism of Reagan's "Morning in America." Jessie cannot participate in the upbeat "shining city on a hill" because her reality provides scant reason for optimism. Mae tries to take matters into her own hands, but this proves impossible because Henry and Lloyd interfere. Home for Jessie is a bitter experience. Her future is no more than knitting, watching TV, overeating, and gossiping with Mother. Approaching old age without promise, Jessie faces a grim reality: her husband has left; prospects for romance are nil; her son is a junkie and thief; her job is unsatisfying; her limited education foreshortens her career; and her epilepsy ties her to medication. The daily grind takes its toll. She is out of step with the triumphalist spirit of the times. Both plays limn portraits contradictory to the prevalent media message. During an age saturated by stereotypical glamour and a world agog with patriotism, Norman and Fornes cast their opposition. In Mae, who lives in the "dark," and in Jessie, "who didn't make it," Fornes and Norman create characters framed by limitations and bristle against convention. Norman and Fornes belong to the period's undercurrent in American arts and letters epitomized by William Kennedy's proletarian novel *Ironweed* (1983). *'night, Mother* and *Mud* also encapsulate an anti-consumerist and feminist representation that has its intellectual forebears. Playwrights Sophie Treadwell, Susan Glaspell, Lillian Hellman, and Gertrude Stein established a twentieth-century trend characterizing female agency. Sophie Treadwell's *Machinal* (1928) cleared a path for *'night, Mother* and *Mud* in its depiction of an alienated character raging against power that binds her will.

Jessie and Mae, from the outset, rebel against the selfless availability they are expected to maintain. Out of a sense of emptiness they seek to challenge their conditions. Jessie has settled her scores and decides to end her life. Mae chooses to fantasize. Norman and Fornes rise to the challenge of creating sympathetic characters lacking eloquence. Jessie may be garrulous and Mae seeks education, but neither demonstrates sophistication. Their language is unpolished and their behavior awkward; yet their down-to-earth sincerity reveals vulnerability deserving compassion. Dying from a gunshot wound inflicted by Lloyd, Mae utters her final words: "Like the starfish, I live in the dark and my eyes see only a faint light. It is faint and yet it consumes me. I long for it. I thirst for it. I would die for it. Lloyd, I am dying" (40). Jessie explains the rationale for her suicide: "That's what this is about. It's somebody I lost, all right, it's my own self. Who I never was. Or who I tried to be and never got there. Somebody I waited for who never came. And never will. So, see, it doesn't much matter what else happens in the world or in this house, even. I'm what's worth waiting for and I didn't make it" (76). Mae pays for attempting to escape her fusty life, and Jessie abandons her wait for a promising future. Yet "starfish" and "not making it" are deliberately awkward expressions. The tragic dimension of these plays is not the upshot of some apocalyptic image or grandiose speech but derives from the simple emotions of plain-speaking women. This simplicity is in itself poetic, and by their negating actions – death and escape – they militate against false heroism. Mae and Jessie carve out their own nobility by rejecting what is expected of them as dramatic protagonists. At stake are the moral imperatives raised by their anti-heroism; Jessie and Mae challenge the handed-down assumption of heroic tragedy, inducing a reexamination of values defining the tragic genre inasmuch as it is dependent on "action," eloquence of speech, and an actor at center stage. For Jessie and Mae there is little opportunity for "action" personifying the traditional tragic hero. Their language is blunt and they avoid showmanship. They are therefore removed from the heroic model of tragedy such as Lear versifying in the storm or Willy Loman caterwauling against his fate. Jessie and Mae instead retrieve their tragedy in an unheroic fashion – by literally *leaving the stage*.

Norman and Fornes deal with the troubling tensions of their time: women's lack of agency, the treatment of women as mere caretakers, and the place of "tragedy" in women's theatre. Their plays take up feminist resistance to conformity by radically redefining the normative assumptions of tragedy. Tragedy attempts to bestow dignity and nobility on human suffering; men assume center stage as fate demolishes their lives. We observe men losing "everything"; pity is bestowed as one thing after another is stripped away. But Jessie and Mae have nothing to lose; what can they inveigh against when their lives amount to zero? Jessie and Mae demand attention because as women they are accorded little dignity and nobility in world affairs. Their denunci-ation of the heroic code through the act of leaving the stage signals a rebellion against the relevance of "heroic action." Leaving the stage is profoundly anti-climactic, yet it supplies a vital rebellion against tra-dition and establishes a new mode of tragedy. Mae and Jessie must extricate themselves from decay, but they must also assert an anti-heroic position. Herbert Blau writes that "rottenness spreads through" *Mud*, with Mae "struggling against it, like an existential condition." However, "in the accretion of reality around her, its grievous tedium, the ironing, the protoplasmic irritation, it is as if there is something else she has forgotten: something very sick, something is rotting away, somebody is going to die."[33] The same can be said of Jessie: the accretion of boredom, endless ironing, her mother's insufferable palaver, and the giving without receiving make life unbearable. Conversely, Christopher Bigsby's description suffices for Mae when he says that Jessie "is a woman who has woken up to the fact that she is living a life without true meaning or purpose and has the power to end such a pointless existence, thereby paying herself the respect of believing that she is at least the author of her own fate."[34] Mae and Jessie assess the authorship of their lives in different ways, but their desire for authorship makes them soulmates.

Mamet and Shepard share the theme of characters seeking a return. The stage space may contain violence, and escape is often the goal, but inside (onstage) is typically better than outside (offstage). Movement onstage is directed inward. In her book *Woman's Theatrical Space*, Hanna Scolnicov observes that, "Conversely, from a woman's point of view, and especially in modern times, the problem is how to escape the restrictive space of the house." For female characters, the interior is confining and the action is "to sever her bonds and abandon the house."[35] Three dramatists – Wendy Wasserstein, Beth Henley, and Tina Howe – take up the notion of space but differ in how it is to be regarded. They portray characters with conflicting relationships to place, home, and theatre. Wasserstein's *Uncommon Women and Others* (1977) examines college friends who come to maturity at the onset of the women's liberation movement. The play begins in a restaurant as five of the eight principals enjoy a reunion. The plot moves back and forth from their alma mater Mount Holyoke College to the same restaurant. The women take account of their lives and aspirations. Wasserstein delineates several unique characters. Rita is the sexually liberated rebel who believes she will be "amazing" when she hits her stride. The rainbow for her is always just over the horizon. Kate is the prim-and-proper future lawyer. Holly is bright, Jewish, and resistant of her parents' expectations. But her inner conflict inhibits her ability to make decisions. She makes lists of things to do, but the numerous options lead to vacillation. Samantha, destined to marry early, is sanguine of her fate. Muffet is both charming and charismatic. Susie is dressed in pink and always beams. Carter is the detached intellectual. Leilah is a shy do-gooder, traveling to Iran on an archeological expedition. The play galvanizes competing urges: to enjoy the new-found opportunities women's liberation has made available, and to seek past certainty and single-minded direction. Each character internalizes the struggle without the expectation of resolution.

The need to escape restrictions and expectations comprises the plots for Wasserstein's *Isn't It Romantic* (1981), *The Heidi Chronicles* (1988), and *The Sisters Rosensweig* (1992), as well. *Isn't It Romantic* concerns a conflict between women opting for career or marriage. It repeats the notion of "having it all." The term signifies both a blessing and a curse. Characters are overwhelmed by their options. Overbearing parents press the protagonist to marry. Janie recoils from unpacking her boxes, symbolizing her feelings of rootlessness and fear of permanency. *The Heidi Chronicles* deals with a liberal feminist art historian, Heidi Holland. It begins with her involvement in Eugene McCarthy's presidential campaign of 1968. Although a leftist, Heidi (played with charismatic charm by Joan Allen) is hardly a radical. Her encounters set her apart from her colleagues, who are at first 1970s radicals but rejoin the establishment by the 1980s. Heidi is like most of Wasserstein's protagonists, drawn to a career and also of a domestic frame of mind. In the end she adopts a child. The play develops Heidi's friendship with Peter, a gay doctor, and Heidi's sometime relationship with Scoop Rosenbaum.

If Wasserstein's focus is on New York Jewish women, Beth Henley focuses on women of the South. Despite their differences, both authors take up women's coming of age independent of men. Henley's *Crimes of the Heart* (1981) and *Miss Firecracker Contest* (1984) use the salty epigrams and gothic idioms of Southern literature. *Crimes of the Heart* concerns three sisters: Babe Magrath, the youngest, accused of attempting to murder her husband; Meg Magrath, the eldest, who spends her time reading novels of disease; and Lennie, who has escaped to Hollywood. Babe has an adulterous affair with a 15-year-old African American, Willie Jay, prompting her outraged husband to threaten them both. Babe shoots him in retaliation. The trial brings Lennie back home. Their mother had committed suicide, and the sisters try to understand why. In the end the three achieve a better understanding of themselves and their past.

Few playwrights examine space as intensely as Tina Howe. Her characters are not seeking escape as much as a reconciliation of desires and demands. Her play *Museum* (1978) takes place in the trendy art world. Its large canvas explores the pretensions of the art scene. *The Art of Dining* (1979) is hyper-realistic, situated in a kitchen onstage, and explores the action of eating and dining. In doing so it reveals the characters' desires and comestible expectations. *Painting Churches* (1983) continues Howe's examination of art. The three-character play centers on Margaret Church and her attempt at drawing a portrait of her parents. The play takes place in a Beacon Hill drawing room of a Boston Brahmin family. Margaret's effort to complete the painting parallels her effort to finish the picture of her life. *Coastal Disturbances* (1987) is set on a New England beach. Like *Museum*, it is a collage. The settings for Howe's plays are in themselves characters influencing the protagonists. *Approaching Zanzibar* (1989) dwells on a family's automobile journey that becomes a metaphor for self-discovery. The moving relationship between grandmother and granddaughter at the play's conclusion creates a closure of sorts for a family seeking understanding.

David Mamet's *Glengarry Glen Ross* (1984) presents a hostile setting. This tightly constructed play deals with Chicago real estate salesmen selling Florida land. Act I is in three scenes in a Chinese restaurant. It exposes the characters' hustling and scams. Act II takes place in the real estate office following a robbery the night before. The salesmen use guile, wit, cunning, deception, and bribes for the best leads. The play is *Death of a Salesman* without sentiment; unlike Willy Loman, Mamet's salesmen know that the product they sell is phony. The characters operate in Darwin's jungle; for them, selling is joyless survival. The game-of-the-week is to sell enough shares to earn a Cadillac. Demolishing your colleague is inconsequential. In describing the play, Mamet articulates a theory in which competition is symbolic of national identity: "Your extremity is my opportunity. That's what forms the basis of our economic life, and this is what forms the rest of our lives. That American myth: the idea of something out of nothing." He adds, "One can only succeed at the cost of, the failure of another, which is what a lot of my plays – *American Buffalo* and *Glengarry Glen Ross* – are about. That's what Acting President Reagan's whole campaign is about. In *Glengarry Glen Ross* it's the Cadillac, the steak knives, or nothing. . . . Why should I control my sense of fair play when the other person may not control his sense of fair play? So hurray for me and to hell with you."[36]

In the play Mamet presents a microcosm of the business world. Four salesmen, Levene, Roma, Moss, and Aaronow, are on a losing streak, though Roma is gaining ground. They vie for the best leads from the office manager, Williamson. In the opening scene Levene supplicates himself to Williamson in order to obtain his leads. Williamson is hardly above a kickback if the price is right. In the next scene (another table at the same restaurant), Moss plans to steal the leads. He tries enlisting Aaronow in the scheme. The final scene reveals Roma's oozy skills. He persuades a stranger, James Lingk, to invest. The scene is a portrayal of a chiseler plying his trade; the hypnotic Roma's blandishment is literally "chiseling" away Lingk's skepticism. Roma begins his huckster pitch with: "all train compartments smell vaguely of shit."[37] The "shit" metaphor reappears at the end of the scene. Roma offers to buy another round of drinks for Lingk and reveals the Florida investment.

> ROMA: I want to show you something. (*Pause.*) It might mean nothing
> to you . . . and it might not. I don't know. I don't know anymore.
> (*Pause. He takes out a small map and spreads it on a table.*) What is that?
> Florida. Glengarry Highlands. Florida. "Florida. *Bullshit.*" (50–1)

Roma calls the item "*Bullshit*" but herein lies his talent. The notion of "carefully wrought bullshit," in Harry Frankfurt's account of "bullshit," differentiates bullshitting from lying. Bullshit involves "a certain inner strain. Thoughtful attention to detail requires discipline and objectivity. It entails accepting standards and limitations that forbid the indulgence of impulse or whim." The liar is concerned with the truth even if the intent is to suppress it. The bullshitter, Frankfurt contends, admits that "the truth-values of his statements are of no central interest to him; what we are not to understand is that his intention is neither to report the truth nor to conceal it. This does not mean that his speech is anarchically impulsive, but that the motive guiding and controlling it is unconcerned with how the things about which he speaks are true."[38] The characters in *Glengarry* are bullshitters of the efficient and artistic sort, because being the best at sales is tantamount to bullshitting most artfully.

However, for Mamet, being the best salesman – the best bullshitter – is hardly trouble free. Levene, Moss, and Aaronow are Jews in their early fifties facing middle age gracelessly. Mamet is influenced by realism Chicago-style, with its gritty toughness, working-class machismo, and down-to-earth urban vernacular. He is also a moralist conscious of the plight of working-class Jews. Yiddish words like *dreck* (shit), *meshugass* (nuttiness), and *schmuck* (prick) are mixed with street argot, creating a muscular poetry and the pathos of aging Jewish salesmen down on their luck. Much has been written about Mamet's syntax – the stichomythia, rhythmic vulgarity, and razor-sharp riposte. These talents are never more evident than in this play. In his 2005 review of the Broadway revival, John Lahr says that *Glengarry Glen Ross* is a "three-card monte of verbal manipulation," which employs a language that has "lost its meaning; words are merely husks of feeling that decoy self-interest and connect the speakers to nothing but their own craven desire."[39] The staccato rhythm masks deception. But there is more to the play than language, and there is more to Mamet's indebtedness to Arthur Miller than the play's being another salesman story. The father–son relationship between the over-the-hill Shelley Levene and the oily-slick Ricky Roma mirrors the father–son mentoring relationship of Willy Loman and his sons Biff and Happy (as well as Donny and Bobby in *American Buffalo*). In Act II Levene bursts into the office with his prize, the eighty-two-thousand-dollar property sale to Bruce and Harriet Nyborg. The nearly 15 percent commission earns Levene twelve thousand dollars. Roma, self-involved and admiring no one but himself, nevertheless looks up to Levene. Although Roma is now behind Levene in sales, he exudes pride in his mentor's success. This subtle but important father–son, teacher–student relationship embodies the play's tragic dimensions. Roma listens intently to Levene's sales story; Roma is the only colleague who refers to his idol as "Shelly 'the Machine' Levene"; and Roma even boasts about Levene to Moss, who is uninterested ("Fuck the Machine," Moss says). Roma defends his mentor against Moss, and following Moss's exit he urges Levene to continue. Levene picks up where he left off: "That's what I'm *saying*. The *old* ways. The *old* ways . . . convert the motherfucker . . . *sell* him . . . *sell* him . . . *make him sign the check*" (72). Roma, for all his shallowness and con artistry, admires Levene; Levene, in turn, is the only character who calls Roma by his first name, Ricky. Their dialogue occupying the central part of Act II underscores a bond. Within their ruthless environment, this relationship is as close to tenderness as Mamet allows.

The relationship of Roma and Levene carries into the next moment. Roma had sold shares to Lingk; Roma, however, must allow three days before he can be assured of the sale's finality. A client is allowed to withdraw his deposit within that time. Roma sees Lingk coming to the office. He surmises that Lingk has had second thoughts and wants to wiggle out of his commitment. His suspicion is confirmed; he winks

at Levene, and they hastily construct a plan. Levene instantly imper-
sonates Roma's satisfied client anxious to complete a deal and depart.
This "game" is meant to avoid Lingk and remove Roma from the
office. Mamet creates a verbal dance between Roma and Levene; the
con artistry is a linguistic *pas-de-deux*. Roma must chauffeur "Levene
the client" to the airport, putting Lingk off till tomorrow (when it will
be too late to rescind the check). Lingk persists, forcing Roma to tell
him that he has yet to cash the check. This will, hopefully, keep Lingk
at bay. But the game is undermined by Williamson, who, in an effort
to help, tells Lingk that he has cashed the check. Williamson fails to
understand the bluff; he thinks he is doing Roma a favor by stepping
in and assuring Lingk that, despite the office break-in, the deal has
been consummated. Lingk exits when he understands that he must
stop the check immediately. Roma then turns on Williamson. His rage
stresses the theme of the play: know "the shot." Roma calls Williamson
a "stupid fucking cunt," who cost him six thousand dollars. More
importantly, he says: "Whoever told you you could work with *men*?
[. . .] What you're hired for is to *help* us – does that seem clear to
you? To *help* us. Not to fuck us up . . . to help *men* who are going *out*
there trying to earn a *living*. You *fairy*. You company man" (96). Roma
ends his diatribe with this: "You want to learn the first rule you'd
know if you ever spent a day in your life . . . you never open your
mouth till you know what the shot is. (*Pause.*) You fucking *child*"
(96–7). Williamson fails to measure up to Roma's idea of manhood
because he fails to understand the "shot." Ironically, Roma's mentor,
Levene, makes the very same blunder.

Levene in fact makes two mistakes: first, he fails to remain silent,
and second, he fails to do what any novice would do: confirm a client's
reliability. Levene's tragic flaw is that he neither stops talking nor
knows the "shot." In defense of his protégé (Roma has exited to be
interrogated by the police investigating the break-in), Levene hurls
invectives at Williamson. He concludes by saying: "You're going to
make something up, be sure it will help or keep your mouth closed"
(98). Levene exposes himself. Williamson, in fact, had failed to deposit
Lingk's check, even though he told Lingk otherwise. Williamson lied
because he thought he understood the "shot" – he thought he was
aiding Roma. This slip flummoxes Levene. Williamson realizes that only
someone *who broke into the office and saw the check on his desk* would
know that he "made it up." Caught, Levene is forced to confess. He

tries bribery, telling Williamson that he will split his commission if he will stay mum. Yet the Nyborg deal is Levene's second mistake. For all his "experience" – his nickname, Shelly "the Machine" Levene, underscores his professional reputation – he fails to examine the Nyborgs' history.

> WILLIAMSON: Where have you been, Shelly? Bruce and Harriet Nyborg. Do you want to see the *memos* . . . ? They're nuts . . . they used to call in every week. When I was with Webb. And we were selling Arizona . . . they're nuts . . . did you see how they were *living*? How can you delude yours . . .
> LEVENE: I got the check . . .
> WILLIAMSON: Forget it. Frame it. It's worthless.   (103–4)

Levene has tragically misjudged. His tragedy, however, is not in the classical sense. In classical tragedies we observe a fall of significant people from some high place. Levene is washed up already. Yet he shares with Oedipus and Lear the flaw of having made choices he has warned others against. Like Lear, he is convinced that his experience and age have gained him unimpeachable knowledge. Mamet additionally provides Levene with a world outside the play. Levene mentions "his daughter" three times. We know little about her other than that she is supported financially by him. Still, this embellishes his circumstances – he has much to lose. The play's conclusion stresses the tragic. Roma enters, having been interrogated by the police. Levene sits silently, knowing that Williamson is informing on him. Roma, who does not know of Levene's imminent demise, says: "I swear . . . it's not a world of men . . . it's not a world of men, Machine . . . it's a world of clock watchers, bureaucrats, officeholders . . . there's no adventure to it. (*Pause.*) Dying breed. Yes it is. (*Pause.*) We are the members of a dying breed" (105). Levene is one of a "dying breed" in more ways than Roma realizes. His tragic flaw is in his succumbing to desperation. He makes critical errors, but we are to understand that these errors result from powerful outside forces.

Mamet's rage against selfishness and greed influenced two plays of the 1980s: David Rabe's *Hurlyburly* (1984) and Lanford Wilson's *Burn This* (1987), as well as his own *Speed-the-Plow* (1988). *Speed-the-Plow* takes up Hollywood greed. Rabe's *Hurlyburly* focuses on the lives of marginal Hollywood players – casting directors and out-of-work actors

– who fill their lives with meetings, drugs, booze, and women, all of which are as disposable as the work they do. The meetings they attend are about deals and future deals; the drugs and alcohol dull the pain; and women come and go like the movies they make. Hollywood in Rabe's play is a cocaine-fueled mirage of deception and cynicism: like Mamet's *Speed-the-Plow*, it shows us its tawdry side. Eddie, the protagonist of *Hurlyburly*, tells Phil, a tough-looking actor and his best friend, that he is little more than a "prop," a supernumerary providing thuggish backdrop for movies in need of "reality." His acting career is barely noticed window dressing. As a result of depression, Phil takes his own life. In Lanford Wilson's *Burn This*, four characters – Anna, Burton, Larry, and Robbie – live in the same apartment. Robbie's accidental death brings Pale, Robbie's straight brother, into the scene. The New York backdrop in *Burn This* is as vapid as Los Angeles is in *Hurlyburly*. Robbie's pointless death, likewise Phil's suicide in *Hurlyburly*, adds to the volatility and emptiness that already permeate the characters' lives. Though Pale and Anna, and Larry and Burton, find a way to bond, the overarching experience is that of rage and despair. Like *Hurlyburly*, *Burn This* incorporates the mid-1980s experience of cocaine-induced anger against the superficialities of Hollywood and New York. The protagonists of both plays are coke-snorting, Quaalude-dropping, disenfranchised characters living on the margins. Both Eddie and Pale offer hyper-drive outbursts, but their speeches spiral in abrupt shifts and circuitous turns. They try to reach beyond their feckless times by establishing a viable relationship with reality; yet their efforts fail because they fall back on their own insular self-protection. They are like characters in a 1987 Bruce Springsteen song: "You end up like a dog that's beat too much / Till you spend half your life just covering up."[40] They rebel against me-generation attitudes, and yet they succumb to them. Eddie speaks of living beneath the shadow of a nuclear holocaust, while Pale rages against oppressive parking conditions in New York. Both substitute targets disguising deeper concerns. In both plays characters more or less collide rather than meet. Figures enter and exit like passing ships. Eddie and Pale have come to believe that emotional distancing and defensive rage are the best ways of dealing with superficiality. But their detachment mixed with vitriol and drugs ultimately fails to quell their desire for human contact. Eddie and Pale are soulmates in bitterness, disillusionment, and anger.

Lanford Wilson's "Talley Trilogy" comprises three plays exploring the history of the Talley family: *Fifth of July* (1978), *Talley's Folly* (1979), and *Talley & Son* (1985, originally *A Tale Told*, 1981). Wilson's lyrical dramas are a cross between Tennessee Williams and Anton Chekhov, turning toward the intimate, domestic, introspective lives of Midwesterners. The plays deal with small enigmas and hurtful moments as characters struggle to avert repercussions of life's pain. *Talley's Folly* is a two-handed love story, the type of play popularized during this time by John Patrick Shanley's *Danny and the Deep Blue Sea* (1984) and Terence McNally's *Frankie and Johnny in the Clair de Lune* (1984). Shanley and McNally, however, depict post-one-night-stand plays portraying angry, displaced characters desperate for love. These plays present screeds about life's shortcomings, but are ultimately love stories set in an age of selfishness. Wilson's inclination toward the lyrical brings together Matt Friedman, a Jew amidst anti-Semites, and Sally Talley, whose infertility makes her unwilling in matters of romance. Wilson's most Chekhovian play, *Fifth of July*, weaves together several post-sixties radicals. The central characters are the gay couple, Kenneth Talley, Jr., a Vietnam veteran amputee, and Jed Jenkins. The insouciant Gwen Landis, the coke-snorting wife of the Talleys' childhood friend John, expresses the cynicism of these former activists, calling attention to similarities between this play and *Kennedy's Children*:

> GWEN: Oh, please. I was stoned. [. . .] Also it was such a crock, really. You go to an antiwar, end-the-war rally, right? You march to the White House. [. . .] Five hundred thousand people, speaker's platforms, signs thick as a convention, everybody's high, we're bombed, the place is mobbed, everybody's on the lawn with their shirts off, boys, girls. [. . .] How straight do you have to be to see that nothing is going to come from it?[41]

Gwen's words reflect Christopher Lasch's remarks in his *Culture of Narcissism* that radicalism "had become so unfashionable, and so pernicious in the support it unwittingly provides for the status quo, that any criticism of contemporary society that hopes to get beneath the surface has to criticize, at the same time, much of what currently goes under the name of radicalism."[42] The characters in Wilson's plays, as well as Kathleen Tolan's *A Weekend Near Madison* (1983), display the cynicism accompanying disappointed expectations.

Cynicism and anger underscore many African American dramas. Charles Fuller's *A Soldier's Play* (1981) incorporates these conditions, but with an interesting twist. The play's backdrop is World War II. During the war African Americans served honorably and in great numbers in the United States military. Although the war was fought for the purpose of spreading democracy, racial discrimination called attention to the double standard. The three branches of military service remained rigidly segregated, with black soldiers subjected by an officer corps dominated by white Southerners. Most African Americans who were sent overseas were relegated to menial tasks; even the few elite black units, like the Tuskegee Airmen, were conspicuous by their absence from media reportage. Segregation of Red Cross blood donations was strictly enforced, and the black press was dissuaded from emphasizing the "phony war" for freedom. Yet, many African Americans understood the link between military service and their place in society; during the Civil War, World War I, and World War II blacks clamored for combat, which they saw as a stepping stone to equal rights. Fuller's plot revolves around the murder of Sargent Waters, the platoon sergeant of a Negro company eagerly awaiting deployment. A black officer, Captain Davenport, is assigned to investigate the murder, which at first appears to be the work of white racists. However, as soldiers are interrogated, flashbacks reveal that Waters (played forcefully by Adolph Caesar) had his enemies, both black and white. Fuller calls attention to the depth of self-effacement and internalized hatred among the soldiers. He creatively uses the Nazis as a kind of concomitant metaphor for Waters. Waters's most brutal act was to contrive to have a soldier, C. J., arrested for shooting a white man. Waters, like the Nazis, wants to eliminate "undesirables." For Waters, the "geechy" (a person of the South Carolina Geechy Islands who retained much of his African heritage) is in need of "cleansing."

WATERS: Them Nazis ain't all crazy – a whole lot of people just can't fit into where things seem to be goin' – like you, C. J. The black race can't afford you no more. There used to be a time when we'd see somebody like you, singin', clownin' – yas-sah-bossin' – and we wouldn't do anything. (*Smiles.*) Folks liked that – you were good – homey kinda' niggah – they needed somebody to mistreat – call a name, they paraded you, reminded them of the old days – cornbread bakin' greens and ham cookin' – Daddy out pickin' cotton,

Grandmammy sit on the front porch smokin' a pipe. (*Slight pause.*) Not no more. The day of the geechy is gone, boy – the only thing that can move the race is power.[43]

If Fuller's play pivots on internal conflicts and self-loathing, August Wilson's important ten-play cycle representing each decade of the twentieth century illuminates the nature of these conflicts without sacrificing a sense of community. With the exception of *Ma Rainey's Black Bottom*, which takes place in Chicago, Wilson's plays are located in the lower Hill District of Pittsburgh. The twentieth-century cycle accords with Wilson's efforts to communicate African American history. His plays juxtapose Afrocentric and Christian religious traditions, take up the scars of slavery, examine the folkways of the rural South and Northern urban life, and are concerned with the effects of incarceration, father–son relationships, and the backdrop of events dictated by each decade. Equally significant subjects in Wilson's plays are individuals defining themselves within the social order, the impact of migration and rootlessness, the importance of the oral tradition (the griot storyteller), and memory as a link to Africa and the South. Situating the plays historically requires viewing them through the spectrum of what Wilson calls "blood memory," connecting displaced people to the continent that was once their origin. A feeling of transience and "placelessness," what Germans call *Unheimlichkeit*, undergirds the collective psyche of Wilson's characters, whose blood memories (or, in some cases, actual memories) recall transplantation from Africa to the American South, and then migrating to the North.

Wilson is under the influence of what Mark William Rocha dubs the "Four B's": collage artist Romare Bearden, Amiri Baraka and the Black Arts Movement, novelist Jorge Luis Borges and his magic realism, and great blues and jazz composers.[44] Wilson writes about African American history because, as he says, "I see myself as answering James Baldwin's call for a profound articulation of the black experience, which he defined as 'that field of manners and ritual of intercourse that can sustain a black man once he has left his father's house.' I try to concretize the values of the black American and place them on a stage in loud action to demonstrate the existence of the above 'field of manners' and point to some avenues of sustenance."[45] For our immediate purposes, the focus will be on *Ma Rainey's Black Bottom* (1984), *Joe Turner's Come and Gone* (1986), and *Fences* (1987), with the next chapter taking up *The Piano Lesson* (1990) and *Two Trains Running* (1992).

Wilson's *Ma Rainey's Black Bottom* takes place in 1927 in a white-owned Chicago record studio. Ma Rainey and her band are recording their music. The popularity of "race records" during the Harlem Renaissance had afforded a limited but new opportunity for African Americans. Few succeeded, but many tried. Ma Rainey (a surrogate of the real-life Bessie Smith) serves as the nexus around which the play's action takes place, but her band – Cutler, Toledo, Irvin, and Levee – dominate the stage. Levee, the recalcitrant trumpeter, confuses his "talent with his skills."[46] Levee has cause for rage; he watched as his father was murdered and his mother raped. However, his anger becomes misdirected as he repines against the status quo. Levee's ambition removes him from his community and even from the members of his band. The tension between Levee's desire for independence and the needs of the ensemble is exacerbated. He tries in vain for rapid success by ingratiating himself before the white producers, Irvin and Sturdyvant. Levee is seduced by an unstable desire for material possession; he takes a "whole week's pay and puts it on some shoes." Shoes give Levee status. He compares his shoes with Toledo's: "Nigger got them clodhoppers! Old brogans! He ain't nothing but a sharecropper!" (31). His anger is understandable, given his history. But Levee's hubris is that in his effort to erase his past, he has become disconnected from his roots. He sells out to the commercial "white" music industry in exchange for success, describing the work of his fellow band members as "nothing but old jug band music" (18). When his music is rejected by the white producers, he turns on his friends. Toledo accidentally steps on his shoes, and is killed by an enraged Levee.

Wilson's language captures the nuance of African American vernacular. It is a mixture of Southern accent and urban syntax, and is predicated by well-known call-and-response patterns. It is blues and urban. Reminiscent of Stevie Wonder's song "Living for the City," Wilson's dialogue articulates the difficulties that accompany urban life. Farah Jasmine Griffin supplies an interesting conflation, saying that Wonder's music "embodies both the sacred and the profane ministers of the black experience: the preacher and the blues performer."[47] The same may be said of Wilson's language and characters. Wilson stresses both the sacred and profane, emphasizing values of the dispossessed coming in contact with the sacred retention of African American heritage. When Levee, Slow Drag, and the others deny their African roots, Toledo reminds them that "Naming all those things you and Cutler done together is like trying to solicit some reefer based on a bond of kinship. That's African. An ancestral retention. Only you forgot the name of the gods" (24). Wilson's characters wander about bewildered, clinging to the material when they ought to be searching out the spiritual.

Humanist values torn from the body politic are emphasized most clearly in Wilson's deeply spiritual play, *Joe Turner's Come and Gone*. Characters in *Joe Turner* are adrift. For Wilson, the Middle Passage (the diaspora across the Atlantic) was traumatic. But what interests Wilson is the twentieth-century Great Migration to the North as a "second" diaspora. Southern African Americans were agrarian; despite the fact of slavery, the South had been home for 300 years. Migration to the city replaced the agrarian home. This displacement left African Americans in a situation twice removed from Africa. In *Joe Turner's Come and Gone*, Wilson describes the condition:

> From the deep and the near South the sons and daughters of the newly freed African slaves wander into the city. Isolated, cut off from memory, having forgotten the names of the gods and only guessing at their faces, they arrive dazed and stunned, their hearts kicking in their chest with a song worth singing. They arrive carrying Bibles and guitars, their pockets lined with dust and fresh hope, marked men and women seeking to scrap from the narrow, crooked, cobbles and the fiery blasts of the coke furnace a way of bludgeoning and shaping the malleable parts of themselves into a new identity as free men of definite and sincere worth.[48]

Joe Turner takes place in the rooming house of Seth and Bertha Holly in 1911. Henry Loomis arrives with his daughter, Zonia. Loomis has spent seven years on a chain gang run by Joe Turner. Joe Turner the character is derived from a legendary blues song about Joe Turney, the real-life brother of the Tennessee governor who used his political connections to operate a chain gang for profit. Loomis searches for his wife, Martha Pentecost, having lost touch with her while serving on the "rock." He comes across the denizens of the rooming house. Bynum, who lives there, is a conjurer and a doctor of sorts who uses homeopathic roots and herbs. Bynum describes Loomis's ailment: "Cause you lost from yourselves and where the places come together, where you're supposed to be alive, your heart kicking in your chest with a song worth singing" (22). The key – finding one's "song" – expresses a greater desire. According to Wilson, African American people have lost their "song." Like Levee cut loose from his community, Loomis wanders in Odysseus-like peregrination for his wife and his "song."

In the powerful Act I climax, the occupants of the house come together for singing and dancing the "Juba." During the nineteenth century, Henry "Juba" Lane (ca. 1825–1852) was a well-known African American dancer who competed in contests against white minstrel dancers. Juba was on his way to becoming an international star when he died aboard ship en route to London. Although dead by age 27, Juba's legend endured through ages, his style being the source of future buck-and-wing, Virginia essence, soft shoe, and tap dancing. According to Wilson's stage directions,

> The Juba is reminiscent of the Ring Shouts of the African slaves. It is a call and response dance. Bynum sits at the table and drums. He calls the dance as others clap hands, shuffle and stomp around the table. It should be as African as possible, with the performers working themselves up into a near frenzy. The words can be improvised, but should include some mention of the Holy Ghost. (52)

The movement and singing combine two fundamentals of black spiritualism: Afrocentricity and Christianity. Like the name of Loomis's wife, Mary Pentecost, the American Pentecostal religion (as well as Baptist and Methodist) has been enriched by African American contributions. Loomis, however, becomes obstreperous on hearing the festivities. He enters enraged.

> LOOMIS: (*In a rage.*) Stop it! Stop!
> (*They stop and turn to look at him.*)
> > You all sitting up here singing about the Holy Ghost. What's so holy about the Holy Ghost? You singing and singing. You think the Holy Ghost coming? You singing for the Holy Ghost to come? What he gonna do, huh? (52)

Like Levee, Loomis at first disdains spiritual and community matters. Yet he becomes possessed; he speaks "in tongues"; he writhes. He tries to resist but is thrown to the floor by spirits he fails to understand. Bynum presses him to describe his vision. Loomis replies: "I done seen bones rise up out of the water. Rise up and walk across the water. Bones walking on top of the water" (53). Wilson incorporates

Afrocentric religious expression (slaves rising from the sea) with Christianity (resurrection and baptism). Loomis tries to stand but his legs give way. The language and physical intensity evoke parallels with Christianity in the guise of Loomis, who suffers for the sins of others. At the conclusion Loomis meets his wife, only to realize that he cannot remain with her and his child. He knows he must find his purpose in life – his song – before he can rejoin his family.

Wilson's next play, *Fences*, takes place in 1957. It revolves around Troy Maxson, a 53-year-old sanitation worker who at one time enjoyed a successful but brief career in the Negro Baseball League. Because his experience in baseball preceded Jackie Robinson and integration, the middle-aged Troy carries an unshakeable anger. Like Levee and Loomis he is bitter, but unlike them he tries to set down his roots. He builds "fences." The "fence" symbolizes Troy's attempt at insulation, and it reminds him of his ability to hit balls over the "fence." He has been forced to observe Jackie Robinson earn the fame he feels he deserves. Robinson's success rankles with him even more because Troy believes he was a superior ballplayer. Troy's wife Rose and his friend Bono try to assuage his anger. Bono says: "Times have changed, Troy. You just come along too early." Troy replies: "There ought not never have been no time called too early!"[49] Wilson's use of multiple negatives ("not," "never," "no") is indicative of the African American rhetorical strategy of emphasis and resistance. Geneva Smitherman maintains that in Lonne Elder's play *Ceremonies and Dark Old Men*, "there is a debate between the central protagonists in which one Brotha, articulating a key theme in the drama, says to another, 'Don't nobody pay no attention to no nigga that ain't crazy!' Because European American language stigmatizes the use of double negatives, African American language goes one better and uses multiple negation (a characteristic feature of African American linguistic grammar)."[50] Troy uses this construction to justify a rage that will never subside:

> TROY: I done seen a hundred niggers play baseball better than Jackie Robinson. Hell, I know some teams Jackie Robinson couldn't even make! What you talking about Jackie Robinson. Jackie Robinson wasn't nobody. I'm talking about if you could play ball then they ought to have let you play. Don't care what color you were. Come telling me I come along too early. If you could play . . . then they ought to have let you play. (Troy *takes a long drink from the bottle.*) (10)

Troy gets promoted to the position of driver of a trash-collecting truck which, until Troy speaks to his boss, was a position formerly reserved for white men. Bono reminds Troy that he neither has a driver's license nor knows how to drive. To this Troy replies: "Driving ain't nothing. All you do is point the truck where you want it to go . . . The man ain't got to know my business. Time he find out, I have two or three driver's licenses" (45). Within a system in which they struggle to find a place, Wilson's characters learn to craft their own opportunities. Yet Troy is acutely aware that the system has its obstacles. The hierarchy that destroys Troy's spirit is the same one Troy manipulates in order to dominate his family. Troy demands of those around him – Rose, Bono, his eldest son from a previous marriage, Lyons, his other son Cory, his brother Gabriel, and even his daughter from an affair – that they fall within his orbit. Troy provides the imposing means of familial stability. But his presence is also oppressive. Troy cannot see beyond the limits of his life; even though it is 1957, he still believes Jim Crow segregation will snatch defeat from the jaws of victory. The world for Troy is unfair to the point of shutting out his own loved ones.

Allusions to Judeo-Christianity and classical drama are frequent in *Fences*. Troy's brother is named Gabriel, and Gabriel (a wounded World War II veteran who lives with a steel plate in his head) refers often to St. Peter. Troy speaks of wrestling with the angel of death, holding his baseball bat as a minatory weapon to strike at death whenever he feels it close. Troy almost died of pneumonia, leaving him profoundly sensitive to the prospect of dying. But the play is about more than fear of death; Troy symbolizes the inner strength of Biblical heroism and that of Greek tragedy. The play contains an overriding sense of Troy as Moses and Abraham: Moses, whose power and authority strengthen others, and Abraham, the father required by God to sacrifice his son. Troy's own name evokes the powerful city felled by overweening pride. It is this hubris – the characteristic "flaw" of Greek tragic figures – that instigates Troy to prevent his son from playing football. He tells Cory, "The white man ain't gonna let you get nowhere with that football noway. You go on and get your book-learning so you can work yourself up in that A&P [grocery store] or learn how to fix cars or build houses or something, get you a trade" (35). Rightfully believing that he has been cheated by segregation, Troy sacrifices Cory's chance for a football scholarship. He goes to Cory's high school, informs the coach that Cory has withdrawn from the team, and dismisses the college recruiter. His reasoning is that sports will only disappoint. Cory, Troy believes, has a better chance elsewhere. Like Abraham, Troy sacrifices his son. Troy's blindspot – and tragic flaw – is owing to the social circumstances beyond his power to change.

Fences is filled with history. References to Jackie Robinson, as well as the great Negro League baseball player Josh Gibson, blend fact and fiction. Wilson deliberately uses historical events to motivate his characters because he is interested in the way history shapes people's lives. History for Wilson is not an abstraction but something real. He shares with the German playwright and theorist Bertolt Brecht a commitment to historicizing dramatic situations. Baseball's injustice is layered into the play as Troy compares Josh Gibson and a backup white player, Selkirk. Selkirk, a below-average athlete, is a Major Leaguer while Troy and Gibson struggle in the Negro Leagues. Troy extends the comparison: "I saw Josh Gibson's daughter yesterday. She walking around with raggedy shoes on her feet. Now I bet Selkirk's daughter ain't walking around with raggedy shoes on her feet! I bet you that!" (9). Wilson's Troy is a derivation of Russell Parker in *Ceremonies and Dark Old Men*, and John Williams in *River Niger* – all three are middle-aged black men railing against injustice and missed opportunity. The irony is that for them, civil rights was a case of too little, too late.

Wilson's characters seek ownership of "things" that they hope will define their identity. This is well illustrated in several of his plays: jitney cab drivers owning their cab station in *Jitney*, Levee owning his music, Loomis seeking to own his "song," Troy owning his fences, Berniece and Boy Willie owning the piano in *The Piano Lesson*, and Risa owning her body in *Two Trains Running*. There is, at root, an overwhelmingly felt need to create an identity informed by history, using objects such as a piano or a song as possession rituals emblematic of the spirit and of the past. The title of Harry Elam's book on Wilson, *The Past as Present in the Drama of August Wilson*, conveys the core fact of the past as it informs the present.[51] Like Baraka, Kennedy, and Bullins before him, Wilson realizes that one of the tragic consequences of oppression is the erasure of cultural history. He understands that in the absence of roots, frustration and anger compensate. Individuals will lash out randomly. The past is more than what mere data can provide; for Wilson, as well as historian and sociologist W. E. B. Du Bois, it provides a source of understanding and renewal. Cultural history makes the present whole. Italian political philosopher Antonio Gramsci may best make sense of Wilson's plays; cultural history, Gramsci remarks, is "organization of one's inner self, a coming to terms with one's own personality; it is the attainment of a higher awareness, with the aid of which one succeeds in understanding one's own historical value, one's own function in life, one's own rights and obligations."[52] Among Wilson's talents is his skill at creating the internal and external content of African American domestic life. He is, perhaps, America's finest domestic dramatist, surpassing even Arthur Miller and Eugene O'Neill as the quintessential dramatic recorder of America's quotidian existence. His works present ordinary yet complex characters shadowed by history and caught up in domestic strife. His plays take place in one setting, always a communal gathering place (boarding house, recording studio, taxi cab station, family parlor, lunch counter, backyard, front porch) where family and work coincide. Wilson uses these places inventively and with a psychological twist.

Not all African American plays of the period took serious situations for plots. George C. Wolfe's *The Colored Museum* (1986) is a collection of eleven scenes defined as museum "exhibits." It is a "tour" through black history. Stereotypes are held up for scrutiny and sacred cows are risibly brought down. One example is "The Last Mama-on-the-Couch Play," which sends up Hansberry's *A Raisin in the Sun* and Shange's *for colored girls*. Wolfe's comedy is mainly a celebration of black life, warts and all. Other comedies surfaced during this era. Among the most noteworthy are plays by Neil Simon, Albert Innaurato, A. R. Gurney, Christopher Durang, and Charles Ludlam. Simon's plays are autobiographic dramas which include *Brighton Beach Memoirs* (1982), *Biloxi Blues* (1984), *Broadway Bound* (1986), and *Lost in Yonkers* (1991). They resemble the work of Clifford Odets, with perhaps less political edge. Albert Innaurato's *The Transformation of Benno Blimpi* (1976) and *Gemini* (1977) take up overeating and Italian American life. The main character, Benno Blimpi, is literally eating himself to death. The popular dramatist A. R. Gurney offered notable plays such as *Scenes from American Life* (1971), *The Middle Ages* (1977), and *The Dining Room* (1981). Gurney explores the world of the upper middle class. One of America's finest satirists, Christopher Durang's plays mix stand-up comic routines with absurdist situations. *The Vietnamization of New Jersey* (1977), *A History of American Film* (1978), *Beyond Therapy* (1981), *Sister Mary Ignatius Explains It All for You* (1981), *Baby and the Bathwater* (1983), *The Marriage of Betty and Boo* (1985), and *Laughing Wild* (1987) represent anger-fueled comedy targeting pretension and life's petty injustice. *Beyond Therapy*, perhaps his best-known work, pokes fun at the New Age healing fad. A love story, Bruce is uncertain of his sexuality, while Prudence exudes a gee-whillikers charm. Charles Ludlam and fellow actor (and partner) Everett Quinton create a camp-style melodrama incorporating drag. Their most popular play, *The Mystery of Irma Vep* (1984), produced by the Ridiculous Theatre Company, is a potpourri of characters imitating the high melodramatic style of a murder mystery. The production requires quick-change of costume and gender imper-sonation. Ludlam's drama is the theatre of the outrageous, the fabulous, and certainly certifies the rising status of gay drama.

Unlike the time where *Boys in the Band* was produced with apologetic overtones, the 1980s witnessed militant gay and lesbian theatre never seen before on the American stage. The groundswell arose partly from the 1969 uprising by gays and lesbians in New York known as "Stone-wall." This was followed by the AIDS epidemic and the political apathy toward the crisis by the Reagan administration. William Hoffman's *As Is* (1985) and Larry Kramer's *The Normal Heart* (1985) mark the begin-ning of gay awareness dramas depicting the slow death from AIDS and a public's refusal to react to the disease. Hoffman and Kramer set a tone of outrage toward a government that refused to acknowledge anything gay-related. Harvey Fierstein's *Torch Song Trilogy* (1982) is the story of a gay and Jewish female impersonator and his encounters. Fierstein played the lead role, its content largely autobiographical. The play was produced at the Glines, one of the leading theatres produc-ing gay and lesbian drama. Martin Sherman's *Bent* (1979) examined the largely overlooked persecution of homosexuals in Nazi Germany. Jane Chambers's *Last Summer at Bluefish Cove* (1980) was also produced at the Glines. It takes place at a summer beach resort on Long Island. The play follows a pattern similar to *Boys in the Band*; a group of lesbians confront a straight character. However, in *Bluefish Cove*, Eva the "straight" character falls in love with Lil. Unfortunately, Lil is dying of cancer. Like Rita Mae Brown's autobiography *Rubyfruit Jungle* (1973), *Bluefish Cove* is a coming-of-age drama in a realistic setting.

Realism would hardly describe one of the most important and endur-ing lesbian theatre groups, Split Britches. Represented by performers and playwrights Lois Weaver, Peggy Shaw, and Deborah Margolin, Split Britches began at the WOW Café in New York. Like the Glines, the

WOW Café became a leading resource for gay and lesbian dramatic works. The Glines generally produced conventional realistic plays, while Split Britches and WOW sought to "deconstruct" realistic devices. *Split Britches* (1981), *Beauty and the Beast* (1982), *Upwardly Mobile Home* (1984), *Little Women* (1988), *Belle Reprieve* (1991), and *Lesbians Who Kill* (1992) are, as these titles suggest, rejoinders to popular plays, fiction, and fairy tales.

John Patrick Shanley, Emily Mann, Philip Kan Gotanda, Michael Christopher, Mark Medoff, Preston Jones, Dennis McIntyre, and Eric Bogosian add to this generation of angry playwrights. Shanley's *Danny and the Deep Blue Sea* (1984), *Savage in Limbo* (1985), *Women of Manhattan* (1986), and *Italian American Reconciliation* (1988) develop complex characters in conflict. Mann's politically charged *Still Life* (1981) is a docudrama examining the after-effects of the Vietnam War. Gotanda's *Yankee Dawg You Die* (1989), like David Mamet's *A Life in the Theatre* (1977), is a relationship play between an older, cynical actor and a younger, rebellious one. Gotanda explores the demands of Asian actors forced into stereotypes. Christopher's popular play *The Shadow Box* (1977) examines three groups of people in a hospice, the themes in each case being the impending death of a character. It explores coming to terms with death and dying. Medoff's drama of the hearing impaired, *Children of a Lesser God* (1980), is a love story that showcased Phyllis Frelich's acting range in the leading role. Frelich's character rails against injustice. Preston Jones's *Texas Trilogy* (1976) is a three-play cycle interweaving events. Each play sheds light on small-town Southern life, focusing on a former cheerleader, a shell-shocked veteran, and the Klan-like organization now little more than a bunch of aging good-old-boys. Jones, like the prolific Horton Foote, chronicles Southern life in the style of Flannery O'Connor and William Faulkner. Dennis McIntyre and Eric Bogosian stand out among this group, creating hard-edged, unsparing dramas. McIntyre's *Modigliani* (1980) traces the self-destructive life of the modernist painter. His *Split Second* (1984) is the story of an African American policeman who confronts a white racist. The opening scene, one of the most powerful in American drama, takes place between the policeman Val and Willis. In making the arrest, Willis spews a tirade of racist epithets that pushes Val over the edge. Val shoots Willis. The opening scene has a potent, unnerving effect. The remainder of the play deals with Val's confrontation with his father, a former cop, and the guilt induced by his "split second" mistake.

Known as a solo artist, by the mid-1980s Bogosian developed full-length dramas. *Talk Radio* (1987) is prescient in its use of a radio talk show host ("bloggers" as they will later be called). His drama *SubUrbia* (1994) examines disillusioned youth, anticipating the "Goth" style of the early twenty-first century.

The 1980s experienced the rise of one-person shows. Vaudeville and stand-up comedy made the form common, but money added to the rise of this genre during the 1980s. One-person shows are financially viable, often requiring little if any set, and are easily transported. Bogosian was one of the period's best-known performers. Holly Hughes, Tim Miller, and Karen Finley emerged as leading gay and lesbian solo performance artists. The nonpareil monologist is Spalding Gray. A founding member of the Wooster Group theatre, his early work was developed under the aegis of Wooster Group director Elizabeth LeCompte. Gray's *Rhode Island Trilogy* (1978) is a collage of personal narrative mixed with sound effects and screen projections. He became well known for sitting behind a desk recording his life story. Part script and part improvisation, Gray's close attention to trivial details enables him to abstract the extraordinary from the ordinary. His most well-known play, *Swimming to Cambodia* (1985), recounts his experience as an actor in the film *The Killing Fields*. His combination of storytelling and first-person narrative marks the period's interest in a new kind of realism and mimesis. This experiment helped give way to the work of Anna Deavere Smith and the hyper-realism of the Tectonic Theatre Company of the 1990s.

This chapter closes with four plays that might be loosely called "postcolonial." Postcolonialism describes the way cultures reset themselves following World War II. There is marked weakening of colonial power while emerging new cultures reassert their values. Its literature is often associated with India's Salman Rushdie, Trinidad's V. S. Naipaul, Kenya's Ngúgú wa Thiong'o, and Nigeria's Wole Soyinka, among others. Eric Overmyer's *On the Verge, or The Geography of Yearning* (1985), Richard Nelson's *Principia Scriptoriae* (1986), Wallace Shawn's *Aunt Dan and Lemon* (1985), and David Henry Hwang's *M. Butterfly* (1988) represent dramas examining a changing perspective of colonial rule. *On the Verge* is a comic journey of three American "lady adventurers" who set off in 1888 to explore Africa, the Himalayas, and Terra Incognita. The safari takes the "sister sojourners" on an intrepid trek, one which portrays ingenuity and fortitude in the face of danger. The doughty women explore their independence – they debate whether or not to wear pants – and discover foreign lands with an open mind, subdued by an occasional residual degree of Victorian prejudice. For instance, Mary, the anthropologist of the three, makes journal entries which sometimes call attention to her superior attitude.

> MARY: I am an anthropologist. I traveled extensively amongst the Indigos. Cannibals – but lively. Anthropophagii tend to be sluggish, you know. I found them no bother to me at all. Of course, you had to keep them from eating your porters. Frequently head counts were the order of the day. There are two sorts of folks in the world. The sort you drink with, and the sort you eat with. Cannibals you drink with.[53]

Overmyer's admiration of these women fails to rule out criticism. Their insensitivity and disregard for cultural difference are put in the cross hairs. Overmyer's point is that the women must learn to shed preconceived notions. The process of postcolonialization is in fact a discarding of threadbare notions and outworn ideas. The women can also be insightful. Alexandra remarks on the term native: "Funny word, native. Assuming he is a native. Everyone is a native of somewhere, when you think about it" (17). Fanny is the journalist who reports to her newspaper, the *True Trek*. She is the conservative, a Midwesterner with restraint. Alexandra is the youngest and, according to Overmyer, the "most modern, most out of place in the Victorian world" (83). Pride in the power of their words and the eloquence of their language envelops the play. Ideals of successful communication come to have an almost sacred meaning for them. They also use language humorously. One such occasion is when Fanny describes her hacking away through the jungle: "Ah, the familiar chop chop swack swack. Takes me back. The cloud forest of Orinoco. Now there is a jungle, ladies. Spiders the size of flapjacks! They flop on you out of the trees! You have to get 'em on the fly! Cut 'em in half mid-air! Thwack! Spider blood splatters!" (11). Reverence for language and its sometimes comic cadence bond the characters. The play stresses different sides of the women as chroniclers, poets, interlocutors, journalists, and witnesses.

Richard Nelson is an American playwright who has enjoyed success primarily outside the United States. His *Principia Scriptoriae* takes place in a Latin American jail and occurs in divided frames, 1970 and 1985. It mostly concerns the relationship between Bill Howell, a backpacking garrulous American writer, and Ernesto Pico, a more taciturn Latin American author. Pico is a mentor of sorts to Howell. They are joined in an undisclosed prison, unaware of their crime, and go through the play in a Kafkaesque haze. They talk compulsively about revolution, yet their notion of revolution's meaning is ambiguous. Bill, for instance, praises the speeches of radicals in front of the local mall, yet he also has his doubts: "God can some of them talk, Ernesto. You should have heard them speak at the Mall. (*Pause.*) You couldn't really hear them at the Mall. But God could they talk."[54] Their dialogue focuses on the subject of writing and whether it can have a significant political effect. The incarceration is evidence that their writings have some impact, but they are unsure if this is the sort of thing they intend. Their prison cell is not the only carceral location. Ernesto's home at the play's conclusion is claustrophobic. They have been released and sit together on "two rusted lawn chairs" (54) on Ernesto's porch. Instead of coming to a mutual understanding, they have become further removed from one another. Bill's boyish charm and Tom Sawyeresque outlook is out of place in Ernesto's world of political intrigue. Nelson calls attention to the dangerous necessities of intercultural dialogue and the complexities of a postcolonial world.

Wallace Shawn's *Aunt Dan and Lemon*, like *Principia Scriptoriae*, develops a mentor–mentee relationship. Lemon's emulation of her Aunt Dan (Danielle) undergirds their bond. The allure of Dan's power drives Lemon from her immediate family. Lemon is a narrator serving both as theatrical tour guide, inviting the audience into her London flat, and as guide to her memory (the story is told in flashbacks). In an unassuming and charming manner, we observe the way Lemon learns from Aunt Dan first to appreciate power, then to admire Henry Kissinger's killing of the Viet Cong, then to enjoy Dan's description of a prostitute blackmailing and killing men, and finally to share Dan's admiration of the Nazis. The rationale behind this gradual descent into morbid attraction is deliberately ambiguous. In his review of the 2004 revival of *Aunt Dan and Lemon*, Hilton Als remarks that "Shawn is one of the few American playwrights to eschew psychological background as a means of explaining character; he prefers the audience to draw its own conclusions from the character's behavior."[55] Nevertheless, Shawn stacks the deck in favor of Lemon. We sympathize with her despite her politics. She is frail; she drinks only fruit juice; she is unassuming; and she emulates Aunt Dan in an affectionate way.

Shawn shows how quickly and easily attitudes of repression and bigotry can be absorbed. Some of the play's most memorable passages deal with moral contamination conveyed as effervescent logic. Shawn wants to reveal how easy it is to be tempted into becoming an accomplice to atrocities and colonialism.

David Henry Hwang's protagonist in *M. Butterfly*, Rene Gallimard, gives an account of how self-deception and lust for power can be rationalized into an obsession. The play takes place during the Cold War and deals with a French diplomat, Gallimard, who falls in love with a Chinese opera singer who is in fact a Communist spy, Song Liling. Gallimard is also duped by Song in ways other than political. Song is male, though Gallimard is unaware of this fact for two decades. Song dresses in drag and seduces him. Hwang capitalizes on the stereotypes of Chinese women as perceived by Western men. Song "acts" the role of Gallimard's desires. Song describes to the judge at Gallimard's trial for treason how he was able to disguise himself:

> SONG: As soon as a Western man comes into contact with the East – he's already confused. The West has sort of an international rape mentality towards the East. Do you know rape mentality?
> JUDGE: Give me your definition, please.
> SONG: Basically, "Her mouth says no, but her eyes say yes." The West thinks of itself as masculine – big guns, big industry, big money – so the East is feminine – weak, delicate, poor . . . but good art, and full of inscrutable wisdom – the feminine mystique.[56]

The play uncovers myths of both East and West. But using the theatricality of role-playing, Hwang reveals how gender is a performance. Song's performance of a specifically "Asian" woman acting the way Western men expect is so convincing that Song is able to carry out the deception for two decades. Song dispels any notion that Gallimard is gay; sex is only performed in the dark, with Song supine and face down. The deception depends on Gallimard's belief in the stereotype; Song gambles that Gallimard is so convinced by the myth of passive Asian woman that he will miss the obvious. It succeeds. Song is able to gather vital information while serving as Gallimard's mistress. For Gallimard, Song's "body" is less fact than fantasy, a fulfillment of his desires. This is made clear when Marc, Gallimard's boyhood buddy, describes women to a shy Gallimard, while Song "mimes attending to her toilette" in the backdrop. As Song's "robe comes loose, revealing her white shoulders," Marc says to Gallimard:

> MARC: All your life you've waited for a beautiful girl who would lay down for you. All your life you've smiled like a saint when it's happened to every other man you know. And you see them in magazines and you see them in movies. And you wonder, what's wrong with me? Will anyone beautiful ever want me? (25)

Hwang explains that the "impossibility" of such a story is highly plausible owing to the "degree of misunderstanding between men and women and also between East and West." Hwang adds that the stereotypes of "rice queens," meaning a "gay Caucasian man primarily attracted to Asians," and "Yellow Fever," heterosexual "Caucasian men with a fetish for exotic Oriental women," create a "pattern of relationships" that are codified and accepted (98). Hwang challenges the colonial conception of gender and race manufactured to maintain dominance. For Hwang, the body's representation and performance aid Song's duplicity once the stereotype has been ingrained in Gallimard's delusion. The notion of the body as a theatrical representation will come to occupy playwrights of the next decade.

CHAPTER 5

The Body in Pain: American Drama, 1990–2000

Roy: *This is . . . this is gastric juices churning, this is enzymes and acids, this is intestinal is what it is, bowel movement and blood-red meat – this stinks, this is* politics, *Joe, the game of being alive. And you think you're . . . What? Above that? Above alive is what? Dead! In the clouds! You're on earth, goddamnit! Plant a foot, stay a while.*

Tony Kushner, *Angels in America* (1992)[1]

Sterling: *Wolf say you put them scars on your legs yourself. Wasn't you scared you was gonna bleed to death?*
Risa: *They didn't bleed much.*

August Wilson, *Two Trains Running* (1992)[2]

Craver: *In our bunker at night, Remzi used to read the names out loud to us, and it calmed us down. He must have read that weapons manual a hundred times. All those ways to kill the human body.*

Naomi Wallace, *In the Heart of America* (1994)[3]

Dr. Cantway: *Then two days later I found out the connection and I was . . . very . . . struck!!! They were two kids!!!! They were both my patients and they were two kids. I took care of both of them. . . . Of both their bodies. And . . . for a brief moment I wondered if this is how God feels when he looks down at us. How we are all his kids. . . . Our bodies. . . .*

Moisés Kaufman, *The Laramie Project* (2000)[4]

Pain resists description. Elaine Scarry contends that pain "does not simply resist language" but "actually destroys it, bringing about an immediate reversion to a state anterior to language, to the sounds and cries a human being makes before language is learned."[5] A silent body onstage can generate an intense relationship with an audience. When it is represented as a body in pain it can embrace empathy and amplify passion. This idea is nothing new, but what made the 1990s different was its emphasis on the representation of pain. This emphasis reflected a period of introspective self-involvement. It was a time of material gain, but also a time of self-reflection. The go-go stock market, dot.com economy, relative peace, body consciousness, and Bill Clinton's peccadilloes created an age of frivolity. Any celebration of individuality was soon inverted into commercialism, inspiring marketers to keep pace with or even create fads. Yet it was also a contemplative decade enriched by a focus on history, memory, and nostalgia. Seven playwrights in particular – Anna Deavere Smith, John Guare, Paula Vogel, Josefina López, Suzan-Lori Parks, August Wilson, and Tony Kushner – inaugurate the decade's preoccupation with these notions.

Anna Deavere Smith's *Fires in the Mirror: Crown Heights, Brooklyn and Other Identities* (1993) centers on a fatal car accident that occurred in August 1991. Crown Heights is an ethnic cheek-by-jowl amalgam of African Americans, Jamaicans, and Hasidic Jews. A car driven by a Hasidic group crashed onto the sidewalk. The accident killed Gavin Cato, a 7-year-old from Guyana, and injured his cousin. A private ambulance attended to the injured passengers but neglected Cato, who was pinned between the car and a tree. His death ignited a riot, leading to the stabbing of Yankel Rosenbaum, a 29-year-old visiting Hasidic scholar from Australia. The deaths of Cato and Rosenbaum unleashed already simmering tensions. The riot itself symbolized the closing of black–Jewish relations dating from the Scottsboro trials of the 1930s and into the civil rights–voter registration era of the 1960s. The 1964 murder of three civil rights workers in Mississippi – James Chaney, Andrew Goodman, and Michael Schwerner – illustrated Jewish involvement in the Civil Rights Movement. The marching arm-in-arm of Reverend Doctor Martin Luther King and Rabbi Abraham Joshua Heschel in protest of the murders marked the highpoint of black–Jewish relations. The Crown Heights catastrophe marked its low.

Fires in the Mirror, like Kennedy's *Funnyhouse of a Negro* and Hansberry's *The Sign on Sidney Brustein's Window*, examines black–Jewish relations. However, Smith's approach to playwriting departs from tradition. She interviews people closely associated with the event and reenacts their response. *Fires in the Mirror* is a one-person show in which Smith performs all roles. She belongs to a group of many 1980s and 1990s quick-change artists in the crowded field of solo multi-character shows. Smith is concerned not only with history, but also with memory; she wants to uncover how an event is remembered. For Smith, each portrayal exposes the anguish accompanying the violence. Her goal is to reenact the body language and speech with a minimum of costume changes (a mere wig, sweater, or jacket to indicate change). Avoiding any temptation to editorialize, she becomes an observer rather than an interpreter. Actors usually speak through their characters, but Smith's characters speak through her. This performance style allows for portrayals otherwise unavailable to many a black actress. Smith asks: "Who has the right to see what? Who has the right to say what? Who has the right to speak for whom?" These questions, Smith contends, "have plagued the contemporary theater. These questions address issues of employment equity and issues of *who is portrayed*. These questions are the questions that unsettle and prohibit a democratic theater in America. If only a man can speak for a man, a woman for a woman, a Black person for all Black people, then we, once again, inhibit the *spirit* of theater, which lives in the *bridge* that makes unlikely aspects *seem* connected."[6] Instead of taking sides in the debate among competing groups, Smith makes use of the theatre's ability to cast the entire issue in one body. This enables audiences to observe a multiplicity of ideas; instead of stark lines drawn between ethnicities, we observe a symphony of voices. *Fires in the Mirror*, like Smith's *Twilight: Los Angeles, 1992* (1996) and *House Arrest* (1999), is an intimate theatrical work that brings into proximity the experience of loss.

Like *Fires in the Mirror*, John Guare's *Six Degrees of Separation* (1990) is social criticism. It, too, is based on actual events. *Six Degrees of Separation* takes place in the upper-middle-class New York apartment inhabited by two WASPs, Flan and Ouisa Kittredge, who buy and sell art. They wine and dine Geoffrey, a South African art dealer. When asked why he remains in South Africa, he replies condescendingly: "One has to stay there and educate the black workers and we'll know we've been successful when they kill us."[7] The Kittredges had assisted a young African American, Paul, the night before. Paul claimed to have been mugged in Central Park; he had entered their home covered in blood. They believe him to be Sidney Poitier's son, and with good reason. Paul has conned them: not only can he recite details of Poitier's life and career, but he also concocts a story that his "father" plans to attend the musical *Cats* with the intent of turning it into a movie. He convinces the Kittredges because they want to be convinced. As liberals, they feel obliged. Guare illuminates the way craven desire for celebrity status can skew judgment. Like Tom Wolfe in his novel *Bonfire of the Vanities*, Guare satirizes the liberal duplicity of caring for the maligned without upsetting a rich and famous lifestyle.

Guare, Gene Plunka remarks, "acts as a sociologist who probes a troubled, conflicted, angst-ridden contemporary American society," positing that society "has become dehumanized, interested more in commercialization of celebrity than the value of life."[8] The radical chic world of New York's Upper East Side is revealed as Paul wends his way into the Kittredges' home. Paul also bamboozles two naïve Midwesterners, Rick and Elizabeth, whom he meets in Central Park, by claiming the Kittredges are his parents. He seduces Rick and then steals his money, but eventually Paul is arrested. He disappears into the legal system despite efforts by Ouisa to track him down. Paul comes from a tradition of American mountebanks such as Elmer Gantry who exploit weaknesses through charm and guile. However, Paul is himself vulnerable; beneath the deception is a lonely drifter. Exposed as a fraud, he reveals himself.

> OUISA: What did you want from us?
> PAUL: Everlasting friendship.
> OUISA: Nobody has that.
> PAUL: You do.   (99)

Ouisa, however, does not. She and her husband live superficially and like it that way. Paul's machinations momentarily expose Ouisa's desire for deeper connections. She says to the audience, "I read somewhere that everybody on this planet is separated by only six other people. Six degrees of separation. . . . Six degrees of separation between me and everyone else on this planet. But to find the right six people" (81). Her belief in six degrees of separation depends on bonds no matter how circuitous. Paul's revolving-door appearance trades on the Kittredges' white liberal guilt. Their relationship is quid pro quo: he hopes to awaken the Kittredges' desire for fame, and they in turn serve Paul's need for family. Paul's body becomes as a vessel fulfilling the Kittredges' longings: connected vicariously to the "son" of a famous actor; helping a troubled youth; and the satisfaction of aiding a "victim."

Paul is a compulsive liar, and once exposed he is useless to them. Paul even stabs himself to elicit their sympathy. He wants companionship in the same way Jerry in Albee's *The Zoo Story* does. At the conclusion Ouisa comes as close as she can to understanding her situation, saying to her husband: "We were hardly taken in. We believed him – for a few hours. He did more for us in a few hours than our children ever did. He wanted to be your child. Don't let that go. He sat out in that park and said that man is my father. He's in trouble and we don't know how to help him" (117). In his two finest plays, *House of Blue Leaves* and *Six Degrees of Separation*, Guare discloses the cost of rubbing elbows with the high and mighty.

Connections, or lack thereof, are at the root of Paula Vogel's work. Whereas Guare is interested in connections between people, Vogel is concerned with connecting past and present. The themes here include memory, nostalgia, and trauma. In *The Baltimore Waltz* and *How I Learned to Drive*, Vogel explores the memory of a dead brother and the molestation of a child by her uncle, respectively. In *The Baltimore Waltz* (1990) we discover Anna and Carl, sister and brother, on a trip through Europe in search of a cure for what is believed to be her fatal illness. However, it is in fact Carl who is dying of AIDS. The play occurs in Anna's recollection of her relationship with her brother (the story is based on the author's own experience). The memories, however, are fantasy – the trip to Europe never occurred – producing a sublevel representation of grief. In her memory Anna reverses the roles of caretaker and afflicted. Comedy and playful intrigue supply an unexpected response; instead of arousing grief, their journey is humorous. Scenes depict the siblings encountering secret-spy shenanigans, lighthearted affairs, and entangled schemes that playfully recreate a character from the movie *The Third Man*, a film noir dealing with the illegal drug trade. The play loosely follows the pattern of Ambrose Bierce's short story *An Incident at Owl Creek Bridge* (1961, made into TV's Twilight Zone episode, *An Occurrence at Owl Creek Bridge*, in 1962), in which a Civil War soldier who is about to hang fantasizes his escape seconds before dying. Denial is the force which drives both Bierce's and Vogel's characters. Vogel explores the way in which memory plays tricks. In the play the "Third Man" would have us recall Elizabeth Kübler-Ross's well-known "stages of grief," in which "the terminal patient travels in the course of her illness."[9] *Baltimore Waltz*'s camp style – the sendup of a serious subject – provides a refreshing perspective on

AIDS. In contrast to the powerful but overwrought AIDS "rage" dramas of the 1980s such as *Normal Heart* and *As Is*, Vogel's play renders bodily functions comic through toilet jokes. Vogel not only satirizes the belief, prevalent in the 1980s, that people could contact AIDS through toilet seats, she is also seeking to understand the role of nostalgia.

Nostalgia fills a void. In *Future of Nostalgia*, Svetlana Boym defines it as "a longing for a home that no longer exists or has never existed. Nostalgia is a sentiment of loss and displacement, but it is also a romance with one's own fantasy." Boym adds that "nostalgia is a double exposure, or a superimposition of two images – of home and abroad, past and present, dream and everyday life."[10] For Vogel, fantasy (nostalgia) competes with reality (trauma) along the lines of Boym's dual images (home–abroad, past–present). Yet Vogel, in a creative twist, considers nostalgia for an event that never happened. This in itself complicates the relationship of nostalgia and fantasy. The trip to find a cure is a way for Anna and Carl to avoid the reality of death. Anna and Carl shuttle from home to abroad, past to present, sharing their dream-like experience. They live a might-have-been situation. The results are fragmentary, with Vogel arranging the play's narrative accordingly. This "patchwork quilt of a play," observes Ann Pellegrini, "breaks open cramped notions of time and space and loosens propriet-ary understandings of kinship and affiliation."[11] Trauma resists causal unfolding from event to memory because it is both insufficiently grasped at the time of its occurrence and inadequately processed in the archive of memory. Trauma may be recalled at will, but more likely it rears up unexpectedly and intrusively. Unsettling and disturbing, trauma departs from the strictly linear, zigzagging across the panoptic lines of reality and illusion. In an atmosphere of trauma, Vogel's play is suffused with a soft luminosity and a gentle recollection of the past. The sibling relationship is, from the outset, selfless and sincere. The play catches us by surprise; the brother is depicted as caretaker, fulfilling the role the sister has failed to assume. Amidst the void created by her brother's death, Anna's fantasies transform emptiness into plenitude. It is as if to say, "This is how I imagined it to be, or how I would have liked it to be."

The play is divided into "lesson plans." Each examines language and the body. The doctor, for example, describes Anna's illness in medical gibberish. Carl says: "Lesson Seven: Basic Vocabulary. Parts of the body" (23). Anna notes: "I feel so alone. The ceiling is pressing down on me.

I can't believe I am dying. Only at night. Only at night. In the morning, when I open my eyes, I feel absolutely well – without a body" (26). During a comic affair with the "Munich Virgin," Anna says: "The human body is a wonderful thing. Like yours. Like mine. The beauty of the body heals all the sickness, all the bad things that happen to it. And I really want you to feel this. Because if you feel it, you'll remember it. And then maybe you'll remember me" (41). For Anna her brother resembles a fading photograph; the story is her effort to keep the picture in focus. In the final moment, Anna tries to awaken her brother. The background music is Strauss's *The Emperor Waltz*. Anna wants to dance with him. She forces him to sit, but his body stiffens. He rises and falls, puppet-like. Carl *"mechanically springs forward. Then suddenly, like a doll in E. T. A. Hoffman, the body of Carl becomes animated, but with a strange, automatic life of its own. Carl begins to waltz with Anna"* (56). Anna gets him to dance but his doll-like movements are ungainly. The final scene with Anna and the doctor occurs after her brother's death. The beauty of their relationship is contrasted with Anna's blunt comment: "I never would have believed what sickness can do to the body" (57). The doctor produces Carl's personal items, one of which is a brochure for a trip to Europe – a journey that never happened.

Despite the focus on loss, the play avoids the sentimental. There is a sense of the whimsical and an unstable sense of identity through a variation of role-playing. Though Vogel may render processes of identification and sympathy inapplicable by demonstrating that identity is in flux, the breakdown of stable identity through playfulness is not frivolous. The illusions, role-playing, and role reversal are an appraisal of grief. Vogel's fusion of grief and humor renders uncertain the boundary separating tragedy and comedy. This blurring of genres captures something fundamental to mourning – a physical and social need to alternately grieve and deny, fantasize and accept. Her technique of destabilizing identity trades on an unsettling amplification of physical dislocation, which acts metaphorically for disintegrating memory. In many ways Vogel's portrayal is the opposite of Sam Shepard's sibling relationships; her siblings reject "rivalry." Closeness for Shepard is threatening; for Vogel it is exhilarating. Her examination of trauma and memory continues throughout her work, especially in what is, perhaps, her finest play, *How I Learned to Drive* (1997).

Like Anna, Li'l Bit, the central character in *How I Learned to Drive*, is caught between past and present. The play is essentially a two-character relationship story of Li'l Bit and her Uncle Peck, with a chorus of other actors playing subordinate roles. Like *The Baltimore Waltz, How I Learned to Drive* is framed around a "lesson plan," in this case driving lessons. Driving represents control; Li'l Bit's relationship to her uncle is based largely on his teaching her to drive, but it also includes sexual abuse. Still, theirs is not reduced to a one-dimensional victimizer and victim relationship. Peck and Li'l Bit are bonded despite their roles as predator and victim. For Li'l Bit, untangling and deciphering the lines of involvement are not easy. She longs for her innocent past, inspired by her memory of Uncle Peck. She says, tongue-in-cheek: "Even with my family background, I was sixteen or so before I realized that pedophilia did not mean people who loved to bicycle."[12] The play alludes to pedophilia, but it is not until Peck places Li'l Bit on his lap for one of his many driving lessons that it becomes evident. Driving is not merely functional – it imparts meaningful lessons of life. It is the bond between them, and Li'l Bit cannot, or will not, divorce the benefit she has accrued from the abuse she has endured.

Li'l Bit's life unfolds in memory by suggestion rather than certainty. We know that she was dismissed from a "fancy school in 1970," but the reasons are vague. There are hints of a lesbian relationship: "Some say I got caught with a man in my room. Some say as a kid on scholarship I fooled around with a rich man's daughter" (21). The last affair recalls Oscar Wilde's relationship with a wealthy man's son. The sequence of scenes moves back and forth as Li'l Bit's narration commences on a memory driving tour. She reveals the sense of power that comes from driving.

> Li'l Bit: What I did, most nights, was cruise the Beltway and the back roads of Maryland, where there was still country, past the battlefields and farm houses. Racing in a 1965 Mustang – and as long as I had gasoline for my car and whiskey in me, the nights would pass. Fully tanked, I would speed past the churches and the trees on the bend, thinking just one notch of the wheel would be all it would take, and yet some . . . reflex took over. My hands on the wheel in the nine and three o'clock position – I never so much as got a ticket. He taught me well. (21)

Uncle Peck did, indeed, teach her well. The implication of suicide ("one notch of the wheel would be all it would take") and being saved by Uncle Peck's "lessons" complicate their relationship. Nostalgia for her Maryland upbringing and Uncle Peck, David Savran asserts, "conjoins her with the past, with the land, and with the body (both the material body and her own), as she imagines herself miraculously whole again through the power of memory. But as Li'l Bit knows all too well – and as anyone who has become a subject can tell you – this primordial wholeness cannot last, and the remainder of the play shows her being taken for a ride that will lead – or rather, has led – her into another realm."[13] Li'l Bit's "learning" is connected to Peck; the healing process requires unlearning what is painful as well as useful. "There's something about driving," Peck says; "when you're in control of the car, just you and the machine and the road – that nobody can take from you. A power. I feel more myself in my car than anywhere else. And that's what I want to give you" (50). Peck teaches her to anticipate the moves of others. Li'l Bit not only learns how to drive, but also receives in the process lessons on life. However, for Li'l Bit, "education" entails disassociation from her body. In the penultimate scene, she is seated on his lap. Peck touches her breasts while teaching her to drive. The final scene has Li'l Bit driving years after the first of several incidents of molestation: "That day was the last day I lived in my body. I retreated above the neck, and I've lived inside the 'fire' in my head ever since" (90). Li'l Bit feels most alive behind the wheel of a car: "The nearest sensation I feel – of flight in the body – I guess I feel when I'm driving" (91). The play ends with the sound of a screeching car driving away. Li'l Bit's "cure" requires separating her sexual experience from driving, something she is unwilling to do. Vogel's works – including *And Baby Makes Seven* (1984), *The Oldest Profession* (1990), *Desdemona, A Play about a Handkerchief* (1993), *Hot 'N' Throbbing* (1993), *The Mineola Twins* (1997) – non-simplistically examine relationships, nostalgia, and sexuality with frankness.

The body is associated with the marginalized in Josefina López's *Real Women Have Curves* (1990), one of the most produced plays written by a Chicana playwright (it eventually became an HBO film). It is about Ana and her sister Estela. They work with other women in a sewing factory in East Los Angeles. This slice-of-Chicana-life creates a community in microcosm. Through their interrelationships we learn of loves, struggles, and ambitions. The main conflict involves Ana's desire to leave the barrio and attend college. The play, Jorge Huerta asserts, "is about expectations – what society, especially Mechicano culture, expects of its women and how women might negate those expectations on a path towards liberation from the patriarchy."[14] The play is also about Ana's body. Being overweight in a culture that glorifies the svelte further marginalizes her. Yet Ana resists the usual paradigms of beauty, celebrating her "curves." She ends the play in hortatory fashion, encouraging solidarity among women.

Suzan-Lori Parks's *Imperceptible Mutabilities in the Third Kingdom* (1989), *The Death of the Last Black Man in the Whole Entire World* (1992), and *The America Play* (1993) create language and gesture that keep disengaging from the very actions they call forth. One way Parks accomplishes this is a performing style calling attention to the fact that the actors are "play acting." Vaudeville routines, for instance, create for Parks a rich quarry of acting styles. In *The America Play*, the first act consists in the repetition of a vaudeville theme park routine in which a black man portrays Abraham Lincoln and the fairground patrons pay to reenact the assassination. The character of Lincoln is named "The Founding Father as Abraham Lincoln." Though black, he does in fact resemble Lincoln; when dressed in fake beard, top hat, and long coat, he is often mistaken for "the great man." The patrons step up to the "shooting gallery," reenacting the actions of John Wilkes Booth. Lincoln assumes his place at "Ford's Theatre" and chortles. Fairground patrons take turns circling to his rear. Once shot, the patron – in this instance A Man – jumps from the balcony and shouts John Wilkes Booth's exhortation:

A MAN: Ready.
THE FOUNDING FATHER: Haw Haw Haw Haw (*Rest.*) HAW HAW HAW HAW.
(*Booth shoots. Lincoln "slumps in his chair." Booth jumps.*)
A MAN: (*Theatrically.*) "The South is avenged!"[15]

Parks's plays have a desultory, pseudo-allegorical sense that we are watching a parody of history. "Uh exact replica of thuh Great Hole of History!" Brazil says (179). The "hole" is the missing portion of history. There is the sense that the past is buried in the "Great Hole" of history, one bypassed in the textbooks. Parks also severs the action from speech; the disparity between the message conveyed by the actions and that by the words prevents cohesion. Like Beckett, Parks encourages the reduction of meaning while retaining a sense of the

theatrical. *The America Play* is a self-consciously postmodern challenge
to reality and its fictional depiction. "Postmodern" describes a literary or
dramatic work that features irony, serendipity, non-linearity, indeterm-
inacy, repetition, parody, and celebration of theatricality. Postmodern
drama makes no effort to disguise a play qua play or follow events in
chronological sequence. Playwrights, Parks writes, "are often encouraged to write 2-act plays with traditional linear narrative. Those sorts
of plays are fine, but we should understand that the form is not
merely a docile passive vessel, but an active participant in the sort of
play which ultimately inhabits it" (8). The notion of form is central
to Parks's work. Repetition and revision, what Parks's calls "rep and
rev," are formal devices she employs to highlight the reenactment of
historical episodes. She challenges the dominance of realism as the
accepted conveyor of history. Traditional aspirations of social realism
mean cutting through to a truth behind the appearance; by holding
close to the "facts," realism hopes to peel away obfuscation and get to
the core of reality. This appears shop-worn to Parks and other artists
such as Andy Warhol, whose *Marilyn Monroe, diptych* (1962), *Four Mona
Lisas* (1963), *Orange Car Crash Fourteen* (1963), and *Brillo Boxes* (1971)
invoke repetition by juxtaposing a replicated series of actual people,
objects, or events. Social realism's supposed absolutes collapse in
Warhol's art; by dint of repetition, we see how an image becomes
fixed into our minds. Like Warhol, Parks uses repetition to demonstrate how stultified icons become branded into our subconscious.
Her *America Play* seeks to represent "representation" itself. Lincoln's
assassination – Lincoln himself – is iconic. In the play, Lincoln-as-
black-man reenacting the assassination in a theme park venue playfully disengages the event from the status symbol of the "great white
patriarch and the notorious assassination." Parks's objective is to unpack
history and "deconstruct" its role in America's national consciousness.
Rather than conceiving of history as one-directional, she imagines it
as a palimpsest of past and present. Throughout her writing she posits
a penumbra that asks to be filled, a "hole" in history that signals the
need for revision in the way history is remembered and conceived.
Parks's *America Play* creates an awareness of the fragmentary nature
of African American history, evocative of the image of "digging" in a
"hole" that is yet to be "whole."

Digging into the past and thereby making it complete is a core feature of August Wilson's dramas. In *The Piano Lesson* (1990) the conflict

between siblings for control of the family piano is more than a matter of possession. The piano symbolizes competing notions of African American history. The plot revolves around the return of Boy Willie from the South to Pittsburgh during the Depression, ostensibly to sell watermelons, but actually to reclaim the family heirloom. Boy Willie wants to sell the piano to buy land. His sister Berniece has the piano but refuses to sell it. She lives in Pittsburgh with her daughter and her Uncle Doaker. The richly ornate piano was originally a gift to the wife of slave owner Sutter. Sutter traded "one-and-a-half slaves" in order to buy the piano and make it a gift. One of the slaves was the great-grandmother of Boy Willie and Berniece, and the other – the "half" – their grandfather. Over time Sutter's wife, Miss Ophelia, wanted the slaves back; as Doaker describes it, "Miss Ophelia got to missing my grandmother . . . the way she would cook and clean the house and talk to her and what not. And she missed having my daddy around the house to fetch things for her."[16] But Sutter was unable to return the piano in exchange for the slaves. In lieu of mother and child, Sutter asked the great-grandfather to hand carve the images of his wife and son onto the piano. This way Miss Ophelia would see them every time she played. The great-grandfather went further, drawing not only his wife and son but also the family's history, images of his marriage ceremony, and memories of African rituals. The piano resulted in emblematic status for the family. For this reason Berniece refuses to sell it, even though the piano is "haunted" by Sutter's ghost – a haunting that prevents her from playing.

Conflict of interest rises above sibling rivalry because the piano embodies a legacy of two cultural loci: African and the South. Berniece opposes the sale because the instrument represents African ancestry. The carved artwork of their African past makes it an object of family value and a symbol of African roots. In addition, their father had died trying to regain possession of it. Boy Willie sees it otherwise; for him the sale of the piano will bring in money, allowing for purchase of property once owned by Sutter. The piano becomes a "body," an organism representing two ideals. The images on the piano, notes Kim Pereira, produce "a totemic aura, for it now symbolizes the struggle of one family to survive slavery and sharecropping."[17] For Wilson, black history is rooted in Africa *and* slavery. Africa is home, but the South is where blacks tilled, toiled, and created. To reject the South would be to repudiate not only Negro spirituals, the blues, and the oral tradition, but also the rightful ownership of land. Boy Willie's desire for Sutter's property represents the ethics of black entitlement. As he says:

> BOY WILLIE: I take my hat off whenever somebody say my daddy's name. But I ain't gonna be no fool about no sentimental value. You can sit up here and look at the piano for the next hundred years and it's just gonna be a piano. You can't make more than that. Now I want to get Sutter's land with that piano. I get Sutter's land and I can go down and cash in the crop and get my seed. As long as I got the land and the seed then I'm alright. I can always get me a little something else. Cause that land give back to you. I can make me another crop and cash that in. I still got the land and the seed. But that piano don't put out nothing else. You ain't got nothing working for you. Now, the kind of man my daddy was he would have understood that. (51)

Berniece resists, believing that the piano, as Wilson's biographer Sandra Shannon has suggested, "is a monument to her ancestors, which, by right, ought to be preserved."[18] She responds to her brother by appealing to their mother's love for the piano:

> BERNIECE: You ain't taking that piano out of my house.
> (*She crosses to the piano.*)
> Look at this piano. Look at it. Mama Ola polished this piano with her tears for seventeen years. For seventeen years she rubbed on it till her hands bled. Then she rubbed the blood in . . . mixed it up with the rest of the blood on it. Every day that God breathed life into her body she rubbed and cleaned and polished and prayed over it. (52)

The piano is marked by blood, history, and memory. Devon Boan maintains that the "action of the play is driven by conflict over how best to engage history – as iconographically centered mythology, which would celebrate the *events* of the past, or as foundation for the present, which would seek to fulfill its *promise*."[19] The struggle is manifested in the symbols of seed and blood: Boy Willie wants to plant seeds in Southern roots, while Berniece longs to maintain blood ties to African roots. Both "seed" and "blood" are symbolic; both characters are firm in their moral fortitude and sense of justice; and both fix their demands to these larger considerations. The dramatic structure revolves around past and present, Africa and the South, and the conflict is such that the drama underscores competition of values. For Wilson, the modern world of African Americans is in a constant dialogue with the past. To deny the past is, for him, to break with one's roots.

The past looms large in Tony Kushner's two-part epic, *Angels in America*. The first part is subtitled *Millennium Approaches* (1992) and Part II, *Perestroika* (1993). Kushner weaves a complex tapestry of events using three storylines: the disintegrating marriage of Joe and Harper Pitt; the mentoring relationship between Joe and Roy Cohn (based on the real-life attorney); and the fraught relationship between Louis and Prior. The play takes place in the mid-1980s during the Reagan administration. Joe and Harper are Utah Mormons living in Brooklyn. Joe is a rising young Republican and Harper is addicted to Valium. She senses their marital disintegration as Joe's homosexuality becomes evident. When Joe returns home in the wee hours from wandering alongside Central Park's boathouse (a well-known rendezvous for homosexuals), he sparks the already volatile mix into something considerably more incendiary. His betrayal leads to their separation. Joe is also involved politically with Roy Cohn, an activist lawyer in the Republican Party and a closet homosexual. In another plotline, Prior has contracted AIDS, making Louis uncomfortable. This leads to their break-up. Louis has an affair with Joe. They are bound by a feeling of guilt. Along the way are several secondary characters, among them Belize, a nurse and friend of Louis and Prior; Hannah Pitt, Joe's mother; Prior's ancestors, who appear as ghosts; the Angel, who also appears only to Prior; an Eskimo, who appears to Harper; and Ethel Rosenberg (the real-life figure executed for treason), who appears as a ghost to Roy Cohn (the prosecutor who pressed for Rosenberg's death sentence).

Angels in America is an amalgamation of melodrama and history; realism and camp; dreams and reality; religion and secularism; and flesh and spirit. The play opens with death and the memory of it: how does one remember the dead as a means of continuing life? It proceeds to untangle the knotty politics of AIDS during a time of crisis. Roy Cohn is told by his doctor, Henry, that he has AIDS. Cohn says it is "hemophilia" and must be recorded as such; any implication of AIDS must be avoided. Henry argues against this, but Cohn elides his doctor's equivocation, insisting that AIDS will "label" him a homosexual, a stigma he can ill afford to have.

ROY: Like all labels they tell you one thing and one thing only: where does an individual so identified fit in the food chain, in the pecking order? Not ideology, nor sexual taste, but something much simpler: clout. Not who I fuck or who fucks me, but who will pick up the phone when I call, who owes me favors. [. . .] Homosexuals are not men who sleep with other men. Homosexuals are men who in fifteen years of trying cannot get a pissant antidiscrimination bill through City Council. Homosexuals are men who know nobody and who nobody knows. Who have zero clout. Does that sound like me, Henry? (45)

Though both are afflicted with AIDS, Prior is the antithesis of Cohn. Prior is a "prophet." He is visited by an Angel – a theme Kushner borrows from Walter Benjamin's angel of history – along with Prior's ancestors. Harper's Valium-induced hallucinations also evoke surreal images. In one scene Kushner playfully crisscrosses fantasies: Prior shows up unexpectedly in Harper's dream (see figure 5). Prior, a drag performer, is seated at his make-up table; when Harper enters his "space" we are transported from conventional reality to fantasia (the two-part drama is referred to as a "gay fantasia on national themes"). They commiserate with each other; each has been betrayed by his or her lover. Harper's addiction is revealed.

HARPER: It's terrible. Mormons are not supposed to be addicted to any-
thing. I'm a Mormon.
PRIOR: I'm a homosexual.
HARPER: Oh! In my church we don't believe in homosexuals.
PRIOR: In my church we don't believe in Mormons.
HARPER: What church do . . . Oh! (*She laughs.*) I get it. (32)

Louis's goal is freedom. This entails abstracting himself from inter-est in the body, especially blood. He therefore rationalizes abandoning his lover. At the opening of Act II, Christmas of 1985, Prior is, accord-ing to the stage directions, *"alone on the floor of his bedroom; he is much worse"* (47). He calls for Louis, who is evidently no longer sleeping with him. Louis tries to convince Prior to go to the emergency room, but Prior is afraid. As Louis tries to help him, the stage directions say Prior *"shits himself."*

FIGURE 5   *Angels in America*, by Tony Kushner, 1996; directed by David Krasner, Southern Illinois University, Carbondale. Julie Esposito (Harper) and Justin DeGiacomo (Prior). Reprinted courtesy of David Krasner.

> Louis: This is blood.
> Prior: Maybe you shouldn't touch it ... me ... I ... (*He faints.*)
> Louis: (*Quietly.*) Oh help. Oh help. Oh God oh God oh God help me I can't I can't I can't.   (48)

Louis is unable to incorporate blood, feces, and the deterioration of the flesh into his concept of "freedom." Louis invokes "God," but when that fails he simply states the obvious: "I can't." What he "can't" do is deal with "blood," because blood, flesh, and mortality are antithetical to his idealization of freedom.

Louis's quest for freedom is tied to self-knowledge. But he is ambivalent about the truth and commitment. In discussing law, for example, he says to Prior that law "should be the question and shape of a life, its total complexity gathered, arranged and considered, which matters in the end, not some stamp of salvation or damnation which disperses all complexity in some unsatisfying little decision – the balancing of the scales" (38–9). Louis's point is that a small act (small in his terms) must fall short in the face of larger issues like absolute freedom. This summarizes Louis's rationalization of betrayal; Louis is a free agent, who in his effort to understand himself, creates a protective shell. Prior responds sharply, acknowledging Louis's cold logic: "I like this," he says, "very zen; it's . . . reassuringly incomprehensible and useless. We who are about to die thank you" (39). Prior is aware of Louis's intentions, and counters by bringing up the issue of the body, in this case a dying one.

Louis and Joe share their guilt, the likely basis of their mutual attraction. Joe joins Louis on a park bench during lunch. Joe devours several hotdogs. Joe, a Republican, and Louis, a Democrat, are also attracted to each other despite (or perhaps because of) their differences. Joe admires Louis's "freedom," but he is also petrified, largely because of his fear of coming out. Louis is nonplussed.

JOE: Yes, I mean it must be scary, you . . .
LOUIS: (*Shrugs.*) Land of the free. Home of the brave. Call me irresponsible.
JOE: It's kind of terrifying.
LOUIS: Yeah, well, freedom is. Heartless, too.
JOE: Oh you're not heartless.
LOUIS: You don't know. Finish your weenie. (72)

The play creates images, aphorisms, and metaphors expressive of the American conscience. Its poetic language, sense of humor, and the explosive entrances of angels and ghosts add to the play's carnivalesque design, but Kushner's main objective is to raise awareness about moral authority in an age of AIDS. The body politic – in fact the body itself – is frequently emphasized. Prior's bleeding and Louis's inability to deal with his lover's deteriorating flesh are one example. Prior's fantasy of a dance with Louis is another. It is, as Louis says, only "spectral." It resembles the waltz in Vogel's *Baltimore Waltz*; a touching expression of love and affection. The body and spirit merge, but only briefly and only in the mind. For Cohn, flesh is all. He is a hedonist. His relationship to Ethel Rosenberg's ghost and his impending death is Faustian, or at least Faust-like in his dialogue with the spirits. The play follows certain classical ideas of drama, i.e., the ability of characters to carry on dialogue with the physical and the metaphysical, accomplished in wit and polemics. As in his other works – *A Bright Room Called Day* (1985), *The Illusion* (1988, an adaptation of Pierre Corneille's *L'Illusion Comique*), *Slavs!* (1994), and *Homebody/Kabul* (2002) – Kushner combines the intimate with the grandiose, sublime with largesse.

The world August Wilson puts together in his 1992 play *Two Trains Running* is that of the African American community. The play's locale is a restaurant in Pittsburgh owned by Memphis and run by the waitress, Risa. The rhythms of everyday life are replete with discussions about a funeral parlor, "having children," politics, the "washing of souls," North–South migration, and other themes related to life, death, love, and religion. The time is 1969, a period informed by the Civil Rights Movement. In the backdrop is a rally for slain activist Malcolm X. The offstage boisterous politics contrast with the relative silence of the waitress, Risa. Throughout the play she rarely speaks and moves at a deliberately slow pace. She has mutilated her legs with a razor, leaving visible scars (see figure 6). The scars are a comment on her sexual objectification. If men gaze at her for control, then they must now reckon with a body in pain. The lacerations announce her identity through the unspeakable. Her self-inflicted wounds and her deliberately slow movements evoke Antonin Artaud's "theatre of cruelty," a concept counteracting the nullification of the body prevalent in western theatre. Artaud called for an immediate theatre of the flesh and a rejection of recitation. To be emancipated from the dramatic text – which Artaud sardonically calls "masterpieces" (*"En finir avec les chefs-d'œuvre"*) – requires pronounced physicality of the actor. Artaud expresses contempt for psychological conflicts and glorification of the word at the expense of the body. Risa's mutilation, like Artaud's theatre of cruelty, is an embodied theatrical statement, what Artaud calls "a unique language halfway between gesture and thought (*entre le geste et la pensée*)."[20]

For Wilson the rebellious 1960s occurs offstage, thereby making it secondary to the daily comings and goings in the restaurant. Throughout characters eat, report on events, and pass through. The only significant onstage action is the love story between Risa and Sterling, recently released from the penitentiary. Sterling's hyper-caffeinated behavior – he seems to be eager to engage in any activity and conversation available – and Risa's *largo assai* tempo, provide a dynamic contrast as well as an interesting romance. Sterling declares that he will marry Risa, but she fails to take him seriously. Their romance is

FIGURE 6 *Two Trains Running*, by August Wilson, 2005; directed by Lou Bellamy (artistic director of Penumbra Theatre); set designer Vicki M. Smith. Adolphus Ward (Holloway, left) and Erika LaVonn (Risa, right). Photograph by Don Ipock Photography. Reprinted courtesy of Kansas City Repertory Theatre (formerly Missouri Repertory Theatre).

creatively designed by Wilson; instead of behaving as lovers subsumed by each other, Risa and Sterling discover ways of reaching out without loss of individuality.

Wilson has shaped an impressionistic play, one different in many respects from his previous works. He is concerned with an Afrocentric world view, where funerals, protest, love, eating, politics, and storytelling set the tone. The play is less about conflict and more a slice-of-black-life. More than any other August Wilson play to date, *Two Trains Running* best represents his insight into the black community (*Jitney* can be categorized this way; though written earlier, it was produced later). On the outskirts are whites. No white character enters, though the presence of whites is felt indirectly. They include the owner of most of the property in the Pittsburgh Hill District; the jukebox owner who has yet to repair it; Andrew Mellon, the wealthy Pittsburgh banker; a police officer known for killing African Americans; and the boss of the numbers (an illegal game where the three-digit report of daily horse races acts as a lottery number).

The most significant offstage white character is Lotz. He is intimately bound up with Hambone, an eccentric character with one goal. Hambone enters the restaurant and repeats: "I want my Ham."

> HAMBONE: He gonna give me my ham. I want my ham.
> STERLING: Somebody got his ham.
> (*To Hambone.*)
> Who got your ham, man? Somebody took your ham?
> HOLLOWAY: He talking about Lutz across the street. He painted his fence for him nine . . . almost ten years ago, and Lutz told him he'd give him a ham. After he painted the fence Lutz told him to take his chicken. He say he wanted his ham. Lutz told him to take a chicken or don't take nothing. So he wait over there every morning till Lutz come to open his store and he tell him he wants his ham. He ain't got it yet. (22–3)

On the surface this appears to be a straightforward arrangement: Hambone is shortchanged and demands justice. This can be symbolic of black reparation for slavery. However, Wilson investigates something deeper. He is concerned with human worth: how does one attach "value" to a human being? Memphis chimes in to correct Holloway.

MEMPHIS: That ain't how it went. Lutz told him if he painted his fence he'd give him a chicken. Told him if he do a good job he'd give him a ham. He think he did a good job and Lutz didn't. That's where he went wrong – letting Lutz decide what to pay him for his work. If you leave it like that, quite naturally he gonna say it ain't worth the higher price. (23)

In one sense Memphis is correct; never leave the determination of one's self-worth to another, particularly when it entails whites judging blacks. However, Hambone ought to be credited with seeking human contact and affirmation beyond his own self-valuation. Hambone, likely bereft of his senses even before his incident with Lutz, seeks to be valued in a world that offers him little hope for dignity. Hambone desires the recognition that comes with hard work. The process he stands for is that humans must live together and must regard each other as equals. He represents the 1960s, an age when African Americans were seeking more than mere subsistence; they were after acknowledgment of their contributions. It can be argued that Lutz believes Hambone's work was subpar and therefore he deserved a chicken. But ten years of Hambone's own explanation is hard to counter, and if we are to provide any acknowledgment of Hambone as a legitimate character onstage, he deserves the benefit of the doubt.

Wilson brings into his cycle of plays the character of Aunt Ester, who is over 300 years old and whose name sounds like "ancestor." While unseen in *Two Trains Running*, she is the overarching symbol of the three hundred-plus years of African presence in America (she will appear in Wilson's future plays). Most importantly, she symbolizes history and justice. Prior to the exchange above dealing with the ham and the painting of the fence, Holloway says: "Aunt Ester got a power cause she got an understanding. Anybody live as long as she has is bound to have an understanding" (22). This statement leads to Hambone's declaration of "I want my ham." The arrangement of the dialogue is not coincidental; Wilson is deliberately orchestrating the sequence to amplify Hambone's plea for justification. Aunt Ester's symbolism of justice follows with the request for the ham, representing the ethical goal of Hambone's one-track mission. The play itself is arranged like an African village, where people exchange food rather than cash, and wisdom and understanding supersede selfishness. Had this been an African community, Lutz would likely have seen the value of Hambone's work and acknowledged a job well done. But Wilson's point is that community and humanistic concerns are trumped by penny-pinching and insensitivity. Hambone is not merely seeking redress for a grievance; he is calling for a return to another way of life, one which values human dignity.

Like Kushner, Wilson is a spiritual writer. Kushner's and Wilson's metaphysical speculations belie a religious component. Prior's importance to the gay community is much like Aunt Ester's significance to the black community. Prior is the seer interconnecting politics and history; Aunt Ester's prophecies ramify throughout Pittsburgh's Hill District, symbolizing the enduring continuum of her people. Prior's lineage (hence his name) and Aunt Ester's longevity are suggestive of the hope that the world may endure. For Wilson and Kushner politics is the touchstone of historical understanding, but religion is its soul. Prior signifies redemption through the rubble of a fallen world – Walter Benjamin's angel of history, from which the title of the play derives. The Risa–Sterling love story and Hambone's quest for justice suggest a coming redemption in *Two Trains Running*. For both playwrights the aim is the attainment of understanding through recollection and faith. The end of *Angels in America*, Part II, conjures up a multitudinous revelation of process and change, a day of loving judgment where all, even Roy Cohn in death, will be redeemed. Only Joe is excluded from the "Kingdom of Heaven" scene beneath Bethesda Fountain at Central Park, where Louis, Prior, Belize, and Joe's mother enjoy reconciliation and look to the future with hope. Wilson's and Kushner's Judeo-Christian ethos is strongly present in all their work.

In *Three Tall Women* (1992) Edward Albee revisits the themes that had characterized his earlier plays. Like *A Delicate Balance* and *All Over*, he considers death, aging, and the generational conflicts among women. In addition, *Three Tall Women* takes up a deathwatch; uncertainty in regard to existence; the importance of language in defining identity; animal imagery; vaudevillian dialogue; accidents that affect people's lives; and the body's appendages (reminiscent of his play *The Man with Three Arms*). In the first act three characters named A, B, and C (ages 92, 56, and 26, respectively) are in a room, with A, the eldest, in bed. C, a paralegal, has come to her client's house to oversee the dispersal of A's wealth (a similar action occurs in *Tiny Alice*). B, serving as nursemaid and personal secretary to A, also helps with the details of A's inheritance. At the end of Act I, A suffers a stroke. In Act II, it becomes clear that the three women are one and the same. Albee makes A, B, and C the incarnations of the same "tall women" at different stages of life. C is naïve and gullible, demanding to know what is coming to her. She optimistically asserts her power to change fate. She craves knowledge of her future, but rejects uncomfortable predictions. B is more experienced and conspicuously less forward looking. She is a middle-aged realist whose expectations have been thwarted. A is the matriarch whose blunt truths provide a contrast to the illusions and cynicism of others. She is heartbroken over the estranged relations with her son, yet she is too proud to wear her heart openly.

In the 1990s David Mamet turned toward nostalgia and politics. *The Cryptogram* (1995) and *The Old Neighborhood* (1997) reflect on childhood memories. His 1992 play *Oleanna* raises controversy by critiquing political correctness. This two-character play is set in a university teacher's office. John is soon to be tenured; in anticipation he buys a home. Carol, a student, enters without appointment, wanting to know why she is failing. During the first act John's attention is divided between Carol and the telephone, where he is conducting the business of obtaining a mortgage. Tension escalates as Carol demands his undivided attention. She wants to improve her grade and John condescendingly placates her. Both are being coy, and there is more to her agenda. Carol accuses John of sexual harassment. In the second act she is on the offensive, trying to force John to sign a document produced by her "group." She will withdraw her charges if he meets her demands.

The play examines power dynamics and authority. Mamet's trademark is his use of language and action. What people say sets in motion a series of actions that return to haunt them. The second act reexamines the experiences of the first. Did John place his hand on her? How did he do it? Were his intentions sexual or mere friendliness (or both)? What did John mean when he said, "I like you"? Audiences must rethink what they saw in Act I, referring to the previous gestures and language for confirmation. Mamet uses the stage as a microcosm of the larger issues of power. Whether it is sexual dominance (*Sexual Perversity in Chicago*), staking a place in Don's junk shop (*American Buffalo*), breaking into a real estate office to steal the leads (*Glengarry Glen Ross*), demanding attention (*Edmond*), a child asserting his place in an adult world (*The Cryptogram*), or a middle-aged man trying to find his roots (*The Old Neighborhood*), Mamet's characters seek control. The stage for Mamet is a place where actors jockey for "position."

Oleanna examines the concept of "language" ownership. John's home-buying is more than an offstage catalytic event; it accentuates the fact that John is trying to learn the language of real estate in the same way Carol is trying to negotiate the language of academia. For all her modesty and frustration, Carol is actually a fine student. She learns intellectual bullying from John, as well as the use of language to reach her goals.

A less contentious student–teacher relationship play is Donald Margulies's *Collected Stories* (1997). This was one of many "intimate relationship" plays that surfaced in the 1990s. Like his *Sight Unseen* (1992) and *Dinner with Friends* (1999), Margulies's works concern reconnection to passion. The artist in *Sight Unseen* returns to his former lover for inspiration. Although successful, he has lost his desire to paint. *Collected Stories* examines the life of two writers, one older and jaded, the other young, enthusiastic, and seeking a key to good writing. *Dinner with Friends* is a foursome study involving the break-up of one couple and the impact it has on the other. It explores how marital passion is sustained (or not) by those approaching middle age. One of the most prolific American dramatists, Terrence McNally, also portrays intimate relationships in his *Lips Together, Teeth Apart* (1991) and *Love! Valour! Compassion!* (1994). In the former, two couples share a Fourth of July weekend at a beach house in a gay community. Sally has inherited the summer home from her brother who died of AIDS. The two straight couples put up an affable front, but their relationships are tenuous. The truth gradually emerges. In *Love! Valour! Compassion!*, McNally depicts a gay community at a summer home. Jill Dolan reminds us that, in a similar way to Jane Chambers's *Last Summer at Bluefish Cove*, the group "constructs their community through their relationships." She writes: "After narrating a series of personal, artistic, and health crises, the play's bittersweet epilogue describes how the couples bravely live out their lives together (for whatever length of time) in comfortable, domestic ways."[21] Like most of McNally's work, *Lips Together, Teeth Apart* and *Love! Valour! Compassion!* revolve around a secret, usually sickness or sadness, which comes to light during the play. Another stalwart American dramatist is Horton Foote. His *The Young Man from Atlanta* (1995) is, like many of his plays, a Southern gothic tale combining realism and sentiment. Kenneth Lonergan's *This is Our Youth* (1998) is a three-character play about the meanderings of drug-addled, twenty-something miscreants struggling for direction. Eric Bogosian's *SubUrbia*

(1994) also centers on aimless youth. This dark play takes place in a parking lot outside a 7–11, a gathering place for teenage urchins who drink beer, smoke pot, and seek a reason to live. Like Lonergan, Bogosian has a sharp ear for dialogue and empathy for those enjoying few breaks in life.

Richard Greenberg's *Three Days of Rain* (1997) explores intimacy and memory. The first act takes place in a contemporary downtown Manhattan loft. Walker and his sister, Nan, rummage through their deceased father's "things." Their father had been a famous architect. His will leaves everything to his old partner's son, Pip. The second act takes place in 1960. The same three actors assume the roles of their parents and Pip's father. Many of the issues raised by the children in the first act are answered by their parents in the second. Greenberg has a writer's love for a well-turned phrase. Like John Robin Baitz in *The Substance of Fire* (1991), he probes generational conflicts and moral decisions with Oscar Wildean language. Although selfish, the characters in Greenberg's and Baitz's plays express wit and intelligence that prove to be their redeeming virtues. Another memory play is Warren Leight's *Side Man* (1998). It examines the life of a second-string musician, often called "side men" during the big band era. Flashbacks draw the protagonist to his father, Cliff, and Cliff's romance with Terry. Cliff is the unreliable musician who keeps late hours; Terry is the Catholic girl hoping for a closely knit family. Leight captures the atmospheric details of a musician's life in his secondary characters. These musicians make do with their status as back-ups. Lynn Nottage's *Crumbs from the Table of Joy* (1995) is also a reflective play that recalls the life of a young black woman growing up in Brooklyn during the early 1950s. The Civil Rights Movement by then had finally begun. The conflict between the widower Godfrey Crump and his two daughters, just arriving from the South, and his sister-in-law, Lily Ann "Sister" Green, shapes this cross-generational play. "Sister" Green is inspired by the Civil Rights and women's liberation movements, bringing these notions into the household. Her radical ideas chafe against Crump's old-fashioned way of thinking. Like McNally, Greenberg, Baitz, and Leight, Nottage captures the characteristics of her community. Cheryl West's dramas, *Before It Hits Home* (1992), *Holiday Heart* (1995), and *Jar on the Floor* (1999), also concern life in the black community. West's especially poignant play, *Before It Hits Home*, examines how AIDS affects the African American community. Constant Congdon's *Dog Opera*

(1995) deals with AIDS as well as a friendship between a heterosexual female and a gay man. Scott McPherson's *Marvin's Room* (1991) considers the life of a caretaker, Bessie, who aids her invalid father and aunt. The relationship central to the play is that between Bessie and her sister, Lee, a divorcée with two children. Lee has left Bessie the caretaker's role, creating a conflict that is later resolved. McPherson's promising career ended abruptly when he died of AIDS a year after the play's successful opening. Atmosphere and community are the basis of Pearl Cleage's *Flyin' West* (1992) and *Blues for an Alabama Sky* (1995). Cleage follows the tradition set in place by Ed Bullins and August Wilson, both of whom explore twentieth-century African American life. In *Flyin' West*, Cleage takes up black pioneers who were women seeking a new life in Kansas at the end of the nineteenth century. Harlem of the 1930s is the backdrop for *Blues for an Alabama Sky*.

One of the exemplary plays of "intimate relationship" is Diana Son's *Stop Kiss* (1998). Superficially, it is the story of two women who fall in love. The play moves back and forth in time, the central incident being an assault. The protagonists, Callie and Sara, sit on a park bench in Greenwich Village at 4 a.m. to kiss. They are confronted by a homophobe. Sara is the worse for the attack. Beaten badly into a coma, with the help of Callie she is brought back to health. What makes the play exceptional is the way the two women come together. Son is attentive to the beauty of small details that evolve into love. Before Sara, Callie had been merely living. She reports traffic from a helicopter, a metaphor signaling her distance from "real" life. Her one relationship is with George, but only for sex. She is satisfied with this arrangement. It is a measure of Callie's disconnection from people that when she receives physical intimacy other than sex with her smoothie lover George, she flinches under his touch. It is only with Sara's recovery that Callie moves from withdrawal to compassion. In the penultimate scene Callie dresses Sara. The actresses, Son observes, "made those heartbreaking, involuntary sounds and gestures that would fill the silence, because the silence was excruciating." This intimacy, Son remarks, "can only happen in the theatre."[22]

José Rivera's *Marisol* (1993) and Theresa Rebeck's *The Family of Mann* (1994) are thematically similar. Their protagonists are caught out of place. *Marisol* occurs in New York City. Its protagonist is an educated Puerto Rican in her mid-twenties living a dual existence. She lives in her Bronx apartment in her Hispanic community, and she is also a working professional Manhattanite. Her inability to reconcile these two worlds results in her "double consciousness." Rivera's gambit constructs a surrealistic account of Marisol's murder on the subway. It is uncertain if the murdered woman is the same Marisol Perez, or someone with the same name, but the symbol is clear: Marisol's soul is under siege. The play carries an element of the absurd. Marisol's friend and colleague, June, disappears. She sets out to find her. She encounters "Scar Tissue" and other surreal figures. Scar Tissue accuses Marisol of being dead, but she denies this. In her defense, she asserts her split identity.

> MARISOL: I lived in the Bronx . . . I commuted light-years to this other planet called – Manhattan! I learned new vocabularies . . . wore weird native dress . . . mastered arcane rituals . . . and amputated near sections of my psyche, my cultural heritage . . . yeah, clean easy amputations . . . with no pain expressed at all – none! – but so much pain kept inside I almost choked on it . . . so far deep inside my Manhattan bosses and Manhattan friends and my broken Bronx consciousness never even suspected.[23]

The Family of Mann takes place in Los Angeles. Its protagonist, Belinda, like Marisol, is an educated professional. She is a television sitcom writer with a doctorate. Unable to reconcile her artistic ambition with her pedestrian job, Belinda struggles to find her place. For Rivera and Rebeck the glamour of New York and Los Angeles no longer conjures up utopia; paradise has become hell, overrun by hypocrisy and commercialism. Marisol and Belinda live a nightmare, constantly drawn to and repelled by the pretense permeating their lives. They are idealistic vagabonds on a quest that is doomed to disappointment.

William S. Yellow Robe's *The Independence of Eddie Rose* (1990) presents an idealist torn between home and escape. The 16-year-old Eddie Rose must choose whether to remain on the Reservation (referred to as the "Rez"), or leave for Seattle with his friend, Mike. Neither alternative offers much reward. Life on the Rez is one of poverty and boredom; however, leaving without money would be irrational. Eddie is beset by the problems of a dysfunctional home centered on an alcoholic mother. The action revolves around his mother, Katherine Rose, her abusive boyfriend, Lenny Sharb, and his 10-year-old sister, Theia, who falls victim to Lenny's temper. Eddie is helped by his aunt, Katherine's sister, Thelma. Still, Thelma provides little reason for believing that life will improve if he remains; Eddie sees nothing but the hopelessness of dead-end jobs. His friend Mike, who has trouble with the law, tries to persuade Eddie to leave with him. Mike tells him that the big city holds adventure, and along with it at least possibilities for a better life. Mike is at one point being harassed by the Reservation's truant officer. Though his crimes are petty – occasional marijuana and loitering – he is badgered by Sam Jacobs, who finds Mike sexually attractive. Sam has Mike incarcerated in order to "make a deal." Mike wants to escape but neither he nor Eddie has money (they are hoping to "borrow" a car), nor any real experience outside the Rez.

The plot has Eddie struggling with the decision whether to remain on the Rez and protect his younger sister from Lenny or abandon her for the big city. But there is more to the play than the depiction of a trouble-laden youth. The drama chronicles his metamorphosis from naïveté to awareness. Eddie Rose comes to the realization that escape cannot reconcile his divided consciousness. Unlike other minorities that experience roots in two places, Native Americans are true "natives." Leaving the Rez will not reunite a divided self, making "escape" oxymoronic. Yellow Robe's dramas, like those of other Native American playwrights such as LeAnne Howe and Ray Gordon's *Indian Radio Days* (1995), Drew Hayden Taylor's *Only Drunks and Children Tell the Truth* (1996), Diane Glancy's *The Woman Who Was a Red Deer Dressed for the Deer Dance* (1995), John Neihardt's *Black Elk Speaks* (1995), Victoria Nalani Kneubuhl's *The Story of Susanna* (1998), and the collective Spiderwoman Theatre of Lisa Mayo, Gloria Miguel, and Muriel Miguel, examine the frustration invested in the notion of "escape."

Nicky Silver has a screwball director's sense of timing. His play *The Food Chain* (1995) is a superb period comedy. Like his *Pterodactyls* (1993) and *Raised in Captivity* (1995), *The Food Chain* is a zany look at relationships and contemporary culture. Amanda Dolor's husband has been missing for three weeks. She calls a crisis hotline, but Bea who works at the crisis center has an even larger crisis on her hands. "Amanda," Bea says, "loneliness is my oxygen. I breathe loneliness. I'm Bea, and you don't know what loneliness is until you've walked a mile in my shoes."[24] The long, bizarre phone call ends with the return of her husband, Ford. Amanda now talks non-stop. She accuses Ford of making her feel "fat," even though Ford has said nothing. The metaphor of weight and the body recurs throughout the play. In scene two, Serge is visited by his past overweight lover, Otto, who shows up unexpectedly. Otto, one of the most outrageous characters in American drama, is a hyper-charged compulsive eater who literally plunges onto the stage. His dialogue scatter-shoots from one subject to another, creating a whirligig meant to keep others off balance.

> OTTO: You're afraid to try new things, *that's* your problem. I like your hair. Are you combing it differently, or at all. Slim-Fast is delicious! It goes fabulously with pretzels! (*He pulls a can of Slim-Fast out of his bag.*) I'm not thirsty yet. Maybe later. – You'd love me again, if I was thinner. I told my analyst that I was going to come and see you and you know what she did? She laughed! She burst into gales of laughter! She told me she was crying. She cries all the time. I don't think she's happy. I think she's got serious problems. Would you love me again if I weighed a hundred pounds? Would you love me if I weighed fifty pounds? Would you love me if I looked like one of those living corpses in the photographs from the liberation of Auschwitz? (33)

Silver captures not only the sense of our multi-tasking society, but the dynamics of relationships which reverse suddenly. In a Silver play it is often hard to tell who is in charge. The author traffics in unstable and absurd situations, making a mockery of our national sacred cows such as beauty, love, and marriage. David Ives's *All in the Timing* (1994), *Don Juan in Chicago* (1995), *Ancient History* (1996), and *Mere Morals and Others* (1997) also pillory social pretensions. With few exceptions his plays are short and even though more vaudeville than drama, they express the intensity of the successful comic. Douglas Carter Bean's *As Bees in Honey Drown* (1997) concerns the first novel by a gay author who is swept up in celebrity circles. Like John Guare, Bean explores the lure of celebrity status. David Lindsay-Abaire's *Fuddy Meers* (1999) examines the comic potential in amnesia. A. R. Gurney's *Sylvia* (1995) is a story about a man's love for his dog. Craig Lucas's *Prelude to a Kiss* (1990) examines what happens when a ghost takes over the body of a couple about to be married.

Although American drama has rarely felt comfortably yoked to the abstract, it has however produced a few homegrown absurdist creators. Richard Foreman's longstanding and prolific presence in avant-garde theatre deserves mention. Known as a conceptual artist, his Ontological-Hysteric Theater investigates the relationship between art and its reception. In his pivotal essay, "Foundations for a Theater," Foreman characterizes "character, empathy, narrative" as indices of "straightjackets imposed on the impulse so it can be dressed up in a fashion that is familiar, comforting, and reassuring for the spectator." Foreman creates theatre that "frustrates our habitual way of seeing, and by doing so, frees the impulse from the objects in our culture to which it is invariably linked." His plays yield "an art that focuses on changing the perceptual environment within which we see objects and problems," refusing "to analyze objects and problems using the terms insisted upon by our socially enforced perspectives."[25] From the mid-1970s through the end of the century, Foreman shaped the avant-garde New York theatre scene. His trademarks are unique costuming, lighting, sound effects, slapstick, cabaret, vaudeville, and Grand Guignol. Similarly, but on a much broader canvas, Robert Wilson's prodigious output exploits visual and sensual theatrical images. He uses space, music, shapes, color, and movement slowed in tempo to promote new ways of seeing. Like Foreman, he is on the cutting edge of new wave art, incorporating the works of musician John Cage and choreographer Meredith Monk. Wilson's plays are often long, with movement slowed in order to allow visualization of transformation. He merges installation art with theatre, creating a three-dimensional perspective and motion. Among other progressive theatres during the 1980s and 1990s were Mabou Mines and the Wooster Group. The later produced two outstanding directors, Elizabeth LeCompte and Reza Abdoh; Abdoh's brief but creative life produced stark political dramas on gay themes.

Gay and lesbian theatre continued to flourish during the 1990s. Five Lesbian Brothers and Pomo Afro Homos furnished dramas from the groups' experiences. These two collectives revel in razor-sharp satire, nudity, ribald humor, and commentary on homophobia designed to prick the conscience of society. The Five Lesbian Brothers – Lisa Kron, Peg Healey, Moe Angelos, Babs Davy, and Dominique Dibbell – create parodies of film noir and space travel in such plays as *Voyage to Lesbos* (1989), *Brave Smiles* (1992), *The Secretaries* (1994), and *Brides of the Moon* (1997). Pomo Afro Homos (Postmodern African American Homosexuals) is a San Francisco-based group founded in 1990 by Djola Bernard Branner, Brian Freeman, and Eric Gupton. Their first play, *Fierce Love: Stories from Black Gay Life* (1991), premiered in San Francisco's Castro District. Their most popular play, *Dark Fruit* (1994), celebrates the lives of gay black men. One of the most outspoken lesbian dramatists is Cherrie Moraga, whose plays *Heroes and Saints* (1992) and *Giving Up the Ghost* (1994) are personal stories of growing up lesbian amidst hostility. For Moraga, the "personal is the political," with each drama exploring lesbianism as a political statement.

Among the era's developments are plays of social protest. Mac Wellman's *7 Blowjobs* (1991) challenges the censorship of gay solo performing artists. Steve Tesich's *The Speed of Darkness* (1991) portrays Joe, a successful businessman, and Lou, homeless. Both are Vietnam veterans. Lou's unexpected appearance symbolizes Joe's conscience. Both committed atrocities that Joe wants to forget, but Lou will not let him. Naomi Wallace's *In the Heart of America* (1994) critiques the first Iraqi war. Robert Schenkkan's two-part *Kentucky Cycle* (1993) is a social drama on a large canvas. The play concerns three families from Eastern Kentucky who can trace their history back to the American Revolution. Russell Lee's *Nixon's Nixon* (1995) is an intimate two-hander examining the relationship between Richard Nixon and Henry Kissinger prior to Nixon's resignation. Political and social issues are also the themes of Elizabeth Wong's *Letters to a Student Revolutionary* (1990). The play examines the life of a Chinese American and her letters to a Chinese revolutionary caught up in the 1989 repression in Tiananmen Square.

One political play which attracted considerable attention is Eve Ensler's *Vagina Monologues* (1999). Like Smith's *Fires in the Mirror*, Ensler interviewed women, recording their thoughts and feelings about genitalia. She recreated their words into monologues. Ensler's work has a duel concern: to purge the derogation and shame associated with female anatomy and to celebrate the vagina's multiple uses. Rape, masturbation, childbirthing, sexual encounters, sexual discovery, and the words used to describe the organ are explored. Monologues alternatively express embarrassment or pride, but with the intention of liberating the word "vagina" from shame and opprobrium. Like *Vagina Monologues*, Robbie McCauley's *Sally's Rape* (1992) deals with abuse. The play involves two characters, Robbie (black) and Jeannie (white). It begins with a conversation over tea. The characters role-play: one is the slave, the other the slave auctioneer. Robbie stands naked on the auction block as Jeannie asks the audience to "bid" on her. Another role is that of Sally, Thomas Jefferson's mistress. Kai Corthron is a dramatist who captures the language of the underclass. Not since Ed

Bullins has there been a playwright who writes urban-street vernacular with such intensity. *Come Down Burning* (1993) and *Breath, Boom*
(1997) explore the lives of a handicapped hairdresser and street gangs,
respectively. In *Come Down Burning* Corthron considers the grim vicis-
situdes of being poor without access to abortion. Skoolie, a hairdresser
unable to walk, cares for her sister, Tee. At the play's end Tee aborts
herself with a wire hanger, causing hemorrhage and death. The characters' hardscrabble background informs their behavior, but Corthron
never succumbs to simple-minded conceptions of victimization.

Among the riskier and challenging plays of the decade are Rita
Dove's *Darker Faces of the Earth* (1996) and Rebecca Gilman's *Spinning
into Butter* (2000). Both Dove and Gilman confront race in American
history, one exploring the past, the other political correctness. Dove, a
poet, creates a classic tragedy based on *Oedipus Rex*. The setting is pre-
Civil War South Carolina. Offended by her husband's philandering,
Amalia seeks revenge by bearing a child from a slave. The child is
supposedly killed, but he is in fact saved by a conscientious doctor.
Like Oedipus, Augustus Newcastle returns ignorant of his parentage. He
organizes a slave rebellion while carrying on an affair with his mother
Amalia (unbeknownst at the time). The truth comes full circle. The
love story between Augustus and Amalia is shrouded in taboo, but it
also sheds light on the complexities of race and sex. The protagonist of
Gilman's *Spinning into Butter*, Sarah Daniels, is thrust into a dilemma.
As the dean of students at a liberal arts Vermont college, she must
investigate a racially charged incident. An anonymous racist letter has
been pinned on the dorm-room of an African American student. The
largely white college is unable to cope with the incident; the administration holds forums on racial sensitivity, but primarily they pass the
responsibility of coping on to Daniels. Daniels, like Augustus and
Amalia, is caught in the dicey web of America's race relations. Her
colleagues recite politically correct platitudes and homilies, but have
little if any understanding of minorities attending a predominantly
white school. The play's end reveals that the African American student
(who is never seen) has written the letters himself. Though Daniels
does not condone the action, she empathizes with him.

Two plays proved intellectually stimulating as well as emotionally engaging: Mary Zimmerman's *Metamorphoses* (1998) and David
Auburn's *Proof* (2000). Zimmerman creates a collage of nine scenes
based on Greek myths and morality tales. What lifts this production

from the ordinary is the staging. Zimmerman's set is occupied by a square pool of water. Actors dive in and out during the scenes. The result is that set and text combine to produce intellectual rigor and intense sensuality. Catherine, *Proof*'s protagonist, is the 25-year-old daughter of a brilliant mathematician, Robert, now deceased. She is a math genius in her own right, but is too inhibited to be assertive. Robert appears to her as a ghost. Both are melancholy and both are haunted by the specter of insanity. Robert laments that his best work was at age 25, when he contributed heavily to game theory, algebraic geometry, and non-linear operator theory. Catherine senses that she too is at her peak mental capacity and facing a future much like her father's descent into madness. Catherine's sister Claire visits and offers to pay for her hospital stay. Hal is a math student with a crush on Catherine. He searches through Robert's notebooks trying to find unfinished solutions to math problems. Catherine's fears loom large: how much of her father's genius and madness did she inherit, and how can she distinguish between madness and genius? Her resentment at having to play caretaker to a former genius adds to her anxiety: "I spent my life with him. I fed him. Talked to him. Tried to listen when he talked. Talked to people who weren't there . . . Watched him shuffle around like a ghost. A very smelly ghost. He was filthy. I had to make sure he bathed. My own father."[26]

In *Regarding the Pain of Others*, Susan Sontag encourages a framework for dealing with the way we view suffering: "One can feel obliged to look at photographs that record great cruelties and crimes. One should feel obligated to think about what it means to look at them, about the capacity actually to assimilate what they show."[27] Two plays, Margaret Edson's *W;t* (1999) and Moisés Kaufman's *The Laramie Project* (2000, written with the members of the Tectonic Theater), bring forth the artistic incarnation of pain, the body, and how they should be viewed. In *W;t*, Edson portrays Vivian Bearing, a 50-year-old English professor who specializes in the seventeenth-century metaphysical poet John Donne. She has been stricken with terminal cancer. The play moves along two trajectories: her experiences with doctors and hospitals, and her teaching (conveyed through flashbacks). These worlds collide; pain starkly reminds her of physical deterioration, while teaching enables her to cling to high ideals and escape the body's encroachment. Vivian brings these two themes – physical and metaphysical – together in her discussion of language: "So imagine the effect that the words of John Donne had on me: ratiocination, concatenation, coruscation, tergiversation. Medical terms are less evocative. Still, I want to know what the doctors mean when they . . . anatomize me."[28]

Vivian's encounters with doctors and their treatments reveal a breakdown in communication. Since the doctors consider her case nearly incurable, they convince her to try painful experimental drugs. She is resentful but relents. Aside from a sympathetic nurse, she feels dehumanized by the doctors who make her pain a public affair. A brief visit from a former teacher, the one who inspired her love of poetry, provokes a touching interlude from hospitals and medical testing. Vivian retreats into the past, recreating lectures and recalling her hero Donne.

> VIVIAN: The poetry of the early seventeenth century, what has been called the metaphysical school, considers an intractable mental puzzle by exercising the outstanding human faculty of the era, namely *wit*. The greatest wit – the greatest English poet, some would say – was John Donne. [. . .] In his poems, metaphysical quandaries are addressed, but never resolved. Ingenuity, virtuosity, and a vigorous intellect that jousts with the most exalted concepts: these are the tools of wit. (48)

Vivian can analyze the literature, but it is of no help in articulating her suffering. The "horrible pain," as the stage directions note, is beyond description.

> VIVIAN: (*Trying extremely hard.*) I want to tell you how it feels. I want to explain it, to use *my* words. It's as if . . . I can't . . . There aren't . . . I'm like a student and this is the final exam and I don't know what to put down because I don't understand the question and I'm *running out of time.* (70)

Never one to lose her "wit," Vivian adds: "I apologize in advance for what this palliative treatment modality does to the dramatic coherence of my play's last scene. It can't be helped." Following a pause, she remarks: "Say it, Vivian. *It hurts like hell. It really does*" (70).

Vivian knows that language works by trying to connect words with objects, feelings, states, ideas, and people. Donne's metaphysical poetry was derived as an attempt to express his feelings at the death of his wife. Vivian is attracted to Donne's elegiac verses, which are meant to make sense out of inscrutable loss. The metaphysical poets – Donne in particular – approached philosophy and spirituality with reason, meditation, and faith in the word. But as Vivian discovers, language is not up to the task of describing pain. She realizes that if thought is embodied, then thinking about death and pain is ipso facto embodied. At the play's conclusion she stands naked, expressing her body proudly and without words. Words are insufficient; she has embodied her pain.

If Edson constructs the representation of pain in the flesh – in the body of the actress – the pain in Kaufman's *The Laramie Project* flows from the absent body of Matthew Shepard. Like *Fires in the Mirror*, the text of *The Laramie Project* is taken from tapings. People involved with the murder of Shepard in Laramie, Wyoming in 1998 are interviewed and recorded. They are either residents of Laramie, or they have some connection with the crime. Shepard's death was an incident of "gay bashing." Two men lured him into their car and drove him to the edge of town. They beat him unconscious, tied him to a fencepost, and left. He was later discovered in a coma. His murder became a flashpoint of protest. Kaufman and the actors from the Tectonic Theater Company came to Laramie and interviewed those who lived in this Western town, which had been thrust into the national spotlight.

Both *W;t* and *Laramie Project* are elegies: one deals with the visible body, the other concerns its absence. In *Laramie Project*, the "protagonist" Shepard is never present but his presence is no less important. The language of *Laramie Project* demonstrates the desperate attempt on the part of the mourners to connect with Shepard and, in making contact, prove that his loss had meaning. Elegy intertwines loss and gain; mourners fill the void simultaneously as the emptiness appears. *The Laramie Project* acts as a commemorative monument to Shepard in dramatic form similar to the AIDS quilt or the Vietnam Veterans Memorial Wall. It carries with it a tension between the desire to honor Shepard and an attempt to do so with a lack of knowledge about him. Before his murder, Shepard was an ordinary citizen of Laramie, an undistinguished student at the University of Wyoming, a face in the crowd. Once a corpse, he rises to the status of martyr. The emotion between the reality of his death and the promise of consolation moves from speaker to speaker: some describe the brutal murder in detail, some attempt to find meaning and hope, and some even condemn Shepard's lifestyle as the catalyst for his demise.

Like *W;t*, *The Laramie Project* is concerned with death and the body. What sets it apart from *W;t* and other such plays is the absence of the victim. Matthew Shepard is described, discussed, and symbolized, but we never see him. A "representation" of the crime would fall short; an enactment of Shepard's beating would fail to have sufficient impact. In drama enactment is a representation; a "dead" actor takes a curtain call, calling attention to the representation over the reality. By keeping him offstage but always "present," Kaufman elevates Shepard into a kind of "everyman" martyr. Yet, despite the national attention of Shepard's death, no political action against hate crimes was taken. Jonas Slonaker, living in Laramie, reports: "You know, it's been a year since Matthew Shepard died, and they haven't passed shit in Wyoming . . . at a state level, any town, nobody anywhere, has passed any kind of laws, antidiscrimination laws or hate crime legislation, nobody has passed anything anywhere. What's come out of it? What's come out of this that's concrete or lasting?" (99).

At the close of the play a resident of Laramie calls attention to the town and Shepard. Doc O'Connor knew him; he operated a car service and once took Shepard to a gay bar in Colorado. He describes the drive and the place where Shepard's life ended:

> DOC O'CONNOR: I remember to myself the night he and I drove around together, he said to me, "Laramie sparkles, doesn't it?" And where he was up there, if you sit exactly where he was, up there, Laramie sparkles from there, with a low-lying cloud . . . it's the blue lights that's bouncing off the clouds from the airport, and it goes *tst tst tst tst* . . . right over the whole city. I mean, it blows you away. . . . Matt was right there in that spot, and I can just picture in his eyes, I can just picture what he was seeing. The last thing he saw on this earth was the sparkling light. (99)

This chapter begins and ends with death: the deaths of Gavin Cato, Yankel Rosenbaum, and Matthew Shepard. In each case, death followed from intolerance. American drama since World War II may be described as a succession of strategies for enlarging public awareness. Drama may not always change public policy, but it may, at times, sparkle where there is darkness.

Notes

Dramas, once cited in the endnote, are recited in the text with page number. Secondary texts that are not included in the Selected Bibliography receive full citation.

Chapter 1   Politics, Existentialism, and American Drama, 1935–1945

1   C. Odets, *Waiting for Lefty and Other Plays* (New York: Grove, 1979), 31.
2   T. Wilder, *Three Plays* (New York: Perennial Classics, 1957, 1998), 111.
3   T. Williams, *The Glass Menagerie* (New York: New Classics/New Directions, 1945), 5.
4   T. Dreiser, "What is Americanism?" *Partisan Review and Anvil* 3.3 (April 1936): 3.
5   Cotkin, *Existential America*, 2.
6   M. Denning, *The Cultural Front* (London: Verso, 1997), xviii.
7   J. Dinerstein, *Swinging the Machine: Modernity, Technology, and African American Culture between the World Wars* (Amherst: University of Massachusetts Press, 2003), 5.
8   L. Hellman, *Six Plays by Lillian Hellman* (New York: Vintage, 1979), 70.
9   Odets, *Waiting for Lefty and Other Plays*, 37.
10 R. Wainscott, *The Emergence of the Modern American Theater, 1914–1929* (New Haven: Yale University Press, 1997), 4.
11 Odets, *Waiting for Lefty and Other Plays*, 62.
12 Henderson, *Mielziner*, 87.
13 *Three Comedies of American Family Life*, ed. J. Mersand (New York: Washington Square Press, 1960), 126.
14 Ibid., 308.

15 Wilder, *Three Plays*, 26.

16 R. Sherwood, *The Petrified Forest* (New York: Dramatist Play Service, 1935, 1961), 16, 37.

17 Fearnow, *The American Stage and the Great Depression*, 61.

18 D. M. Kennedy, *Freedom from Fear: The American People in Depression and War, 1929–1945* (New York: Oxford University Press, 1999), 365; Stevens, in M. Szalay, *New Deal Modernism: American Literature and the Welfare State* (Durham: Duke University Press, 2000), 11.

19 W. Saroyan, *Three Plays* (New York: Harcourt Brace, 1939), 19.

20 Wilder, *Three Plays*, 125.

21 Cotkin, *Existential America*, 81, 82.

22 D. Schwartz, "Does Existentialism Still Exist?" *Partisan Review* 15.12 (December 1948): 1361.

23 In C. L. Greenberg, *Or Does It Explore? Black Harlem in the Great Depression* (New York: Oxford University Press, 1991), 43.

24 Cotkin, *Existential America*, 163, 167.

Chapter 2 Money is Life: American Drama, 1945–1959

1 T. Williams, *The Glass Menagerie* (New York: New Classics/New Directions, 1945), 122.

2 A. Miller, *Death of a Salesman* (New York: Viking, 1949), 126.

3 E. O'Neill, *Long Day's Journey into Night* (New Haven: Yale University Press, 1956), 150.

4 L. Hansberry, *A Raisin in the Sun*, in *Six American Plays for Today* (New York: Modern Library, 1961), 345–6.

5 J. T. Adams, *The Epic of America*, in J. Cullen, *The American Dream: A Short History of an Idea that Shaped a Nation* (New York: Oxford University Press, 2003), 4.

6 H. A. Wallace, "The Price of Free World Victory" (1942), in *Democracy Reborn* (New York: Reynal and Hitchcock, 1944), 190–6.

7 B. Holliday and A. Herzog, Jr., "God Bless the Child" (New York: Columbia/Legacy, 1941); *The Definitive Billie Holiday* (Verve Music Group, 2000).

8 Henderson, *Mielziner*, 142.

9 T. Postlewait, "Spatial Order and Meaning in the Theatre: The Case of Tennessee Williams," *Assaph C* 10 (1994): 56, 60.

10 W. Stevens, "Not Ideas about the Thing but the Thing Itself," in *Poems: Selected* (New York: Random House, 1959), 166.

11 E. O'Neill, *The Iceman Cometh* (New York: Vintage, 1946), 79.

12 A. Miller, *All My Sons* (1947), in *American Drama*, ed. S. Watt and G. Richardson (Fort Worth, TX: Harcourt Brace, 1995), 628.

13 C. Isherwood, "A Morality That Stared Down Sanctimony," *New York Times*, February 12, 2005: A15.

14 A. Miller, "Tragedy and the Common Man," *New York Times*, February 27, 1949: 1.

15 G. Lukács, "Die Soziologie des Modernen Dramas" (1914), trans. Lee Baxandall, in *The Theory of the Modern Stage*, ed. E. Bentley (New York: Penguin, 1968), 426, 447.

16 T. Williams, *A Streetcar Named Desire* (New York: New Directions, 2004), 114.

17 A. Miller, "Regarding *Streetcar*," in ibid., x, xi–xii.

18 Savran, *Communists, Cowboys, and Queers*, 91–2.

19 H. W. Smith, "An Air of the Dream: Jo Mielziner, Innovation, and Influence, 1935–1955," *Journal of American Drama and Theatre* 5.3 (Fall 1993): 49.

20 C. Bigsby, *Arthur Miller: A Critical Study* (Cambridge: Cambridge University Press, 2005), 105, 106.

21 R. Williams, *Modern Tragedy* (Stanford: Stanford University Press, 1966), 104.

22 A. Miller, *Timebends: A Life* (New York: Grove, 1987), 184.

23 S. A. Sandage, *Born Losers: A History of Failure in America* (Cambridge, MA: Harvard University Press, 2005), 263.

24 M. Gottfried, *Arthur Miller: His Life and Work* (New York: Da Capo, 2003), 139.

25 T. Williams, *Cat on a Hot Tin Roof*, in *American Drama*, ed. Watt and Richardson, 693.

26 *Selected Letters of Eugene O'Neill*, ed. T. Bogard and J. R. Bryer (New Haven: Yale University Press), 506–7.

27 Berkowitz, *American Drama of the Twentieth Century*, 109.

28 Adler, *American Drama, 1940–1960*, 85.

29 W. Inge, *Four Plays* (New York: Grove, 1958), 64–5.

30 A. Hirsch, *The Making of the Second Ghetto: Race and Housing in Chicago, 1940–1960* (Chicago: University of Chicago Press), 41, 9.

31 R. Ellison, in *Cultural Contexts for Ralph Ellison's Invisible Man*, ed. E. J. Sundquist (Boston: Bedford, 1995), 237.

32 McConachie, *American Theater in the Culture of the Cold War*, 190.

33 T. Kushner, "Kushner on Miller," *The Nation* 280.23 (June 13, 2005): 10.

34 Bigsby, *Modern American Drama, 1945–2000*, 124.

Chapter 3 Reality and Illusion: American Drama, 1960–1975

1 E. Albee, *Who's Afraid of Virginia Woolf?*, in *The Collected Plays of Edward Albee*, Vol. I (New York: Overlook, 2004), 285.

2   A. Baraka [L. Jones], *Dutchman and The Slave* (New York: Apollo, 1964), 21.
3   M. Crowley, *Famous American Plays of the 1960s*, ed. H. Clurman (New York: Dell, 1972), 394.
4   J. Guare, *The House of Blue Leaves* (New York: Samuel French, 1971), 62.
5   F. Chin, *Chickencoop Chinaman and The Year of Dragon: Two Plays by Frank Chin* (Seattle: University of Washington Press, 1981), 8.
6   M. Piñero, *Short Eyes* (New York: Hill and Wang, 1974), 121.
7   J. Poggi, *Theater in America* (Ithaca: Cornell University Press, 1968), 212.
8   Roudané, *America Drama Since 1960*, 6.
9   Cohn, *New American Dramatists, 1960–1990*, 4.
10 M. Esslin, *Theatre of the Absurd* (Harmondsworth: Penguin, 1961), 24, 26.
11 E. Albee, *FAM and YAM: An Imaginary Interview* (New York: Dramatist Play Service, 1962), 84.
12 A. Kopit, *Oh Dad, Poor Dad, Mamma's Hung You in the Closet and I'm Feelin' So Sad* (New York: Hill and Wang, 1960), 62.
13 Bigsby, *Modern American Drama, 1945–2000*, 125.
14 W. T. Lhamon, Jr., *Deliberate Speed: The Origins of a Cultural Style in the American 1950s* (Washington: Smithsonian, 1990), 122–3.
15 E. Albee, *Zoo Story*, in *The Collected Plays of Edward Albee*, Vol. I, 31.
16 A. Baraka, *Conversations with Amiri Baraka* (Jackson: University of Mississippi Press, 1994), 257.
17 A. Baraka [L. Jones], *Blues People* (New York: Morrow, 1963), 227, 228.
18 Z. N. Hurston, *Mules and Men* (New York: HarperCollins, 1990), 1.
19 A. Kennedy, *Adrienne Kennedy in One Act* (Minnesota: University of Minnesota Press, 1988), 7.
20 Robinson, *The Other American Drama*, 130.
21 M. Schisgal, *Luv* (New York: Signet, 1963), 21.
22 Ibid., 15.
23 T. Kushner, "Kushner on Miller," *The Nation* 280.23 (June 13, 2005), 11.
24 A. M. Stenz, *Edward Albee: The Poet of Loss* (The Hague: Mouton, 1978), 40.
25 Davis, *Get the Guests*, 216.
26 E. Albee, *Conversations with Edward Albee*, ed. P. C. Kolin (Jackson: University of Mississippi Press, 1988), 161.
27 E. Albee, *A Delicate Balance*, in *The Collected Plays of Edward Albee*, Vol. II (New York: Overlook, 2005), 109.
28 A. Aronson, *American Avant-Garde Theatre* (London: Routledge, 2000), 67–8.
29 H. Keyssar, "Megan Terry: Mother of American Feminist Drama," in *Feminist Theatre* (Basingstoke: Macmillan, 1984), 53–76.
30 A. Sofer, "Maria Irene Fornes: Acts of Translation," in *Companion to Twentieth-Century American Drama*, ed. Krasner, 443.
31 S. Shepard, *Fool for Love and Other Plays* (Toronto: Bantam, 1984), 147.

32 Ibid., 5.
33 R. Milner, "Black Theater – Go Home!" in *The Black Aesthetic*, ed. A. Gayle (New York: Doubleday, 1971), 291.
34 C. Gordone, *No Place to Be Somebody* (Indianapolis: Bobbs-Merrill, 1969), 113.
35 E. Bullins, *The Theme Is Blackness* (New York: William Morrow, 1973), 11.
36 M. Sell, "The Black Arts Movement: Performance, Neo-Orality, and the Destruction of the 'White Thing,'" in *African American Performance and Theater History: A Critical Reader*, ed. H. Elam and D. Krasner (New York: Oxford University Press, 2001), 57.
37 A. Baraka, "Foreword," in *What the Wine-Sellers Buy: Four Plays by Ron Milner* (Detroit: Wayne State University Press, 2001), 7.
38 E. Bullins, *Goin' a Buffalo*, in *Black Theatre USA*, ed. J. Hatch and T. Shine (New York: Free Press, 1996), 441.
39 K. W. Benston, *Performing Blackness* (London: Routledge, 2000), 55.
40 J. E. Smethurst, *The Black Arts Movement* (Chapel Hill: University of North Carolina Press, 2005), 103.
41 Williams, *Black Theatre in the 1960s and 1970s*, 31; P. C. Harrison, "Mother/ Word," in *Totem Voices* (New York: Grove, 1989), xxiii.
42 In Bigsby, *Contemporary American Playwrights*, 11.
43 D. Kondo, "The Narrative Production of 'Home,' Community, and Political Identity in Asian American Theater," in *Displacement, Diaspora, and Geographies of Identity*, ed. S. Lavie and T. Swedenburg (Durham: Duke University Press, 1996), 100.
44 W. M. Gaines, "The Lone Stranger Rides Again," in *Bedside Mad* (New York: Signet, 1959), 30–50.
45 P. Thomas, *Down These Mean Streets* (New York: Signet, 1967), 9.
46 D. Krasner, "Deviancy in a Deviant Society: The Labelling Process in Miguel Piñero's *Short Eyes*," *Text and Presentation* 19 (1998), 71.
47 R. Patrick, *Kennedy's Children* (New York: Samuel French, 1975), 38.

Chapter 4   Mad as Hell: American Drama, 1976–1989

1 D. Mamet, *American Buffalo* (1975; New York: Grove, 1996), 9.
2 J. Chambers, *Last Summer at Bluefish Cove* (New York: JH Press, 1982), 93.
3 S. Shepard, *Fool for Love and Other Plays* (Toronto: Bantam, 1984), 23.
4 M. I. Fornes, *Plays* (New York: PAJ, 1986), 17.
5 D. Rabe, *Hurlyburly* (New York: Grove, 1985), 153.
6 L. Wilson, *Burn This* (New York: Hill and Wang, 1987), 25.
7 P. K. Gotanda, *Fish Head Soup and Other Plays* (Seattle: University of Washington Press, 1991), 93–4.

8   C. Capozzola, "'It Makes You Want to Believe in the Country': Celebrating the Bicentennial in an Age of Limits," in *America in the 70s*, ed. B. Bailey and D. Farber (Lawrence: University Press of Kansas, 2004), 33–4.

9   D. Horowitz, *The Anxieties of Affluence: Critiques of American Consumer Culture, 1939–1979* (Amherst: University of Massachusetts Press, 2004), 226.

10   G. Troy, *Morning in America: How Reagan Invented the 1980s* (Princeton: Princeton University Press, 2005), 5.

11   Mick Jagger and Keith Richards, "Shattered" (EMI Music Publishing Ltd., 1978); reprint, *Forty Licks* (Virgin Records, 2002).

12   J. L. Austin, *How to Do Things with Words* (Cambridge, MA: Harvard University Press, 1962), 62.

13   G. Lakoff and M. Johnson, *Metaphors We Live By* (Chicago: University of Chicago Press, 1980), 5.

14   N. Shange, *for colored girls who have considered suicide when the rainbow is enuf* (Toronto: Bantam, 1975), 44.

15   In N. Lester, *Ntozake Shange: A Critical Study of the Plays* (New York: Garland, 1995), 26.

16   In Burke, *American Feminist Playwrights*, 184.

17   D. Krasner, "Dialogics and Dialectics: Bakhtin, Young Hegelians, and Dramatic Theory," in *Bakhtin: Ethics and Mechanics*, ed. V. Nolan (Evanston: Northwestern University Press, 2004), 24.

18   S. Cosgrove, "The Zoot-Suit and Class Warfare," *History Workshop Journal* 18 (Autumn 1984): 78.

19   L. Valdez, in *Mexican American Theatre*, ed. Kanellos, 98.

20   J. Huerta, "Introduction," in *Zoot Suit and Other Plays* (Houston: Arte Público Press, 1992), 15.

21   In A. Danto, *Nietzsche as Philosopher* (New York: Columbia University Press, 1965), 201–2.

22   S. Shepard, *Seven Plays* (Toronto: Bantam, 1984), 130.

23   T. P. Adler, "Repetition and Regression in *Curse of the Starving Class* and *Buried Child*," in *Cambridge Companion to Sam Shepard*, ed. M. Roudané (Cambridge: Cambridge University Press, 2002), 114.

24   S. J. Bottoms, *The Theatre of Sam Shepard: States of Crisis* (Cambridge: Cambridge University Press, 1998), 159.

25   Shepard, *True West*, in *Seven Plays*, 48.

26   R. Slotkin, *Gunfighter Nation: The Myth of the Frontier in Twentieth-Century America* (Norman: University of Oklahoma Press, 1998), 10.

27   F. J. Turner, *The Frontier in American History* (New York: Dover, 1996), 30.

28   M. Jay, *Songs of Experience: Modern American and European Variations on a Universal Theme* (Berkeley: University of California Press, 2005), 265–6.

29 M. Robinson, "Joseph Chaikin and Sam Shepard in Collaboration," in *Cambridge Companion to Sam Shepard*, ed. Roudané, 94.

30 Troy, *Morning in America*, 117.

31 M. Norman, *'night, Mother* (New York: Hill and Wang, 1983), 3.

32 J. Dolan, *The Feminist Spectator as Critic* (Ann Arbor: University of Michigan Press, 1991), 35–6.

33 H. Blau, *The Dubious Spectacle* (Minneapolis: University of Minnesota Press, 2002), 213, 214.

34 Bigsby, *Contemporary American Playwrights*, 232.

35 H. Scolnicov, *Woman's Theatrical Space* (Cambridge: Cambridge University Press, 1994), 8.

36 D. Mamet, "Something Out of Nothing," in *David Mamet in Conversation*, ed. L. Kane (Ann Arbor: University of Michigan Press, 2001), 46–7.

37 D. Mamet, *Glengarry Glen Ross* (New York: Grove, 1982), 47.

38 H. G. Frankfurt, *On Bullshit* (Princeton: Princeton University Press, 2005), 22, 55.

39 J. Lahr, "Survivors," *New Yorker*, May 9, 2005: 91.

40 Bruce Springsteen, "Born in the USA" (Columbia Records, 1987).

41 L. Wilson, *Collected Works*, Vol. III (Lyme, NH: Smith Kraus, 1999), 42.

42 C. Lasch, *Culture of Narcissism: American Life in an Age of Diminishing Expectations* (New York: Norton, 1979), xv–xvi.

43 C. Fuller, *A Soldier's Play* (New York: Hill and Wang, 1981), 72.

44 M. W. Rocha, "August Wilson and the Four B's Influences," in *August Wilson: A Casebook*, ed. M. Elkins (New York: Garland, 1994), 3–16.

45 A. Wilson, in Bigsby, *Modern American Drama, 1945–2000*, 293.

46 A. Wilson, *Three Plays* (Pittsburgh: University of Pittsburgh Press, 1991), 16.

47 F. J. Griffin, *Who Set You Flowin'? The African-American Migration Narrative* (New York: Oxford University Press, 1995), 97.

48 A. Wilson, *Joe Turner's Come and Gone* (New York: Plume, 1988), n.p.

49 A. Wilson, *Fences* (New York: Plume, 1986), 9.

50 G. Smitherman, *Talkin That Talk: Language, Culture, and Education in African America* (London: Routledge, 2000), 272.

51 H. J. Elam, *The Past as Present in the Drama of August Wilson* (Ann Arbor: University of Michigan Press, 2004).

52 A. Gramsci, "Working-Class Education and Culture," in *The Antonio Gramsci Reader*, ed. D. Forgacs (New York: New York University Press, 2000), 57.

53 E. Overmyer, *On the Verge, or The Geography of Yearning* (New York: Broadway Play, 1988), 19.

54 R. Nelson, *Principia Scriptoriae* (New York: Broadway Play, 1986), 2.

55 H. Als, "Arrested Development," *New Yorker*, January 5, 2004: 88.

56 D. H. Hwang, *M. Butterfly* (New York: Plume, 1989), 82–3.

Chapter 5 The Body in Pain: American Drama, 1990–2000

1   T. Kushner, *Angels in America, Part I: Millennium Approaches* (New York: TCG, 1992), 68.

2   A. Wilson, *Two Trains Running* (New York: Penguin, 1993), 46.

3   N. Wallace, *In the Heart of America and Other Plays* (New York: TCG, 2001), 111.

4   M. Kaufman, *The Laramie Project* (New York: Vintage, 2001), 38.

5   E. Scarry, *The Body in Pain* (New York: Oxford University Press), 4.

6   A. D. Smith, "Introduction," in *Fires in the Mirror* (New York: Doubleday, 1993), xxviii–xxix.

7   J. Guare, *Six Degrees of Separation* (New York: Vintage, 1994), 10.

8   G. A. Plunka, "John Guare and the Popular Culture Hype of Celebrity Status," in *Companion to Twentieth-Century American Drama*, ed. Krasner, 352, 353.

9   P. Vogel, *The Baltimore Waltz and Other Plays* (New York: TCG, 1996), 26.

10 S. Boym, *The Future of Nostalgia* (New York: Basic Books, 2001), xiv, xiii.

11 A. Pellegrini, "Repercussions and Remainders in the Plays of Paula Vogel: An Essay in Five Moments," in *Companion to Twentieth-Century American Drama*, ed. Krasner, 474.

12 P. Vogel, *The Mammary Plays* (New York: TCG, 1998), 14.

13 Savran, *A Queer Sort of Materialism*, 196.

14 Huerta, *Chicano Drama*, 127.

15 S.-L. Parks, *The America Play and Other Works* (New York: TCG, 1995), 165.

16 A. Wilson, *The Piano Lesson* (New York: Plume, 1990), 43.

17 K. Pereira, *August Wilson and the African-American Odyssey* (Urbana: University of Illinois Press, 1995), 89.

18 S. Shannon, *The Dramatic Vision of August Wilson* (Washington, DC: Howard University Press, 1995), 147.

19 D. Boan, "Call-and-Response: Parallel 'Slave Narrative' in August Wilson's *The Piano Lesson*," *African American Review* 32.2 (Summer 1998), 263.

20 A. Artaud, *Le Théâtre et son double* (Paris: Gallimard, 1964), 137–8.

21 J. Dolan, "Lesbian and Gay Drama," in *Companion to Twentieth-Century American Drama*, ed. Krasner, 497.

22 D. Son, in *Women Who Write Plays*, ed. Alexis Greene (Hanover, NH: Smith Kraus, 2001), 416.

23 J. Rivera, *Marisol and Other Plays* (New York: TCG, 1997), 48–9.

24 N. Silver, *Etiquette and Vitriol: The Food Chain and Other Plays* (New York: TCG, 1996), 7.

25 R. Foreman, "Foundations for a Theater," in *Unbalancing Acts* (New York: TCG, 1992), 4, 25.

26 D. Auburn, *Proof* (New York: Dramatist Play Service, 2001), 16.

27 S. Sontag, *Regarding the Pain of Others* (New York: Farrar, Straus, and Giroux, 2003), 95.

28 M. Edson, *W;t* (New York: Faber and Faber, 1999), 43.

Selected Bibliography

The following is a brief list of books that consider two or more American dramatists from 1935 to 2000. Studies of individual dramatists are too numerous to include here, but a computer search on the Internet should uncover useful resources of material. Two outstanding database resources for dramatic texts are: www.alexanderstreetpress.com/drama/ (Alexander Street Press) and www.proquest.co.uk/products/tcd.html (ProQuest/Chadwyck-Healey).

Adler, T. P. (1994). *American Drama, 1940–1960: A Critical History*. New York: Twayne.

Andreach, R. J. (1998). *Creating the Self in the Contemporary American Theatre*. Carbondale: Southern Illinois University Press.

Aronson, A. (2000). *American Avant-Garde Theatre: A History*. London: Routledge.

Berkowitz, G. M. (1992). *American Drama of the Twentieth Century*. London: Longman.

Bigsby, C. W. E. (1985). *Broadway and Beyond*. Cambridge: Cambridge University Press.

——. (1999). *Contemporary American Playwrights*. Cambridge: Cambridge University Press.

——. (2000). *Modern American Drama, 1945–2000*. Cambridge: Cambridge University Press.

Bloom, C., ed. (1995). *American Drama*. Houndsmills: Macmillan.

Bordman, G. (1996). *American Theatre: A Chronicle of Comedy and Drama, 1930–1969*. New York: Oxford University Press.

Brown-Guillory, E. (1988). *Their Place on the Stage: Black Women Playwrights in America*. New York: Praeger.

Burke, S. (1996). *American Feminist Playwrights*. New York: Twayne.

Cohn, R. (1991). *New American Dramatists, 1960–1990*. Houndsmills: Macmillan.

Cotkin, G. (2003). *Existential America*. Baltimore: Johns Hopkins University Press.

Crespy, D. A. (2003). *Off-Off Broadway Explosion: How Provocative Playwrights of the 1960s Ignited a New American Theatre*. New York: Backstage Books.

Davis, W. A. (1994). *Get the Guests: Psychoanalysis, Modern American Drama, and the Audience*. Madison: University of Wisconsin Press.

Demastes, W. (1988). *Beyond Naturalism: A New Realism in American Theatre*. Westport: Greenwood Press.

———. (1996). *Realism and the American Dramatic Tradition*. Tuscaloosa: University of Alabama Press.

Fearnow, M. (1997). *The American Stage and the Great Depression*. Cambridge: Cambridge University Press.

Gagey, E. (1947). *Revolution in American Drama*. New York: Columbia University Press.

Geiogamah, H. and Darby, J. T., eds. (2000). *American Indian Theater in Performance: A Reader*. Los Angeles: UCLA American Indian Center.

Harris, S. H. (1997). *American Drama: The Bastard Art*. New York: Cambridge University Press.

Hay, S. (1994). *African American Theatre: An Historical and Critical Analysis*. New York: Cambridge University Press.

Henderson, M. C. (2001). *Mielziner: Master of Modern Stage Design*. New York: Backstage Books.

Hischak, T. S. (2001). *American Theatre: A Chronicle of Comedy and Drama, 1969–2000*. New York: Oxford University Press.

Huerta, J. (2000). *Chicano Drama: Performance, Society, and Myth*. Cambridge: Cambridge University Press.

Kanellos, N., ed. (1989). *Mexican American Theatre: Then and Now*. Houston: Arte Público Press.

Krasner, D., ed. (2005). *A Companion to Twentieth-Century American Drama*. Malden: Blackwell.

McConachie, B. (2003). *American Theater in the Culture of the Cold War: Producing and Contesting Containment, 1947–1962*. Iowa City: University of Iowa Press.

McDonald, R. L. and Paige, L. R., eds. (2002). *Southern Women Playwrights: New Essays in Literary History and Criticism*. Tuscaloosa: University of Alabama Press.

Marranca, B. and Dasgupta, G. (1981). *American Playwrights: A Critical Survey*. New York: Drama Book.

Miller, J. Y. and Frazer, W. L. (1997). *American Drama between the Wars: A Critical History*. New York: Twayne.

Porter, T. (1969). *Myth and Modern American Drama*. Detroit: Wayne State University Press.

Robinson, M. (1994). *The Other American Drama*. New York: Cambridge University Press.

Roudané, M., ed. (1993). *Public Issues, Private Tensions: Contemporary American Drama*. New York: AMS Press.

——— . (1996). *American Drama Since 1960.* New York: Twayne.

Savran, D. (1992). *Communists, Cowboys, and Queers: The Politics of Masculinity in the Works of Arthur Miller and Tennessee Williams.* Minneapolis: University of Minnesota Press.

——— . (2003). *A Queer Sort of Materialism: Recontextualizing American Theater.* Ann Arbor: University of Michigan Press.

Schlueter, J., ed. (1989). *Feminist Rereadings of Modern American Drama.* Cranbury: Fairleigh Dickinson University Press.

——— . (1990). *Modern American Drama: The Female Canon.* Cranbury: Fairleigh Dickinson University Press.

Schmidt, K. (2005). *The Theater of Transformation: Postmodernism in American Drama.* Amsterdam: Rodopi.

Smiley, S. (1972). *The Drama of Attack: Didactic Plays of the American Depression.* Columbia: University of Missouri Press.

Sternlicht, S. (2002). *A Reader's Guide to Modern American Drama.* Syracuse: Syracuse University Press.

Williams, M. (1985). *Black Theatre in the 1960s and 1970s.* Westport: Greenwood Press.

Wilmeth, D. and Bigsby, C. W. E., eds. (2000). *The Cambridge History of American Theatre.* Vol. III. New York: Cambridge University Press.

Index

Page references in *italic* are to illustrations.

Abdoh, Reza 176
abstract expressionism 64, 66, 85
absurdism 64, 65–6, 69, 70, 75,
   94, 139, 175
Action (Shepard) 87
Adams, James Truslow 29
The Adding Machine (Rice) 13
Adler, Thomas 56, 109
African American community 59,
   148, 164, 166, 171–2
African American theatre 71–3,
   89–93, 105–6, 131–9, 156–60,
   164–8, 171–2, 178
  Black Arts Movement 24, 89,
    90, 93, 105, 132
  comedies 73, 139
  gay theatre 176–7
  social issue plays 9, 24–6,
    58–61, 67, 69, 70, 90–1, 131–2
Afrocentric religious expression
   132, 135, 136
After the Fall (Arthur Miller) 99
AIDS 140, 152, 160, 161, 163
  in the black community 172
Albee, Edward 65, 66–7, 70–1,
   75–84, 168–9

All Over 83, 84
The American Dream 65, 67, *68*
A Delicate Balance 82–3, 84
FAM and YAM 64
The Man with Three Arms 168
The Sandbox 65
Three Tall Women 83–4, 168–9
Tiny Alice 82, 83, 168
Who's Afraid of Virginia Woolf?
   62, 64, 75–82, *78*, 83
The Zoo Story 64, 65, 66–7, 83,
   151
alienation 5, 20, 87, 118, 120
All My Sons (Arthur Miller) 38–40
All Over (Albee) 83, 84
All in the Timing (Ives) 175
Allen, Joan 123
Allen, Woody 74
Alley Theatre 63
Als, Hilton 144
America Hurrah (Van Itallie) 85,
   86
The America Play (Parks) 156, 157
American Beauty (dir. Mendes) 84
American Buffalo (Mamet) 100,
   101–5, 112, 124, 126, 169

American Dream 28–9, 32, 35, 45, 46, 47, 49, 58, 94, 95
The American Dream (Albee) 65, 67, 68
American Gothic (Wood) 108
American Negro Theatre 25
Ancient History (Ives) 175
And Baby Makes Seven (Vogel) 155
Anderson, Maxwell
  Winterset 14–15
Anderson, Robert
  I Never Sang for My Father 98
  Tea and Sympathy 57
Angelo Herndon Jones (Hughes) 9
Angelos, Moe 176
Angels in America (Kushner) 147, 160–4, *162*, 168
Anna Lucasta (Yordan) 25
anti-consumerism 120
anti-establishment drama 84–5
  see also social issue plays
anti-Semitism 12–13
anti-Vietnam war movement 64, 85, 88
Apocalypse Now (dir. Coppola) 88
appearance–reality division 108, 109
Approaching Zanzibar (Howe) 124
Arena Stage 63
Arent, Arthur
  One Third of a Nation 5
Aronson, Arnold 85
The Art of Dining (Howe) 123–4
Artaud, Antonin 164
Arthur, Timothy
  Ten Nights in a Barroom 19
As Bees in Honey Drown (Bean) 175
Asian American theatre 96–7, 145–6, 177
Auburn, David
  Proof 178, 179
Aunt Dan and Lemon (Shawn) 142, 144–5

Austin, J. L. 104
avant-garde theatre 65, 175–6
Awake and Sing! (Odets) 10–12, 13, 59
Axelrod, George
  The Seven Year Itch 38

Baby and the Bathwater (Durang) 139
Bad Habits (McNally) 86–7
Baitz, John Robin
  The Substance of Fire 171
Baldwin, James 132
The Baltimore Waltz (Vogel) 151–2, 163
Balzac, Honoré de
  Cousin Bette 31
Bancroft, Anne 38, 57
Baraka, Amiri 67, 69–71, 91, 132, 138
  Dutchman 62, 64, 65, 67, 69, 70, 71
  Slave Ship 93
Barefoot in the Park (Simon) 75
barrooms and patrons 19, 20, 35–6, 37, 90
Barry, Philip
  The Philadelphia Story 15
The Basic Training of Pavlo Hummel (Rabe) 88, 89
Bean, Douglas Carter
  As Bees in Honey Drown 175
The Beard (McClure) 84, 85–6
Bearden, Romare 132
Beat poets 64, 65, 66
Beattie, Ann 84
Beauty and the Beast (Split Britches) 141
Beck, Julian 63, 65
Beckett, Samuel 64
  Endgame 109
  Krapp's Last Tape 65
  Waiting for Godot 23, 24, 86

Before It Hits Home (West)   171
Bellamy, Lou   *165*
Belle Reprieve (Split Britches)   141
Benjamin, Walter   161, 168
Benston, Kimberly   92
Berkowitz, Gerald   55
Beyond Therapy (Durang)   139, 140
Bierce, Ambrose
   An Incident at Owl Creek Bridge
   151
Bigsby, Christopher   2–3, 49, 61,
   65–6, 122
Biloxi Blues (Simon)   139
Birdsall, Jim   *111*
black aesthetic   89
Black Arts Movement   24, 89, 90,
   93, 105, 132
Black Elk Speaks (Neihardt)   174
Black Power   89
Blau, Herbert   121
Blitzstein, Marc
   The Cradle Will Rock   15
blues aesthetic   7, 10, 133
Blues for an Alabama Sky (Cleage)
   172
Boan, Devon   159
Body Indian (Geiogamah)   95
Bogart, Humphrey   18
Bogosian, Eric   141–2
   SubUrbia   142, 170–1
   Talk Radio   142
Bonner, Marita
   Exit: An Illusion   72
   The Purple Flower   72
Borges, Jorge Luis   132
Born on the Fourth of July (dir. Stone)
   88
Born Yesterday (Kanin)   38
Bosoms and Neglect (Guare)   94
Bottoms, S. J.   109
Bovasso, Julie   85
Boyle, Peter   109

Boym, Svetlana   152
Boys in the Band (Crowley)   62, 93,
   140
Brando, Marlon   41
Branner, Djola Bernard   176
Brave Smiles (Five Lesbian Brothers)
   176
Breath, Boom (Corthron)   178
Brecht, Bertolt   138
Brides of the Moon (Five Lesbian
   Brothers)   176
A Bright Room Called Day (Kushner)
   164
Brighton Beach Memoirs (Simon)
   139
Broadway Bound (Simon)   139
The Bronx is Next (Sanchez)   91
Brooks, Mel   74
Brown, Rita Mae   140
Bruce, Lenny   74
Bullins, Ed   90, 91–3, 138, 172,
   178
   Clara's Ole Man   91
   The Duplex   91
   The Fabulous Miss Marie   91
   Goin' a Buffalo   92
   Home Boy   91
   In New England Winter   91
   In the Wine Time   91
   It Bees Dat Way   91
   The Theme is Blackness   93
Buried Child (Shepard)   87, 107–8,
   109, 115
Burn This (Lanford Wilson)   100,
   128, 129
Bus Stop (Inge)   56, 57
Butterflies are Free (Gershe)   98

Caesar, Adolph   131
Caffé Cino   63
Cage, John   176
Calm Down Mother (Terry)   84

Camus, Albert 5
capitalism 50
Capote, Truman 109
Capozzola, Christopher 101
Carmines, Al 63
Carter, Jimmy 102
Casualties of War (dir. De Palma) 88
Cat on a Hot Tin Roof (Williams) 8, 9, 28, 34, 42, 44–5, 51, 53–5, 59
Cazale, John 86
Center Stage 63
Ceremonies and Dark Old Men (Elder) 90–1, 136, 138
Chaikin, Joe 63, 85
Chambers, Jane
Last Summer at Bluefish Cove 100, 140, 170
Chaney, James 148
Chávez, César 97
Chayefsky, Paddy
Network 101, 102
Cheever, John 84
Chekhov, Anton 130
Chicano Movement 97
The Chickencoop Chinaman (Chin) 62, 95, 96–7
Children of a Lesser God (Medoff) 141
The Children's Hour (Hellman) 8–9, 10
Childress, Alice
Wedding Band 91
Wine in the Wilderness 91
Chin, Frank
The Chickencoop Chinaman 62, 95, 96–7
Christianity 37, 132, 136, 137, 168
Christopher, Michael 141
The Shadow Box 141
Cino, Joe 63

Civil Rights Movement 64, 89, 148, 164, 171
Clara's Ole Man (Bullins) 91
Cleage, Pearl
Blues for an Alabama Sky 172
Flyin' West 172
Cleveland Playhouse 63
Clinton, Bill 148
Clurman, Harold 6
Coastal Disturbances (Howe) 124
Cobb, Lee J. 51
Cody, Buffalo Bill 86, 112
Cohen, Lynn 78
Cohn, Roy 160
Cohn, Ruby 64
Collected Stories (Margulies) 170
The Colored Museum (Wolfe) 73, 139
Coltrane, John 69, 70
Come Back Little Sheba (Inge) 56
Come Down Burning (Corthorn) 178
comedy
African American comedies 73, 139
existential comedy 74
Jewish comedy 73–4
romantic comedies 38
Coming Home (dir. Ashby) 88
commodification 49, 73
"common man" 29, 40
communism 25, 56
community 6, 23, 168
see also African American community
Congdon, Constant
Dog Opera 171–2
The Connection (Gleber) 64, 65
consumerism 13, 63, 86
Conversations with My Father (Gardner) 74
Cooper, James Fenimore
Leatherstocking Tales 97

Corneille, Pierre
  L'Illusion Comique 164
corporate success 110
Corthron, Kai 177–8
  Breath, Boom 178
  Come Down Burning 178
Cosgrove, Stuart 107
Cotkin, George 5, 23, 25
Cowboy Mouth (Shepard) 87
The Cradle Will Rock (Blitzstein) 15
Crawford, Cheryl 6
creationism 57
Crimes of the Heart (Henley) 123
Crowley, Mart
  Boys in the Band 62, 93, 140
Crown Heights catastrophe 148
The Crucible (Arthur Miller) 56
Crumbs from the Table of Joy
  (Nottage) 171
The Cryptogram (Mamet) 169
cultural history 138–9
cultural wars 102
Curse of the Starving Class (Shepard)
  87, 107, 109, 115
cycle dramas 91, 132
cynicism 99, 130, 131

Danny and the Deep Blue Sea
  (Shanley) 130, 141
The Dark at the Top of the Stairs (Inge)
  56
Dark Fruit (Pomo Afro Homos)
  176–7
Darker Faces of the Earth (Dove) 178
David, Larry 74
Davis, Miles 69
Davis, Walter 81
Davy, Babs 176
Day, Clarence 15
Day of Absence (Ward) 93
De Kooning, Willem 66
De Niro, Robert 102

Dead End (Kingsley) 15
Dean, Philip Hayes
  The Sty of the Blind Pig 91
death 80, 83, 141, 160, 168
*The Death of the Last Black Man in
  the Whole Entire World* (Parks)
  156
Death of a Salesman (Arthur Miller)
  11, 12, 27, 28, 31, 32, 45–51,
  52, 59, 61, 73, 126
The Deer Hunter (dir. Cimino) 88
DeGiacomo, Justin *162*
A Delicate Balance (Albee) 82–3, 84
Denning, Michael 6
*Desdemona, A Play about a
  Handkerchief* (Vogel) 155
Dibbell, Dominique 176
Dinerstein, Joel 8
The Dining Room (Gurney) 139
Dinner with Friends (Margulies) 170
Dog Opera (Congdon) 171–2
Dolan, Jill 119, 170
domestic drama 139
  see also family relationships
Don Juan in Chicago (Ives) 175
Donne, John 179, 180, 181
Don't You Want to Be Free (Hughes)
  9
Dostoevsky, Fyodor
  Crime and Punishment 25–6
double consciousness 72, 96, 173
Douglas, Kirk 114
Dove, Rita
  Darker Faces of the Earth 178
A Dream Play (Strindberg) 71
Dreiser, Theodore 4
Drexler, Rosalyn 85
Druten, John van
  I Remember Mama 15, 17
Du Bois, W. E. B. 72, 138
Duchamp, Marcel 85
Dunbar, Paul Laurence 70

The Duplex (Bullins)   91
Durang, Christopher   139
   Baby and the Bathwater   139
   Beyond Therapy   139, 140
   A History of American Film   139
   Laughing Wild   140
   The Marriage of Betty and Boo   140
   *Sister Mary Ignatius Explains It All
      for You*   139
   The Vietnamization of New Jersey
      139
Dürrenmatt, Friedrich   64
Dutchman (Baraka)   62, 64, 65, 67,
   69, 70, 71

Edmond (Mamet)   105, 169
Edson, Margaret
   W;t   179–81, 182
*The Effects of Gamma Rays on
   Man-in-the-Moon Marigolds*
   (Zindel)   98–9
El Teatro Campesino   97
Elam, Harry   138
Elder, Lonne
   Ceremonies and Dark Old Men
      90–1, 136, 138
elegy   181
Ellison, Ralph   59
Endgame (Beckett)   109
Ensler, Eve
   Vagina Monologues   177
Esposito, Julie   *162*
Esslin, Martin   64
eternal recurrence   108
ethnic identity, theatre and   95
evolutionary theory   57
existentialism   5, 6, 18–19, 20,
   23–4, 25, 26, 28, 69, 73, 74, 87
Exit: An Illusion (Bonner)   72
experience, rhetoric of   113–14
extended monologue   67, 69, 71,
   72, 90

Eyen, Tom
   The White Whore and the Bit Player
      84, 85

The Fabulous Miss Marie (Bullins)
   91
FAM and YAM (Albee)   64
fame, desire for   94, 150, 175
The Family of Mann (Rebeck)   172,
   173
family relationships   24, 55, 60, 65,
   108
   see also father–son relationships;
      mother–daughter relationships;
      sibling relationships
The Father (Strindberg)   76
father–son relationships   21–2, 47,
   50, 98, 117, 126, 132
Faulkner, William   141
Fearnow, Mark   18
Fefu and her Friends (Fornes)   118
feminist theatre   85, 118–24
Fences (August Wilson)   132, 136–8
Feydeau, George   74
Fierce Love: Stories from Black Gay Life
   (Pomo Afro Homos)   176
Fierstein, Harvey
   Torch Song Trilogy   140
Fifth of July (Lanford Wilson)   130
Finley, Karen   142
*Fires in the Mirror: Crown Heights,
   Brooklyn and Other Identities*
   (Smith)   148–9, 177
The First Breeze of Summer (Leslie
   Lee)   91
Fitzgerald, F. Scott   35
Five Lesbian Brothers   176
   Brave Smiles   176
   Brides of the Moon   176
   The Secretaries   176
   Voyage to Lesbos   176
Flyin' West (Cleage)   172

Fonda, Henry   38
food   87, 109, 115, 139
The Food Chain (Silver)   174–5
Fool for Love (Shepard)   87, 100,
    114–17
Foote, Horton
    The Young Man from Atlanta   170
*for colored girls who have considered
    suicide when the rainbow is enuf*
    (Shange)   105–6, 139
Ford Foundation   63
Foreman, Richard   175–6
Forensic & the Navigator (Shepard)
    87
Fornes, Maria Irene   85, 86, 118
    Fefu and her Friends   118
    Mud   86, 100, 118, 119, 120, 121
    Tango Palace   86
fourth-wall realism   46
*Frankie and Johnny in the Clair de
    Lune* (McNally)   130
freedom   4, 23, 29, 108, 113, 162
Freeman, Brian   176
Frelich, Phyllis   141
Freudian psychology   37, 44, 74
Friedman, Bruce Jay   74
    Scuba Duba   75
    Steambath   75
frontier myth   87, 112–13, 114
Fuddy Meers (Lindsay-Abaire)   175
Full Metal Jacket (dir. Kubrick)   88,
    89
Fuller, Charles
    A Soldier's Play   131–2
Funnyhouse of a Negro (Kennedy)
    64, 65, 68, 71–3, 148
Futz (Owens)   84, 85

Gardner, Herb
    Conversations with My Father   74
    I'm Not Rappaport   74
    A Thousand Clowns   74

Garson, Barbara
    MacBird   84, 85
Garvey, Marcus   24
Garvey Movement   24–5
gay community   93, 170, 181
gay and lesbian theatre   91, 93,
    140–1, 172, 176–7
    one-person shows   142
Geiogamah, Hanay
    Body Indian   95
Gelber, Jack
    The Connection   64, 65
Gemini (Innaurato)   139
gender, performance of   145–6
Genet, Jean   64
Geography of a Horse Dreamer
    (Shepard)   87
Gershe, Leonard
    Butterflies are Free   98
Getting Out (Norman)   118
Gibson, Josh   138
Gibson, William
    The Miracle Worker   57
    Two for the Seesaw   38
Gilman, Rebecca
    Spinning into Butter   178
Gilpin, Charles   9
Gilpin Players   9
Giving Up the Ghost (Moraga)   177
Glancy, Diane
    *The Woman Who Was a Red Deer
    Dressed for the Deer Dance*   174
Glaspell, Susan   120
The Glass Menagerie (Williams)   4,
    27, 28, 29–34, 42, 44, 45, 46
Glengarry Glen Ross (Mamet)   12,
    124–8, 169
Glines   140, 141
Goin' a Buffalo (Bullins)   92
Golden Boy (Odets)   13–14
Goodman, Andrew   148
Gordon, Ray   174

Gordone, Charles
  No Place to Be Somebody   90, 92
Gorky, Maxim
  Lower Depths   95
Gotanda, Philip Kan   141
  Yankee Dawg You Die   100, 141
gothic style   109, 142, 170
Gottfried, Martin   51
Gottlieb, Adolph   66
The Graduate (dir. Nichols)   63, 84
Gramsci, Antonio   139
Gray, Spalding   142
  Rhode Island Trilogy   142
  Swimming to Cambodia   142
Great Depression (1929–41)   4, 5,
  7, 10, 11, 15, 17, 25, 28
The Great God Brown (O'Neill)   13
The Great MacDaddy (Harrison)
  93
Great Society liberalism   101
greed   9, 13, 40, 101, 128
Greek tragic themes   56, 137
Green, Paul   24
Greenberg, Richard
  Three Days of Rain   171
Griffin, Farah Jasmine   133
Group Theatre   6, 10, 13
Guare, John   94–5, 148, 149–51,
  175
  Bosoms and Neglect   94
  The House of Blue Leaves   62, 64,
    94–5, 151
  Landscape of the Body   94
  Rich and Famous   94
  Six Degrees of Separation   149–51
Gupton, Eric   176
Gurney, A. R.   139
  The Dining Room   139
  The Middle Ages   139
  Scenes from American Life   139
  Sylvia   175
Guthrie Theatre   63

The Hairy Ape (O'Neill)   13
Hansberry, Lorraine   19, 28, 29,
  58–61
  A Raisin in the Sun   11, 24, 26,
    27, 28, 49, 58–61, 67, 139
  *The Sign on Sidney Brustein's
    Window*   148
happenings   85
Harlem   90, 91
Harlem Renaissance   24, 89
Harlem Suitcase Theatre   9
Harris, Julie   57
Harrison, Paul Carter   93
  The Great MacDaddy   93
Hart, Moss
  Light Up the Sky   38
Hart, Moss and George S.
  Kaufman
  You Can't Take It with You
    16–17
Healey, Peg   176
Hedda Gabler (Ibsen)   80
Heggen, Thomas and Joshua
  Logan
  Mister Roberts   37–8
Heidegger, Martin   24
The Heidi Chronicles (Wasserstein)
  123
Hellman, Lillian   120
  The Children's Hour   8–9, 10
  The Little Foxes   9
Hemings, Sally   10, 177
Henderson, Mary   15, 33
Henley, Beth   122, 123
  Crimes of the Heart   123
  Miss Firecracker Contest   123
Hepburn, Katharine   15
Heroes and Saints (Moraga)   177
Heschel, Joshua   148
Hirsch, Arnold   58
Hirsch, Joseph   51, 52
Hispanic Movement   97

history   149, 156, 157, 158–9, 160, 167
A History of American Film (Durang) 139
Hoffman, William
   As Is   140, 152
Holiday, Billie   31
Holiday Heart (West)   171
Holliday, Judy   38
Hollywood   128–9
Home Boy (Bullins)   91
Homebody/Kabul (Kushner)   164
The Homecoming (Pinter)   109
homoeroticism   57
homophobia   8, 42, 44, 57
homosexuality   42, 44, 53, 57, 140, 160, 161
   see also gay and lesbian theatre
Hopper, Edward   20
Horovitz, Israel   74
   The Indians Want the Bronx   85, 86
Hot L Baltimore (Lanford Wilson) 88
Hot 'N' Throbbing (Vogel)   155
House Arrest (Smith)   149
The House of Blue Leaves (Guare)   62, 64, 94–5, 151
House UnAmerican Activities Committee (HUAC)   56
How I Learned to Drive (Vogel)   151, 153–5
Howard, Leslie   17
Howe, LeAnne and Ray Gordon
   Indian Radio Days   174
Howe, Tina   122, 123
   Approaching Zanzibar   124
   The Art of Dining   123–4
   Coastal Disturbances   124
   Museum   123
   Painting Churches   124
Huerta, Jorge   107, 155–6

Hughes, Holly   142
Hughes, Langston   9–10, 28
   Angelo Herndon Jones   9
   Don't You Want to Be Free   9
   Limitations of Life   9
   Mulatto   9–10
   The Organizer   9
   Scarlet Sister Barry   9
   Scottsboro Limited   9
   Tambourines to Glory   9
Hughie (O'Neill)   34, 35
humanism   40, 134
Hurlyburly (Rabe)   100, 128–9
Hurston, Zora Neale   70
Hwang, David Henry
   M. Butterfly   96, 142, 145–6

I Never Sang for My Father (Robert Anderson)   98
I Remember Mama (van Druten)   15, 17
Ibsen, Henrik   40
   Hedda Gabler   80
   The Wild Duck   35–6
The Iceman Cometh (O'Neill)   20, 28, 32, 34, 35–7, 90, 103
The Illusion (Kushner)   164
I'm Not Rappaport (Gardner)   74
Imperceptible Mutabilities in the Third Kingdom (Parks)   156
In New England Winter (Bullins)   91
In the Wine Time (Bullins)   91
Incident at Vichy (Arthur Miller)   99
The Independence of Eddie Rose (Yellow Robe)   173–4
Indian Radio Days (Howe and Gordon)   174
Indians (Kopit)   84, 86
The Indians Want the Bronx (Horovitz)   85, 86
individualism   4, 5, 87, 101, 110, 113, 148

Inge, William   28, 56–7, 61
  Bus Stop   56, 57
  Come Back Little Sheba   56
  The Dark at the Top of the Stairs   56
  Picnic   56–7
Inherit the Wind (Lawrence and Lee)
  57
Innaurato, Albert   139
  Gemini   139
  The Transformation of Benno Blimpi
  139
installation art   176
intimate relationship plays   170,
  172
Ionesco, Eugène   64
Iraqi war   177
Irish Catholic fatalism   55
Ironweed (Kennedy)   120
Isherwood, Charles   40
Isn't It Romantic (Wasserstein)   123
It Bees Dat Way (Bullins)   91
Italian American Reconciliation
  (Shanley)   141
Ives, David   175
  All in the Timing   175
  Ancient History   175
  Don Juan in Chicago   175
  Mere Morals and Others   175

Jagger, Mick   102
Jar on the Floor (West)   171
Jay, Martin   113
jazz aesthetic   7, 8, 11, 65, 67,
  69–70
Jefferson, Thomas   10, 177
Jewish theatre   11–12, 73–5
  absurdism   75
  comedy   73–4
  tragedy   73
Jews
  anti-Semitism   12–13
  black–Jewish relations   148

chutzpah   11–12
language   10–11, 125–6
non-conformity   74
working-class Jews   125–6
Jitney (August Wilson)   138, 166
Joe Turner's Come and Gone (August
  Wilson)   132, 134–6
Johnson, Mark   105
Jones, Martin   9
Jones, Preston   141
  Texas Trilogy   141
Jones, Tommy Lee   109
Juba   135
Judson Memorial Church Theatre
  63

Kanin, Garson
  Born Yesterday   38
Kaprow, Allan   85
Karamu Playhouse   9
Kaufman, George S.   15, 16
Kaufman, Moisés
  The Laramie Project   147, 179,
  181, 182
Kazan, Elia   51, 56
Keep Tightly Closed in a Cool Dry Place
  (Terry)   84, 85
Keller, Helen   57
Kennedy, Adrienne   85, 138
  Funnyhouse of a Negro   64, 65, 68,
  71–3, 148
  A Movie Star Has to Star in Black
  and White   72
  The Owl Answers   72
Kennedy, David   19
Kennedy, William
  Ironweed   120
Kennedy's Children (Patrick)   99,
  130
Kentucky Cycle (Schenkkan)   177
Kerouac, Jack   66
Keyssar, Helene   85

Kierkegaard, Søren 23
The Killing Fields (dir. Joffé) 142
King, Martin Luther 148
King, Woodie 63
Kingsley, Sidney
  Dead End 15
Kissinger, Henry 177
"kitchen-sink" atmosphere 60
Kneubuhl, Victoria Nalani
  The Story of Susanna 174
Knott, Frederick
  Wait Until Dark 98
Kondo, Dorinne 96
Kopit, Arthur
  Indians 84, 86
  *Oh Dad, Poor Dad, Mamma's Hung
    You in the Closet and I'm Feelin'
    So Sad* 64–5, 67
Kovic, Ron 88
Kramer, Larry
  The Normal Heart 140, 152
Krapp's Last Tape (Beckett) 65
Kron, Lisa 176
Kübler-Ross, Elizabeth 151
Kushner, Tony 61, 73, 148,
    160–4, 168
  Angels in America 147, 160–4,
    162, 168
  A Bright Room Called Day 164
  Homebody/Kabul 164
  The Illusion 164
  Millennium Approaches 160
  Perestroika 160
  Slavs! 164

La Causa 97
La Mama Theatre 63, 95
LaGue, Michael *78*
Lahr, John 126
Lakoff, George 105
Landscape of the Body (Guare) 94
Lane, Henry "Juba" 135

The Laramie Project (Kaufman) 147,
    179, 181, 182
Lasch, Christopher 130
Last of the Red Hot Lovers (Simon)
    75
Last Summer at Bluefish Cove
    (Chambers) 100, 148, 170
The Late Henry Moss (Shepard) 118
Latino theatre 97–8, 106–7,
    155–6, 172–3
Laughing Wild (Durang) 140
LaVonn, Erika *165*
Lawrence, Jerome and Robert E. Lee
  Inherit the Wind 57
Lawson, John Howard
  Success Story 13
LeCompte, Elizabeth 142, 176
Lee, Canada 25
Lee, Leslie
  The First Breeze of Summer 91
Lee, Robert E. 57
Lee, Russell
  Nixon's Nixon 177
leftist politics 15, 25, 56
Leight, Warren
  Side Man 171
lesbian relationships 91, 140, 154,
    172, 177
  see also gay and lesbian theatre
Lesbians Who Kill (Split Britches)
    141
Letters to a Student Revolutionary
    (Wong) 177
Lhamon, W. T. 66
liberal values 22, 23, 101
A Lie of the Mind (Shepard) 118
Life with Father (Lindsey and
    Kaufman) 15–16
life insurance narrative device 11,
    19, 49, 58, 59
A Life in the Theatre (Mamet) 141
Light Up the Sky (Hart) 38

Limitations of Life (Hughes)   9
Lincoln, Abraham   156, 157
Lindsay-Abaire, David
  Fuddy Meers   175
Lindsey, Howard and George S.
  Kaufman
  Life with Father   15–16
Lips Together, Teeth Apart (McNally)
  170
The Little Foxes (Hellmann)   9
Little Women (Split Britches)   141
Living Theatre   63, 65
Logan, Joshua   37
lone cowboy icon   110
Lone Ranger and Tonto   96–7
Lonely Are the Brave (dir. Miller)
  114
Lonergan, Kenneth
  This is Our Youth   170
Long Day's Journey into Night (O'Neill)
  27, 28, 34, 35, 51, 55
Look Back in Anger (Osborne)   102
López, Josefina   148
  Real Women Have Curves   155–6
Los Angeles race riots (1943)
  106–7
Lost in Yonkers (Simon)   139
Love! Valour! Compassion! (McNally)
  170
Lucas, Craig
  Prelude to a Kiss   175
Luce, Henry   29
Ludlam, Charles and Everett
  Quinton
  The Mystery of Irma Vep   140
Lukács, Georg   40

M. Butterfly (Hwang)   96, 142,
  145–6
Ma Rainey's Black Bottom (August
  Wilson)   132, 133–4
Mabou Mines   176

MacBeth, Robert   63
MacBird (Garson)   84, 85
McCarthy, Eugene   123
McCarthy, Joseph   56
McCarthyism   44, 56
McCauley, Robbie
  Sally's Rape   177
McClendon, Rose   9
McClure, Michael
  The Beard   84, 85–6
McConachie, Bruce   61
McCullers, Carson   109
  The Member of the Wedding   57
Machinal (Treadwell)   13, 120
McIntyre, Dennis   141
  Modigliani   141
  Split Second   141–2
MacLeish, Archibald
  J. B.   57
McNally, Terrence   86
  Bad Habits   86–7
  *Frankie and Johnny in the Clair de
    Lune*   130
  Lips Together, Teeth Apart   170
  Love! Valour! Compassion!   170
McPherson, Scott
  Marvin's Room   172
magic realism   117, 132
Magic Theatre   109
Malcolm X   164
male bonding   103
Malina, Judith   63, 65
Malkovich, John   110
Mamet, David   11, 12, 101–5, 122,
  124–8, 169–70
  American Buffalo   100, 101–5,
    112, 124, 126, 169
  The Cryptogram   169
  Edmond   105, 169
  Glengarry Glen Ross   12, 124–8, 169
  A Life in the Theatre   141
  The Old Neighborhood   169

Oleanna 169, 170
Sexual Perversity in Chicago 103, 105, 169
Speed-the-Plow 12, 128, 129
The Man with Three Arms (Albee) 168
Manhoff, Bill
 The Owl and the Pussycat 98
Mann, Emily 141
 Still Life 141
marginalization 28, 34, 51, 155
 see also outsiders
Margolin, Deborah 140
Margulies, Donald
 Collected Stories 170
 Dinner with Friends 170
 Sight Unseen 170
Marisol (Rivera) 172–3
Marlowe, Christopher
 Tamberlane 65
The Marriage of Betty and Boo (Durang) 140
Marvin's Room (McPherson) 172
Marx, Karl 74
masks 71, 79
materialism 5, 23, 44
 see also consumerism; greed
May, Elaine 74
Mayo, Lisa 174
Medoff, Mark 141
 Children of a Lesser God 141
Melfi, Leonard
 Birdbath 85, 86
melodrama 140, 160
The Member of the Wedding (McCullers) 57
memory plays 29–30, 34, 45, 117, 149, 151, 154, 171
Mere Morals and Others (Ives) 175
Metamorphoses (Zimmerman) 178–9
metaphor 104, 105
Method acting 7, 43

Meyerowitz, Jan 9
The Middle Ages (Gurney) 139
middle-class ennui 82, 84
Midwestern life 9, 88, 130
Mielziner, Jo 15, 33, 46, 47
Miguel, Gloria 174
Miguel, Muriel 174
The Milk Train Doesn't Stop Here Anymore (Williams) 44
Millennium Approaches (Kushner) 160
Miller, Arthur 11, 12, 19, 28, 38–40, 43, 45–51, 56, 61, 74, 139
 After the Fall 99
 All My Sons 38–40
 The Crucible 56
 Death of a Salesman 11, 12, 27, 28, 31, 32, 45–51, *52*, 59, 61, 73, 126
 Incident at Vichy 99
 The Price 99
 Timebends (autobiography) 50
 A View from the Bridge 56
Miller, Jason
 That Championship Season 85, 86
Miller, Tim 142
Milner, Ronald 89–90
 What the Wine-Sellers Buy 89
The Mineola Twins (Vogel) 155
The Miracle Worker (Gibson) 57
Miss Firecracker Contest (Henley) 123
Mister Roberts (Heggen and Logan) 37–8
Modigliani (McIntyre) 141
money 59, 61
 see also capitalism; consumerism; greed; materialism
Monk, Meredith 176
Monk, Thelonious 69
Monroe, Marilyn 99

A Moon for the Misbegotten (O'Neill) 34, 55
Moraga, Cherrie 177
  Giving Up the Ghost 177
  Heroes and Saints 177
moral certainty, decline of 5, 102
"Morning in America" speech
  (Reagan) 102, 112, 118, 119
Moscow Art Theatre 6
mother–daughter relationships 30,
  31, 34, 84, 119–20
*A Movie Star Has to Star in Black and
  White* (Kennedy) 72
Mud (Fornes) 86, 100, 118, 119,
  120, 121
Mulatto (Hughes) 9–10
multiple negation 136
Museum (Howe) 123
The Mystery of Irma Vep (Ludlam and
  Quinton) 140

Naipaul, V. S. 142
Nash, N. Richard
  The Rainmaker 38
Nathan, George Jean 55
National Black Theatre 63
National Organization of Women
  (NOW) 118
Native American theatre 95–6,
  173–4
Native American Theatre Ensemble
  95
Native Son (Wright) 24, 25–6
Negro Ensemble Company 63, 89
Neihardt, John
  Black Elk Speaks 174
Nelson, Richard
  Principia Scriptoriae 142, 143–4
New Deal 19, 29
New Federal Theatre 63
New Lafayette Theatre 63, 89,
  92–3

New Theatre Magazine 6
New York Public Theatre 109
Newman, Barnet 66
Ngúgú wa Thiong'o 142
Nietzsche, Friedrich 37, 108
The Night of the Iguana (Williams)
  44
'night, Mother (Norman) 118,
  119–22
Nixon, Richard 101, 177
Nixon's Nixon (Russell Lee) 177
No Place to Be Somebody (Gordone)
  90, 92
The Normal Heart (Kramer) 140,
  152
Norman, Marsha 118
  Getting Out 118
  'night, Mother 118, 119–22
nostalgia 17, 152, 155, 169
Nottage, Lynn
  Crumbs from the Table of Joy 171
Nuyorican literary movement 97,
  98

O'Connor, Flannery 109, 141
The Odd Couple (Simon) 74–5, 110
Odets, Clifford 10–14, 19, 139
  Awake and Sing! 10–12, 13, 59
  Golden Boy 13–14
  Waiting for Lefty 4, 5, 6, 7–8,
  28
Off-Off-Broadway 63, 64
*Oh Dad, Poor Dad, Mamma's Hung
  You in the Closet and I'm Feelin'
  So Sad* (Kopit) 64–5, 67
oil embargo (1973) 101
The Old Neighborhood (Mamet) 169
Old West theatre 87
The Oldest Profession (Vogel) 155
Oleanna (Mamet) 169, 170
Olmos, Edward James 107
On The Waterfront (dir. Kazan) 56

On the Verge, or The Geography of Yearning (Overmyer) 142–3
One Third of a Nation (Arent) 19
one-person shows 142, 148–9
O'Neill, Eugene 28, 34–7, 51, 55–6, 61, 108, 139
  The Great God Brown 13
  The Hairy Ape 13
  Hughie 34, 35
  The Iceman Cometh 20, 28, 32, 34, 35–7, 90, 103
  Long Day's Journey into Night 27, 28, 34, 35, 51, 55
  A Moon for the Misbegotten 34, 55
Ontological-Hysteric Theater 175–6
Open Theatre 63, 85, 86
oral tradition 132
The Organizer (Hughes) 9
Orpheus Descending (Williams) 44
Osborne, John
  Look Back in Anger 102
Our Town (Wilder) 4, 5, 17
outsiders 20, 26, 28, 37–8, 41, 56, 57, 87, 114
  see also marginalization
Overmyer, Eric
  On the Verge, or The Geography of Yearning 142–3
Owens, Rochelle 85
  Futz 84, 85
The Owl Answers (Kennedy) 72
The Owl and the Pussycat (Manhoff) 98

Pacino, Al 86
Page, Geraldine 38
pain 130, 147–8, 179, 180, 181
Painting Churches (Howe) 124
Papp, Joseph 109
Paris, Texas (dir. Wenders) 117–18
Parker, Charlie 70

Parks, Suzan-Lori 72, 148, 156–7
  The America Play 156, 157
  The Death of the Last Black Man in the Whole Entire World 156
  Imperceptible Mutabilities in the Third Kingdom 156
passage-of-time motif 20
Patrick, Robert
  Kennedy's Children 99, 130
pedophilia 154, 155
Pellegrini, Ann 152
Pereira, Kim 158
Perestroika (Kushner) 160
Period of Adjustment (Williams) 44
The Petrified Forest (Sherwood) 5, 11, 17–19
The Philadelphia Story (Barry) 15
physical handicap 29, 30
The Piano Lesson (August Wilson) 138, 157–60
Picnic (Inge) 56–7
Piñero, Miguel
  Short Eyes 62, 64, 95, 98
Pinter, Harold 104
  The Homecoming 109
Platoon (dir. Stone) 88
Plaza Suite (Simon) 75
Plessy v. *Ferguson* 58
Plunka, Gene 150
Poggi, Jack 63
Poitier, Sidney 60, 149
political correctness 169, 178
political plays 15, 177–8
  see also social issue plays
Pollock, Jackson 66, 85
Pomo Afro Homos (Postmodern African American Homosexuals) 176–7
  Dark Fruit 176–7
  Fierce Love: Stories from Black Gay Life 176

Popular Front   6, 61
populist rhetoric   29
postcolonialism   142–6
Postlewait, Thomas   33
postmodernism   157
Prelude to a Kiss (Lucas)   175
The Price (Arthur Miller)   99
Principia Scriptoriae (Nelson)   142,
   143–4
Prohibition   19
proletarian-style drama   5, 6
Proof (Auburn)   178, 179
protest plays   9, 26
   see also social issue plays
Provincetown Players   63
provincialism   9, 10
Pterodactyls (Silver)   174
The Purple Flower (Bonner)   72

Quintero, José   35
Quinton, Everett   140

Rabe, David   88–9
   The Basic Training of Pavlo Hummel
      88, 89
   Hurlyburly   100, 128–9
   Sticks and Bones   88, 89
   Streamers   88, 89
race records   133
race relations   72
race riots   106–7
racism   9–10, 29, 58, 131
radicalism   130
   see also leftist politics; social issue
   plays
rage   21, 26, 101, 102, 118, 119,
   120, 128, 129, 133, 136, 138,
   140, 152
ragtime   7, 104
The Rainmaker (Nash)   38
Raised in Captivity (Silver)   174

A Raisin in the Sun (Hansberry)   11,
   24, 26, 27, 28, 49, 58–61, 67,
   139
rat-race mentality   12, 16
Reagan, Ronald   102, 113
Real Women Have Curves (López)
   155–6
realism   2, 25, 43, 53, 94, 117, 125
   fourth-wall realism   46
   magic realism   117, 132
   Method acting   7, 43
   social realism   40, 157
Rebeck, Theresa
   The Family of Mann   172, 173
relationship plays   141
   intimate relationship plays   170,
      172
   see also father–son relationships;
      mother–daughter relationships;
      sibling relationships
repetition   72, 157
Rhode Island Trilogy (Gray)   142
Rice, Elmer
   The Adding Machine   13
Rich and Famous (Guare)   94
Ridiculous Theatre Company   140
The Rimers of Eldrich (Lanford
   Wilson)   88
Rivera, José
   Marisol   172–3
Robards, Jason   35
Robbins, Mark   *111*
Robinson, Jackie   136, 138
Robinson, Marc   72, 116
Rocha, Mark William   132
Rockwell, Norman   109
Rollins, Sonny   69
Roosevelt, Franklin   30, 102
rootlessness   92, 96, 132
   see also outsiders
The Rose Tattoo (Williams)   44

Rosenberg, Ethel 160
Rothko, Mark 66
Roudané, Mathew 63–4
Rushdie, Salman 142

Salem witch-hunting trials 56
salesmanship 32, 36, 45, 47, 48,
 103, 124, 126
Salinger, J. D.
 The Catcher in the Rye 81
Sally's Rape (McCauley) 177
San Francisco Actors Workshop 86
San Francisco Mime Troupe 63
Sanchez, Sonia
 The Bronx is Next 91
 Sister Son/ja 91
Sandage, Scott 50–1
The Sandbox (Albee) 65
Sands, Diana 60
Saroyan, William
 The Time of Your Life 5, 19–20,
 28
Sartre, Jean-Paul 5, 23
Savage in Limbo (Shanley) 141
Savran, David 44–5, 155
Scarlet Sister Barry (Hughes) 9
Scarry, Elaine 147–8
Scenes from American Life (Gurney)
 139
Schenkkan, Robert
 Kentucky Cycle 177
Schisgal, Murray
 Luv 64, 65, 73–4
Schulberg, Bud 56
Schwartz, Delmore 24
Schwerner, Michael 148
Scolnicov, Hanna 122
Scopes trial 57
Scorsese, Martin 102
Scottsboro Limited (Hughes) 9
Scuba Duba (Friedman) 75

Seattle Rep 63
The Secretaries (Five Lesbian
 Brothers) 176
Seinfeld 74
self-deception 82
self-obsession 73, 74
selfishness 128, 130
Sell, Mike 90
set design
 Death of a Salesman 46
 The Glass Menagerie 33, 46
 Winterset 15
The Seven Year Itch (Axelrod) 38
Sexual Perversity in Chicago (Mamet)
 103, 105, 169
The Shadow Box (Christopher) 141
Shakespeare, William
 Hamlet 37
Shange, Ntozake 105
 *for colored girls who have considered
 suicide when the rainbow is enuf*
 105–6, 139
Shanley, John Patrick 141
 Danny and the Deep Blue Sea 130,
 141
 Italian American Reconciliation 141
 Savage in Limbo 141
 Women of Manhattan 141
Shannon, Sandra 159
Shaw, Peggy 140
Shawn, Wallace
 Aunt Dan and Lemon 142, 144–5
Sheen, Charlie 88
Sheen, Martin 88
Shepard, Matthew 181, 182
Shepard, Sam 86, 87–8, 107–18,
 122, 153
 Action 87
 Buried Child 87, 107–8, 109,
 115
 Cowboy Mouth 87

Shepard, Sam (*cont'd*)
  Curse of the Starving Class 87, 107, 109, 115
  Fool for Love 87, 100, 114–17
  Forensic & the Navigator 87
  Geography of a Horse Dreamer 87
  The Late Henry Moss 118
  A Lie of the Mind 118
  Paris, Texas (screenplay) 117–18
  Simpatico 118
  Suicide in B Flat 88
  True West 87, 109–12, *111*, 113, 114, 115, 117
  The Unseen Hand 87
Sherman, Martin
  Bent 140
Sherwood, Robert 17–19
  The Petrified Forest 5, 11, 17–19
sibling relationships 110–12, 114, 117, 152, 153, 158
Side Man (Leight) 171
Sight Unseen (Margulies) 170
The Sign on Sidney Brustein's Window (Hansberry) 148
Silver, Nicky 174–5
  The Food Chain 174–5
  Pterodactyls 174
  Raised in Captivity 174
Simon, Neil 74, 139
  Barefoot in the Park 75
  Biloxi Blues 139
  Brighton Beach Memoirs 139
  Broadway Bound 139
  Last of the Red Hot Lovers 75
  Lost in Yonkers 139
  The Odd Couple 74–5, 110
  Plaza Suite 75
  The Star-Spangled Girl 75
Simpatico (Shepard) 118
Sinise, Gary 110
Sister Mary Ignatius Explains It All for You (Durang) 139
Sister Son/ja (Sanchez) 91
The Sisters Rosensweig (Wasserstein) 123
Six Degrees of Separation (Guare) 149–51
skepticism 5
The Skin of Our Teeth (Wilder) 5, 20–3, 24
Slave Ship (Baraka) 93
slavery 134
Slavs! (Kushner) 164
Sleepy Lagoon Murders 107
Slotkin, Richard 112
Smethurst, James Edward 92–3
Smith, Anna Deavere 142, 148–9
  Fires in the Mirror: Crown Heights, Brooklyn and Other Identities 148–9, 177
  House Arrest 149
  Twilight: Los Angeles 149
Smith, Bessie 71, 133
Smith, Harry 46
Smith, Patti 87
Smith, Vicki M. *165*
Smitherman, Geneva 136
social consciousness 5, 6, 8, 28, 29, 40, 59, 149, 177
social issue plays 5, 6, 9, 14, 15, 24–6, 28, 58–61, 67, 69, 70, 90–1, 131–2, 177
social justice 28, 60, 61, 105
social pretensions 175
social realism 40, 157
social relevancy 66
Social Security 19
socialism 25
Sofer, Andrew 86
A Soldier's Play (Fuller) 131–2
Son, Diana
  Stop Kiss 172
Sontag, Susan 179

South Deering Improvement Association 58
Southern life 9, 141
Soyinka, Wole 142
space, metaphor of 83, 122, 123
speech act theory 104
Speed-the-Plow (Mamet) 12, 128, 129
Spiderwomen Theatre 174
spiel 103
Spinning into Butter (Gilman) 178
spinsters, dependent 31, 40–1
Split Britches 140, 141
  Beauty and the Beast 141
  Belle Reprieve 141
  Lesbians Who Kill 141
  Little Women 141
  Split Britches 141
  Upwardly Mobile Home 141
Split Second (McIntyre) 141–2
Springsteen, Bruce 129
stagflation 101
Stanislavsky, Konstantin 6, 7, 43
Stanley, Kim 57
The Star-Spangled Girl (Simon) 75
Steambath (Friedman) 75
Stein, Gertrude 14, 120
Steinbeck, John
  Of Mice and Men 15
Stenz, Anita Maria 79
Steppenwolf 109
Stevens, Wallace 19, 34
Stewart, Ellen 63, 95
Sticks and Bones (Rabe) 88, 89
Still Life (Mann) 141
Stonewall Uprising 93, 140
The Story of Susanna (Kneubuhl) 174
Strasberg, Lee 6
Streamers (Rabe) 88, 89
A Streetcar Named Desire (Williams) 28, 34, 40–4, 45, 46, 48, 53

Strindberg, August
  A Dream Play 71
  The Father 76
student–teacher relationships 169–70
The Sty of the Blind Pig (Dean) 91
The Substance of Fire (Baitz) 171
SubUrbia (Bogosian) 142, 170–1
Success Story (Lawson) 13
Suddenly Last Summer (Williams) 44
Suicide in B Flat (Shepard) 88
Summer and Smoke (Williams) 44
surrealism 66
survival motif 18, 21, 23, 54
Sweet Bird of Youth (Williams) 44
Swimming to Cambodia (Gray) 142
Sylvia (Gurney) 175

Talk Radio (Bogosian) 142
Talley & Son (Lanford Wilson) 130
Talley's Folly (Lanford Wilson) 130
Tamberlane (Marlowe) 65
Tambourines to Glory (Hughes) 9
Tango Palace (Fornes) 86
Taxi Driver (dir. Scorsese) 102
Taylor, Drew Hayden
  Only Drunks and Children Tell the Truth 174
Taylor, Laurette 30, 31
Tea and Sympathy (Robert Anderson) 57
Tectonic Theatre Company 142, 179, 181
Teer, Barbara Ann 63
temperance plays 19
Terry, Megan 85
  Calm Down Mother 84
  Keep Tightly Closed in a Cool Dry Place 84, 85
  Viet Rock 84, 85
Tesich, Steve
  The Speed of Darkness 177

Texas Trilogy (Jones)   141
That Championship Season (Jason Miller)   85, 86
theatre of cruelty   164
théâtre engagé   64
Theatre Genesis   63
theatricality   2, 37, 46, 47, 69, 71, 72, 107
The Theme is Blackness (Bullins)   93
The Third Man (dir. Reed)   151
This is Our Youth (Lonergan)   170
Thomas, Piri
    Bildungsroman, Down These Mean Streets   97–8
Thoreau, Henry David
    Walden   20
A Thousand Clowns (Gardner)   74
Three Days of Rain (Greenberg)   171
Three Tall Women (Albee)   83–4, 168–9
The Time of Your Life (Saroyan)   5, 19–20, 28
Tiny Alice (Albee)   82, 83, 168
Tolan, Kathleen
    A Weekend Near Madison   130
Torch Song Trilogy (Fierstein)   140
tragedy
    heroic tragedy   121
    Jewish tragedy   73
The Transformation of Benno Blimpi (Innaurato)   139
trauma   81, 152, 153
Treadwell, Sophie   120
    Machinal   13, 120
Troy, Gil   102, 118
True West (Shepard)   87, 109–12, *111*, 113, 114, 115, 117
Trumbo, Dalton
    Johnny Got His Gun   88
Turner, Frederick Jackson   112
Turney, Joe   134
Twilight: Los Angeles (Smith)   149

Two for the Seesaw (Gibson)   38
Two Trains Running (August Wilson)   138, 147, 164–8, *165*

Uncommon Women and Others (Wasserstein)   122–3
United Farm Workers (UFW)   97
The Unseen Hand (Shepard)   87
Updike, John   84
upward mobility   28, 29
Upwardly Mobile Home (Split Britches)   141
urban-street vernacular   178

Vagina Monologues (Ensler)   177
Valdez, Luis
    Zoot Suit   106–7
Van Itallie, Jean-Claude   86
    America Hurrah   85, 86
vaudeville   156
Viet Rock (Terry)   84, 85
Vietnam War   88–9, 101, 141
The Vietnamization of New Jersey (Durang)   139
A View from the Bridge (Arthur Miller)   56
Vogel, Paula   148, 151–5
    And Baby Makes Seven   155
    The Baltimore Waltz   151–2, 163
    Desdemona, A Play about a Handkerchief   155
    Hot 'N' Throbbing   155
    How I Learned to Drive   151, 153–5
    The Mineola Twins   155
    The Oldest Profession   155
Voyage to Lesbos (Five Lesbian Brothers)   176

Wainscott, Ronald   13
Wait Until Dark (Knott)   98

Waiting for Godot (Beckett) 23, 24, 86

Waiting for Lefty (Odets) 4, 5, 6, 7–8, 28

Walker, Joseph
  The River Niger 91, 138

Wallace, Henry 29, 40

Wallace, Naomi
  In the Heart of America 147, 177

Ward, Adolphus *165*

Ward, Douglas Turner 91
  Day of Absence 93

Ward, Theodore
  Big White Fog 24–5, 26

Warhol, Andy 157

Wasserstein, Wendy 74, 122
  The Heidi Chronicles 123
  Isn't It Romantic 123
  The Sisters Rosensweig 123
  Uncommon Women and Others 122–3

Waters, Ethel 57

Weaver, Lois 140

Wedding Band (Childress) 91

Weller, Michael
  Moonchildren 98

Wellman, Mac
  7 Blowjobs 177

Wenders, Wim 117

West, Cheryl
  Before It Hits Home 171
  Holiday Heart 171
  Jar on the Floor 171

Wetzsteon, Ross 87

What the Wine-Sellers Buy (Milner) 89

The White Whore and the Bit Player (Eyen) 84, 85

Who's Afraid of Virginia Woolf? (Albee) 62, 64, 75–82, 78, 83

The Wild Duck (Ibsen) 35–6

Wilde, Oscar 74, 154

Wilder, Thornton 20–3, 24
  Our Town 4, 5, 17
  The Skin of Our Teeth 5, 20–3, 24

Williams, Mance 93

Williams, Raymond 49

Williams, Tennessee 40–5, 51, 53–5, 61, 130
  Cat on a Hot Tin Roof 8, 9, 28, 34, 42, 44–5, 51, 53–5, 59
  The Glass Menagerie 4, 27, 28, 29–34, 42, 44, 45, 46
  The Milk Train Doesn't Stop Here Anymore 44
  The Night of the Iguana 44
  Orpheus Descending 44
  Period of Adjustment 44
  The Rose Tattoo 44
  A Streetcar Named Desire 28, 34, 40–4, 45, 46, 48, 53
  Suddenly Last Summer 44
  Summer and Smoke 44
  Sweet Bird of Youth 44

Wilson, August 91, 132–9, 148, 172
  Fences 132, 136–8
  Jitney 138, 166
  Joe Turner's Come and Gone 132, 134–6
  Ma Rainey's Black Bottom 132, 133–4
  The Piano Lesson 138, 157–60
  Two Trains Running 138, 147, 164–8, *165*

Wilson, Lanford 86, 88
  Burn This 100, 128, 129
  Fifth of July 130
  Hot L Baltimore 88
  The Rimers of Eldrich 88
  Talley & Son 130
  Talley's Folly 130

Wilson, Robert 176

Wine in the Wilderness (Childress) 91

Winterset (Maxwell Anderson) 14–15

Wolfe, George C.
  The Colored Museum 73, 139

Wolfe, Tom
  Bonfire of the Vanities 150

The Woman Who Was a Red Deer Dressed for the Deer Dance (Glancy) 174

Women of Manhattan (Shanley) 141

Women's Theatre Council 85

Wonder, Stevie 133

Wong, Elizabeth
  Letters to a Student Revolutionary 177

Wood, Grant
  American Gothic 108

Wooster Group 142, 176

work ethic 22, 23, 110

World War II 5, 21, 29, 59, 131

WOW Café 140–1

Wright, Richard
  Native Son 24, 25–6

Yankee Dawg You Die (Gotanda) 100, 141

Yellow Robe, William S.
  The Independence of Eddie Rose 173–4

Yordan, Philip
  Anna Lucasta 25

You Can't Take It with You (Hart and Kaufman) 16–17

The Young Man from Atlanta (Foote) 170

Zimmerman, Mary
  Metamorphoses 178–9

Zindel, Paul
  The Effects of Gamma Rays on Man-in-the-Moon Marigolds 98–9

The Zoo Story (Albee) 64, 65, 66–7, 83, 151